Our
Fathers'
War

—

Our Fathers' War

Growing Up in the Shadow
of the Greatest Generation

Tom Mathews

Broadway Books

New York

PRINTED IN THE UNITED STATES OF AMERICA

BROADWAY BOOKS and its logo, a letter B bisected on the diagonal,
are trademarks of Random House, Inc.

Visit our website at www.broadwaybooks.com

First edition published 2005.

Book design by Donna Sinisgalli

Louis Simpson, "Carentan O Carentan" and "The Battle" from *The
Owner of the House: New Collected Poems 1940–2001.* Copyright © 2003
by Louis Simpson. Reprinted with the permission of BOA Editions, Ltd.
www.BOAEditions.org.

Library of Congress Cataloging-in-Publication Data

Mathews, Tom.
Our Fathers' war : growing up in the shadow of the greatest generation /
Tom Mathews.—1st ed.
p. cm.
1. World War, 1939–1945—Psychological aspects. 2. Mathews, Tom.
3. Mathews, Thomas Richard, 1922– 4. World War, 1939–1945—
Children—United States—Biography. 5. Fathers and sons—United
States—Biography. 6. Children—United States—Biography. 7. Veterans—
United States—Biography. I. Mathews, Thomas Richard, 1922– II. Title.

D744.55M38 2005
973.92'092—dc22
[B]
2004058602

ISBN 0-7679-1420-1

1   3   5   7   9   10   8   6   4   2

For Lucille

Contents

Our Fathers' War

———

Chapter 1

The Beretta in the Nightstand

Lt. Thomas Richard Mathews,
Camp Hale, Colorado, 1944

My father hated war stories. He was a soldier with a code, a brave man who wouldn't talk about World War II. For a long time after the war, he could bring himself to tell only one story, and that one happened to him on the day he got home. He was crossing the Rockies in a troop train, safely out of the Apennines, glad to be alive. When his train reached Helper, Utah, it stopped to pick up a booster locomotive for the steep haul over the mountains to Salt Lake City. The sun was just coming up, and hundreds of soldiers were still dozing in their seats. Suddenly, just beyond the windows, the dawn erupted in rifle shots, shotgun blasts, and pistol fire. The Japanese had surrendered, and every man in Helper was shooting up the sky.

No one had bothered to tell the soldiers. Aboard the train, every man in uniform hit the floor. If you were a civilian, you might actually believe that World War II was over; if you had seen combat, it would never be over: You would carry it for the rest of your life, wired into your soul and central nervous system. Within Lt. Thomas Richard Mathews, every synapse was still sparking that day as a Union Pacific Challenger coupled itself to the troop train and started to roll, shoving its load of stouthearted men up the last grade and over Soldier Summit, delivering them home to be fathers.

Now, on this hot August day in 1945, it's a few hours later.

On the far side of the mountains, Thomas Richard Mathews Jr. is getting ready for inspection. It's the afternoon before my second birthday. Dressed for a double celebration in clean white shirt, short pants, and scuffed Buster Brown shoes, I am perched on the roof of a garage behind a small brick house on Mill Creek, the safe holding lie where my mother and I have spent the final months of the war. The idea is to get a good look at my father without getting too close too soon. My observation post isn't really a garage, but I don't know that yet. Topping out at about three feet tall, I'm still short on inches and nouns: To me, if a building has a front door and it isn't a house, it must be a garage. I'm also a little vague about the nature of this inspection, not quite sure which of us is on display. All I know is that the war, whatever that is, has ended; a uniform, whatever one looks like, will be on my father; and my father, whatever a father might be, is just about to appear.

"Today's the day, Tommy Two! Today's the day!"

Just a few minutes earlier, my mother had sung her small fanfare as she picked me up and waltzed me across the kitchen of our dark basement apartment. Her joy made me frown. My father and I both have the same name; we are both first sons, alphas to the max; and although I'm still working on my milk teeth, sharing my mother with anyone

*Tommy Two, the view from the
"garage," Salt Lake City, 1945*

bigger than me isn't part of my master plan. None of this I can put into words, of course, but what I am feeling obviously shows on my face.

"Don't you worry, Tee-Two," my mother says gaily, kissing my forehead. "*You* are my golden-haired boy."

I don't know what she's talking about—my hair is not blond; it's dark brown—and now, more than a little suspicious, I'm on top of the garage waiting to get a good look at her soldier. I don't remember anything about the young rock climber and skier who shipped out with the 10th Mountain Division to fight the Germans in northern Italy. He left a few months after my first birthday. I never think about him. To tell the truth, the only thing that piques my curiosity now is his uniform.

From the roof, I have a commanding view of our weedy backyard. Suddenly the door to our subterranean apartment flies open and my father steps out, blinking in the bright August sun. My first impression is this: He is huge. My second impression is that he is a man without a stomach, quite different from my grandfather, whose web suspenders strain against his friendly girth when he hauls himself into his

Chrysler. My father is flat and hard where my grandfather is round and soft, and he is moving toward me at a very fast clip. Pulling up in front of the garage, he opens his arms.

"Jump."

I hesitate, study the distance between us. It is transcontinental. The drop to the ground appears to be fifteen hundred feet. Bottom of the Grand Canyon. Certain death.

"Jump."

Not possible. No, no, no, no, no.

"I said jump." The voice is harder now. But then, for just an instant, he appears to soften.

"It's okay, Tommy," he says. "I'm your father."

Am I supposed to fly? Does he think I'm a bird? Recoiling, I freeze to the roof.

The tanned face flushes. Then the soldier wheels abruptly and storms across the yard, plunging into the basement. For the rest of my life I will hear the screen door's sharp bang and the last thing he said before he turned his back and walked away.

"No son of mine is a coward."

In memory, this first scene always plays out in the present tense, arriving through an odd quantum leap that makes the collision from the past and its impact today coincide in time. I wanted my father's love, he longed for mine; but from the day he came home, the kinetic energy of World War II struck at our center of gravity. To what might otherwise have been the normal, primordial course of battle between fathers and sons, the war added its own peculiar convolutions. In our case, from that first day, my father thought—not without reason—that he was looking at a soft little pain in the neck, and I thought, on balance, that my life would be off to a better start if only the Germans had killed him.

The issue between us wasn't a simple one of who was boss. It was more a question of who was who. I could never quite figure out where he left off and I began. World War II may have been the last war where young men actually sang as they were bound for combat: in their barracks, on the troopship, in the trucks moving them up to the front line. The 10th Mountain Division had a ballad called "Ninety Pounds of Rucksack" about a barmaid who jumped into a skier's bed to keep him warm and wound up with "a bastard in the mountain infantry." The chorus was "Ninety pounds of rucksack, a pound of grub or two. He'll schuss the mountains like his daddy used to do." The big bastard was my father, and the little bastard was me. When I was a small boy, we both thought it was my destiny and duty to follow his smooth, shining track on the hill.

The problem was that the tracks were clear only in light powder snow. The war and what came after made him a hard man to understand. He had grown up during the Great Depression feeling like a boy with empty pockets standing outside a candy store window. After the war, you could never be sure how he felt. My sister once sent me his photograph from Officer Candidate School. In this formal portrait, shot in a studio somewhere near Fort Sill, Oklahoma, he is twenty-one years old. Sewn to his shoulder is a 10th Mountain Division patch: two red bayonets crossed on a field of blue. The stitches on the patch are large, as if he has done the sewing himself. Mercifully, someone with an airbrush has erased the acne that scarred his adolescence. For the first time, he is actually good-looking: hair dark and brushed up in an unmilitary wave, a faint smile, lady-killer eyes.

Before the war swept him into the United States Army, he was a climber on Mount Olympus, Lone Peak, Timpanogos, and Mount Nebo, the craggiest summits of the Wasatch Range. He scrambled aloft from the University of Utah, the first man in his family to go to college and rise so high. Long before the days of Gore-Tex and chairlifts, he was recklessly at ease on rock faces and avalanche slopes, spending his winters on skis and the rest of the year on subversive ideas. From the Arlberg school he got stem christies and his Tyrolean hat; from Ernest Hemingway he developed his sense of style as the grand gesture; from F. Scott Fitzgerald he acquired martinis along with a hangover as big as The Ritz.

As a young man, he once told me, he felt torn between two forces, one physical, the other dreamy: Within the husk of the athlete breathed the soul of a troubadour. He was born in Salt Lake City in 1922, a son of Utah pioneers entitled to full standing in the Mormon Church. But the Mormons had hermetically sealed the Valley of the Saints against troubadours, so he had to reinvent himself. By the time he entered his twenties, he had become a Deseret original, an apostate Jack Mormon sitting behind the wheel of a Model A Ford in Jay Gatsby's suit and shoes. One afternoon in the summer of 1942, he pulled into Fred & Kelly's Drive-In, where a tiny brunette carhop in a bright red uniform took his order. Her name was Bonnie Johnson. When she wasn't hustling burgers and shakes, she was reading Elizabethan plays at the university. Her eyes were brown and piercing, and her intentions were radical. Dodging the advances of the drive-in's owner, hanging up the uniform at the end of the shift, she would light a cigarette and consider the future. "I'd join the Communist Party," she told the other carhops. "But you can't find a cell around this hole."

The troubadour and the revolutionary felt an instant affinity. For their first date, she once told me, my father changed into rough pants and a T-shirt, crammed a loaf of bread and a jug of wine into his rucksack, and took my mother on a hike up Bell's Canyon. Given the choice, she would have preferred a long session with *Das Kapital*. But as she watched my father loping up the trail ahead of her, yodeling to the pines, so young and full of high spirits, she fell in love. At the end of the day they stopped at the A&W to chase the jug of wine with a root beer. When the waiter brought the bill, my father grandly tossed all the loose change to a kid in the next booth. Then he put his head on Bonnie's shoulder and said, "I like you, Johnson."

It was the summer after Pearl Harbor when they started their romance. To save gas he would park the Ford in the garage behind the Fairmount Apartments, where he lived with his parents, and the young couple would neck in the back seat. He didn't know the first thing about sex, she told me. After one particularly clumsy grope, she sent him packing. But the next day he turned up at her door with an armful of flowers and a face so sad, she took him back. Piling into the Ford, they drove to Liberty Park, and there, in the darkness next to the tennis courts, she rendered unto Gatsby what Gatsby always wanted from Daisy. The issue of this shot heard 'round the backcourt was me. When she missed her next period, she spent a few days jumping off a tall chest of drawers in her bedroom, hoping to induce a miscarriage. It didn't work. Then, saying why the hell not, she and my father found a Unitarian minister and got married.

The wedding took place on December 27, 1942. The groom was in an ROTC program at the University of Utah. The following summer, seven months' pregnant, my mother didn't make an appearance at his graduation, but before he left for basic training, the two of them wandered through the old municipal cemetery overlooking the Salt Lake Valley, looking for a boy's name. My mother thought Christopher would be nice—after Marlowe. When they proposed it to my grandmother, a strong-minded Swede, she said, "Christopher—isn't that what *Greeks* call their sons?" Swedes worked on the railroads. Greeks washed dishes in diners behind the Union Pacific depot. This proposal confirmed my grandmother's darkest fear that her son had married a tramp. To mollify her, my parents decided to name me after my father. Two weeks later he left for basic training.

I have another old photograph commemorating this moment. Out in the backyard, my father, rail thin, his khaki tie knotted and crammed into the blouse of his uniform, his hand on his hip, is standing next to my grandfather, who is wearing a straw boater, a white shirt open at the throat, and a belt that would fit around a beer barrel. The young soldier is still so green that he has no insignia on his uniform. The picture was taken just before he set off for Fort Sill. On arrival, according to the form that recorded the results of his Army physical, the doctors found his posture good and his eyes normal; his ears, nose, and throat clear, his bones, joints, muscles, and abdominal viscera all combat ready. He was good to go.

So was I, but in quite a different direction. On the morning of August 16, 1943, just after reveille in Fort Sill, my grandfather came to

Holy Cross Hospital in Salt Lake City with an armload of gladiolus for my mother. He was also trailing a fragrant bouquet of Old Crow. In Oklahoma later that afternoon, Cpl. Thomas Richard Mathews, serial number 0-534107, burst out of his barracks waving a telegram. Running down the dusty street between a long line of identical buildings covered in tar paper, he shouted at the top of his lungs:

"I have a son!"

Fast-forward fifty years.

Fruitland, Utah, at three in the morning is probably as close as any son and father can get to the end of the earth. Sailing above the sagebrush, only a full moon illuminates the pay phone on the wall of the locked grocery next to a ghostly filling station. Seventeen miles back up the dirt road along Strawberry Creek, my father and I have lost the jeep, our fly rods, our fishing vests, and an Igloo cooler full of brown trout.

It is very cold. Shifting from foot to foot in my soggy waders, I watch my father bend over the phone box, muttering to himself. Steam plumes into the Utah darkness as he plugs quarters into the slot. We've been missing in action for twelve hours. Shortly before sunup, my mother pulls into Fruitland. One or two steps ahead of hypothermia, we jump into her car and sit there shivering. Shaking her head, she jacks up the heater and throws the car into reverse. "My God," she says. "What a pair."

Rewind twelve hours.

Huge browns as long as my arm are slashing at the elk hair caddis flies my father and I are presenting in dazzling floats down the riffles on Strawberry Creek. Intent on the rises, we ignore the black thunderheads welling up over the rim of the canyon. Also the first raindrops, then the downpour. Not until the creek starts turning brown do we toss our gear in the back of the jeep and head for home. A perfect day. Then, coming around the first bend, my father slams on the brakes. We are looking at a Great Wall of Mud. Fed by the heavy rain, a flash flood has washed out a cliff, sending a mudslide across the road, over Strawberry

Creek, and halfway up the far canyon wall. There is no way over and no way out. We are sealed into Rattlesnake Canyon.

At least the rain has stopped and there's going to be a full moon. We lock the jeep, pick our way over the slide, and set off on foot, heading for old Highway 40. The hike, under ordinary conditions, would be easy. But today, in addition to the canyon washout and gathering darkness, there is another factor. Earlier that morning, when we set off, I was so eager to get on the road that I grabbed my gear and didn't bother to put on any shoes. Screw it. I'd ride barefoot and pull out my waders when we got there. Now, my father looks down at my feet and shakes his head. "Let's go," he says.

The going is slow and spongy. Three hours later we pick up a ray of hope: a ranch with a security light far off the road in the sagebrush: a phone, rescue. As we pick up speed and cross the cattle guard, a dog starts to bark. We don't hear the door open. What we do hear is a curse and then a rifle shot. The round zings off a rock next to us. We are back-lit against the moon. Retreating full tilt, we sprint over a low hill and sit on the ground for a few moments, breathing hard. My heart is pounding, but when I look over at my father, he seems quite calm. Coming under fire is something new for me, but not for him.

"So much for Western hospitality," he says. "Let's move."

Farther up the road, I notice that while I'm beginning to limp, he is developing a swing to his step, as if he's warming up to the night march. For the first time, after a lifetime on guard, I feel close to him, and I give in to a confessional urge, which is a mistake:

"You know, Pop, there were times over the years I guess I hated you."

He stops, eyes hurt.

"Why?"

Just at the moment I'm about to purge and atone, a pickup comes down the road, a citizens band radio crackling from the dash. A young man and woman jump out. They have heard about the flash floods and are on the way to check on the woman's father, who is probably up the canyon behind us, reloading. Although they are reluctant to interrupt their mercy mission, they take pity on us and give us a ride back to the paved highway. It's too noisy in the bed of the pickup for any more confessions. By the time they drop us off in Fruitland, my father and I are both buttoned up tight and I am developing this unpleasant, through-the-looking-glass feeling of getting lost somewhere out of time.

"What's a coward, Mama?"

We're back in 1945 again, and I'm in the kitchen, alone with my mother, who is peeling carrots. Her soldier has disappeared into the only bedroom.

"What are you talking about, T-2?"

"Uhhhhhh . . ."

"Come on, what is it?"

"Ummmmm, just thinking."

She puts down the peeler, wipes her hands on a dish towel.

"Okay, a coward is someone who is afraid of everything. Why?"

"Uhhh (pointing to the bedroom), HE says I'm a coward."

"What? He says what?"

"I'm a coward."

"Oh, Jesus." Tossing aside the dish towel, she goes into the bedroom and closes the door. For a few seconds I hear angry whispers, then an explosion.

"GODDAMMIT. YOU'VE SPOILED MY SON."

This is terrible. I have to do something. Make it stop. My eyes zone in on our refrigerator, an old Kelvinator. I push a step stool against the kitchen counter, belly my way along it, then climb to the summit of the Kelvinator, five feet above the kitchen floor. The argument in the bedroom stops. The door opens.

"Look, Daddy," I pipe wildly, hurling myself into space. "I am not a coward."

With a sweaty splat, I touch down on the linoleum expecting redemption, but my leap doesn't impress the soldier. He studies me impassively and says nothing as he shuts the door. The point is made. I have disobeyed a direct order from a superior officer, and the consequences will be serious—more serious than either of us even know. For the next thirty or forty years I will spend an astounding amount of energy looking for higher and higher Kelvinators to climb, but after my first flop, none of them will work any better than our first fridge.

All through World War II, I slept in a crib placed against a wall of our one bedroom. Whenever I felt lonely or cold, I could pad across the floor and sneak under the covers with my mother. After getting out of his uniform that first day, the next thing my father did was move my crib into the kitchen. The new location was under the window well. That night after my mother and father had withdrawn beyond the bedroom door, I heard a scratching at the window. Looking up, I saw a face with bristling whiskers and wild eyes. I howled. When my father came steaming out of the bedroom, all I could do was point and yell again. Muttering darkly, he pulled on his pants. A few minutes later, from the far side of the glass, I heard a second scream—this one even more piercing than my own—and the hideous face disappeared. The monster was a porcupine. My father bayoneted it with a garden fork and tossed the body in the woods. Then he came back into the kitchen, leaned over the crib, and said, "Don't ever go near that window well."

Early the next morning, I went out to take a good look and felt a surge of civil disobedience. In my hand I was holding a toy airplane: mustard yellow, a Tootsie Toy Beechcraft Bonanza with a butterfly tail and a silver propeller that whirred when I stuck it out the window of my grandfather's car. Around the window well there was concrete trim about four inches wide, the perfect runway.

Let's see. What if I push my Bonanza along the runway? What if I spin the propeller with my finger? What if I launch the plane across the window well? Surely it will go through the air and land on the other side. What else could happen?

Spin, spin, spin . . . push, push, push . . . wheels up.

Nose-dive.

From the bottom of the window well, my Bonanza was now a splash of yellow on the dirt. I couldn't reach it with my arm. I tried

with a stick, but the metal was too slippery. Monster blood. All else failing, I jumped into the window well. Coming up with the plane in my
fist, I pressed my chest against the concrete runway and tried to pull
myself up; but my legs were too short, and my arms weren't long
enough to swing me out of the hole. Losing strength, I fell back to the
bottom, which is where my father eventually found me.

"I told you not to play there," he said, looming up against the sky
like God.

But, but, but, but, but.

Two acts of insubordination in less than twenty-four hours confirmed every count against me.

"All right, pal. You can stay right where you are."

I'm not sure how long I sat at the bottom of the window well wondering who would come back and get me first, my father or the porcupine. Eventually, after what seemed like several hours, though it was
probably several minutes, my father hove into view and pulled me to
safety. Looking back, I have to admit that he wasn't entirely wrong
about me. As a son I was, at best, a fixer-upper, a boy definitely in need
of work.

He began by taking me to the barbershop in the Newhouse Hotel
on Main Street. The shop had two enormous chairs with padded leather
seats and steel footrests, and it smelled of Vitalis and Barbasol and the
secrets of grown men. While my father watched, the barber ran the
hand clippers ran through my sissy locks, now and then pinching out
entire knots of hair. I got home as shorn as a new recruit, white blotches
all over my scalp. My mother was speechless.

One afternoon not long after the trip downtown, he took my
mother and me out for target practice in the backyard. Over his shoulder he carried an olive drab musette bag. Inside, wrapped in cloth, were
three pistols: a baby-sized Italian Beretta with a beautifully machined
crosshatch grip; a mama-sized German Luger, almost feminine in the
fastidiousness of its heft and form; and a papa-sized .45, enormous and
of Spanish design. First he set a tin can in front of a tree, then he
handed the Luger to my mother. Game but grimacing, she raised the

pistol and yanked the trigger, producing a sharp crack and a spurt of flame. The round whistled through the branches of the tree, six or seven feet above the tin can. Shrinking at the flash and recoil, she said she hated the goddamn thing, handed it back to him, and stalked off the firing range. So he closed the bag, and the following day he went downtown and found a job as a reporter for the *Salt Lake City Tribune*. The paper assigned him to the police shack in the city and county building. Not long after that, he came home and told us he'd sold his pistols to a cop.

The trophies were gone, but my father retained more than enough manly power to dazzle me. Along the banks of Mill Creek, schools of minnows darted through the shallows. During the last few weeks of the war, I tried fishing for them with a safety pin hook, a rod made from an alder twig, and some string from the catchall drawer in the kitchen. I didn't know about casting or bait. I just dropped my naked pin in the water. Drawn to the silvery flash of the metal in the whiskey brown water, the minnows would nose up, then speed away laughing. One day while I was wondering why they refused to impale themselves on my hook, I looked up and saw a real fly rod for the first time. It was attached to my father, who was leaning out our bathroom window above the brook, flicking quick, tight loops over the water. The fly dropped behind a rock and floated for an inch or two, and then a giant trout, Moby-Dick to my minnows, struck at it savagely. My father's rod tip rose, the trout flew out of the water and up through the air wiggling and shimmering into the bathroom. I felt as stunned as the fish. My father was a wizard. There was magic in his wand. Better not to butt heads with him. Stealth, cunning, mutinous silence—that was the way to go.

The war left one clearly visible wound on my father, but that one was superficial; an Army doctor recorded it on an official WD-60 form after his last physical: "Injured right knee April, 1944, at Ft. Sill, Oklahoma, when attempted to catch runaway mule." If anything, he returned from fighting the Germans with an abundance of energy and a determination to get beyond the provincial certainties of Salt Lake City. He had always been a man of action, but now he seemed supercharged. That first winter, when it snowed in the mountains, he called his best friend, Jack Sugden, in wild excitement. Now that they were home, he said to Suggie, who was heading for Chicago to study architecture with Mies van der Rohe, why not treat their wives to a high-altitude winter bivouac, show them the true meaning of endurance?

My mother and Audrey Sugden would have taken the two ski troopers at their word on any claim to mastery in the mountains, but that wasn't the real purpose of the trip. Beyond all the braggadocio, the subzero expedition was about the joy of coming home alive. Together, the four of them climbed to the top of White Pine Canyon two canyons down from Alta. At eleven thousand feet, they pitched a two-man tent, using their body heat to level a patch in the snow. When they broke dinner out of their rucksacks, they discovered that the beef in the canned stew had frozen to stone. After a spectacular sunset, they turned in and spent the night huddling to keep off frostbite. Shortly before dawn, my mother had to get up to relieve what was called in those days a slight pressure of water. Thirty seconds later, she ducked back into the tent, her eyebrows frosted with rime. "All right, you two," she said to Sugden and my father. "Don't ever tell me it ain't a man's world."

Back down in the valley, her drill instructor husband put me through my own survival course. Like a master sergeant confronting a dense recruit, he spelled out the four basic rules of manhood: Don't cry, don't bitch, don't bother me when I'm busy, and never pretend to be sick. The word he used for the last dereliction was "malingering," an Army term. My life, he said, would be full of danger, a constant battle, and in 1945, when the war had vaporized entire cities and extinguished nearly 61 million people, there was no other way to see it. These were good rules. Simple, clear, endlessly pragmatic. For some of them, I can only feel gratitude. When I developed a cough and the doctor presented a diagnosis of asthma, my father said, "He doesn't have asthma and he's not going to get it now." So I didn't. That would have been malingering. The coughing stopped.

Behind the rules was an ethos that my father derived from a single, unswerving Jack Mormon principle: Every man has the right to go to hell in his own handbasket. This particular idea he inherited from my grandfather, Wesley Chase Mathews. A third-generation son of Mormon pioneers, Wes Mathews was born in the Salt Lake Valley in 1887. As soon as he was old enough to enter a saloon, he broke with the church over the basic morality of drinking. Good Mormons didn't, he did. A photo from the Roaring Twenties shows him with his boot on the running board of a Model T, a rumrunner's grin on his face, a crushed Stetson cocked on his head, and a Winchester 12-gauge across his knee. Upended at his feet is a string of seventeen equally blasted prairie hens.

As a young man he ran a railroad track gang out beyond the Bonneville Salt Flats near Wendover. The Utah-Nevada state line ran directly through Wendover, dividing the little town into a dry Mormon sector and a very wet zone of saloons, gambling dens, and whorehouses. A similar division ran through the moral calculus of my grandfather, who transmitted it to my father, who handed it down to me. Among railroad men, a handbasket was a wicker device that road-builders used to blast grades and tunnels. You lowered a basket with a worker in it, usually Chinese, to drill the holes, plant the TNT, and light the fuses. Then you pulled him back from danger. Most of the time the system worked fine. But if anyone was slow on the haul, the man planting the dynamite was blown to hell in his own handbasket. How this could be desirable, or even an entitlement, only a Jack Mormon, torn between loyalties to Brigham Young and Jack Daniel's, could understand. My grandfather invoked it with fundamentalist conviction to justify heavy investments in whiskey, shotgun shells, and fly rods; my father used it to cover gin, skis, and Peal's shoes from London; I used it to warrant just about anything that caught my eye.

World War II enormously increased my father's go-to-hell index. In the family photo album he kept a picture of himself smoking a pipe and sharing a drink with a friend at the Fifth Army Officers Rest Hotel in Florence. With the snapshot, he had scribbled a quick note to his wife: "Please tell mother the battle contains nothing stronger than Chianti." A grand gesture, I told myself for many years: the well-turned phrase, Hemingwayesque, a hard-boiled kiss-off to combat. Then one day quite recently, I examined the note more carefully and saw that the word he had written was not battle, but bottle.

That note for his mother about the octane level of the bottle in Florence was his last after-action report on his own drinking. After he came home, he stopped keeping track. At first the bottle seemed to bring out the best in him; among friends, alcohol supercharged his energy and charm. In the warmest memories I have of him, he is schussing the runs at Brighton, his red nose a blob of white under the zinc oxide, his breath a steamy contrail against the blue sky. At the bottom of the slope I bury my face in the cold crinkles of his parka, breathing in his attar of good whiskey and Hershey chocolate, floating on his euphoria.

For a long time, my battle-bottle slip governed all my what-did-you-do-in-the-war-daddy questions. Since the soldier wouldn't talk about what he had seen or done, I made the battle up for him, tooling the fantasy to meet my needs. I wanted unshakable coolness under fire, sacrifice, heroism, victory: Gary Cooper as Sergeant York, the movie version of the real thing that had struck my father dumb.

The reality he kept at home in a book bound in glacial white leatherette veined with lines of blue. The volume was a combat history of the 87th Mountain Infantry, one of the three regiments that made up the 10th Mountain Division. On its cover an alp rose behind a crossed ski pole and ice ax. Following 154 pages of mayhem, there was a report about the band at the pier that welcomed the survivors back to the United States, the twenty-four-hour layover at Camp Patrick Henry, then the troop trains leaving for home. Nothing about the scare at Helper. But it wasn't hard to see why the soldiers had gone for the floor. During the preceding winter and spring, the 10th Mountain Division had advanced well over 100 miles in Italy in 114 days of fighting with the Germans. Along that path, 4,154 of the division's original 14,000 men and 5,000 replacements had been variously blown up, shot, or mangled, and 975 were killed.

None of this my father ever mentioned. But when I came back

from Kress's dime store with my first toy cap pistol and started shooting up the neighborhood, he broke open the breech and took out the mechanism that moved the roll of paper caps toward the firing pin. When I protested the way he had spiked my martial fantasies, he said, "No guns for you."

After the war, my father rose quickly on the *Tribune*—not the *Deseret News,* the official voice of Mormonism. The *Tribune* was the voice of the opposition in Salt Lake, a morning daily owned and run by Irish Catholics whose fortune came from mines up in the mountains. He preferred Irish Fitzpatricks and Kearnses to dour Mormon Kimbels and Pratts. His Mormon ancestors ran back only three generations; Catholics shared his Celtic genes. Until the first Mormon missionaries discovered the Mathews men in Wales in the 1840s, these men had concentrated on digging coal all day, leaving the nights for drinking and singing; otherwise, they minded their own business. Lured to Utah, they wound up cutting stone for the Mormon Temple, but after two sober pioneer generations, my grandfather and father had backslid from the Book of Mormon to the Book of Kells. My father was pleased when his sister converted and married a hard-drinking Catholic who had gone to Columbia University with Jack Kerouac and Allen Ginsberg. No one else in Salt Lake City had ever heard of them. Catholics were okay. They drank.

Tank topped off with bourbon, my father could seduce a mother superior, but his moods would swing abruptly. Sometimes, late in the evenings, he'd sit in his chair reading Proust, belting gin, brooding. On the bad nights, when his eyes were hooded, he withdrew so far into his gloom you could no longer find him. One time when I asked him why he looked so sad, he studied me through frog eyes and said, "You never know when you'll want to check out."

Another morning, nursing a hangover before setting off for the *Tribune,* he asked me to get a handkerchief for him from the drawer in the nightstand next to his bed. When I pulled open the drawer, I saw the little Beretta, which I had thought was gone forever. Next to it was a steel magazine. After he left for work, I went back to examine the magazine. Before I could find out whether or not there were rounds in it, the front door opened and I heard my mother drop a bag of groceries in the kitchen.

"I'm home, T-2," she called out to me. "Whatcha doing?"

"Nothing, Mom."

That night I sat down next to my father.

"You've got a gun," I said. "I saw it in your drawer."

"Did you touch it?"

"No."

"Don't ever open that drawer again."

"Yes, Dad."

"We're not going to talk about this again, you understand?"

After I went to bed, I heard him out in the living room arguing with my mother. The two of them seldom yelled at each other. If anything, when their feelings rose toward the boil, they lowered their voices, making it harder from the safety of my bunk bed to hear the fight. Only a few muffled bursts made it through the door.

"What the hell do you think you're doing with that thing? You said you sold it."

"Leave it alone, Bonnie."

"He's only a boy, Tom."

"I said leave it alone."

The next day the Beretta in the nightstand was gone, this time for good. Sometimes I have asked myself if the memory could be one of those false ones, something I'd made up or just an artifact from a dream. But a few years ago, I stumbled on an Internet archive of 10th Mountain Division photographs and found a link called Beretta. When I clicked the mouse, up came a snapshot of two soldiers, one with sergeant's stripes, sharing a beer in the ruins of an Italian farmhouse. The sergeant was examining a pistol taken off a dead German officer: a Beretta, identical to the one I'd seen in my father's nightstand.

Picking up the phone, I called my mother and asked her if she re-

membered a fight over my father's Beretta. She remembered every detail. What he had said to her that night in 1948 was this:

"You don't have the guts to kill yourself, Bonnie. I do."

My father stored the rest of his war surplus in a dark closet: a set of
wooden skis painted white, seal climbing skins, two olive drab shelter
halves that could be snapped into a pup tent, a piton hammer, and an
ice ax shaped like a pick but small enough for a boy to swing. About this
time, down at the Utah Theater on Main Street, they were showing re-
runs of Walt Disney's *Pinocchio*. Whenever my own nose was out of
joint, I would retreat to my father's storeroom to discuss weapons and
tactics with Jiminy Cricket, Pinocchio's alter ego and conscience. One
day my father heard me and Jiminy plotting against all senior officers.
When he asked through the door whom I was talking to, I blurted out,
"No one, Dad." After that, my imaginary friend repaid the betrayal by
vanishing and I was on my own.

When a son is as afraid of his father as I was, love can curdle, producing obedience and something close to awe. Boot camp at home rein-
forced this reality. A generation or two later, when "new men" and
"nurturing fathers" entered the vocabulary of "parenting," I could
never work up a willing suspension of disbelief. To me, the natural state
of relations between fathers and sons was a state of war, not an exercise
in psychological piety. How did Isaac feel when Abraham put the knife
to his throat? No one really asked him. If the choice had been his,
wouldn't he have skipped the honor? On the other hand, no one con-
sulted Philip of Macedon on whether his boy Alexander really had to
terminate him before he could conquer the known world. In this zone
of love and hostility, rivalry and suspicion, I could never see the virtue
of the standard biblical and historical analogies. All I know is that at
seven or eight I was deeply afraid of my father, fiercely proud to be his
son, constantly wondering what it would take to bump him off.

His wartime training for winter combat gave him a significant advantage as he moved ahead in his own life, drawing us behind him.

Tom and Bonnie, a love story, Alta,
Utah, 1946

When a small plane lost in a blizzard crashed deep in the Uinta Mountains, he strapped on his skis, joined a rescue team, and headed into the wilderness. After three days in deep snow, he found the survivors, who were so grateful they refused to give their story to anyone but him. With his first scoop, the *Tribune* published a photograph from the rescue. He is wearing a fur-fringed Army parka and looking over his shoulder. This is the face I remember best from those years: daring, indomitable, a man to adore and fear. For years I coveted that parka. When I left for college, he gave it to me as a going-away present. When I dropped out three years later, somehow I lost it.

The *Tribune*'s office was on Main Street next to the Pony Express Memorial. At Christmas, the paper always put up a giant tree. The ornaments were made of rubber and as big as beach balls. I coveted them, too. One year my father and a drinking friend named Elf got lit, climbed the tree late on Christmas Eve, and cut down two ornaments for my brother and me. We could bounce them only indoors because the following day the *Tribune* ran a story saying that vandals had stolen Christmas. On another fine Christmas morning I came into the living room to find my first pair of skis, boots, and poles under a tree lit by electric candle lights that bubbled like the trim on a jukebox.

"Where are the presents?" I asked.

The outfit cost a week's pay. It was generous beyond belief, but as I saw it, I was being called up for advanced military training, not looking at a gift from Santa. Later on, a professional photographer took a picture of my father teaching me how to snowplow. He's wearing his Tyrolean hat, and I'm there between his knees—a small Eisenhower jacket for a parka, a set of tank driver goggles pushed up on my forehead, and a frown of concentration that says, "This is never going to work." Once, when I lost my nerve during a traverse, he ordered me to get into his rucksack. Taking off at high speed, he went twenty yards and fell, and we pinwheeled down the slope. When we finally rolled to a stop, he came up blowing powder snow and laughing. I felt blackly betrayed. He had given an order, I had followed it, he had let down the troops. Many years later a shrink asked me why I didn't simply say no when he told me to get in his rucksack. I had no answer. Disobeying wasn't an option for a soldier's son.

On balance, it seemed a lot safer to steal his girl. The following winter, when I was eight, he disappeared at the top of the new chairlift in Brighton, leaving my mother and me to make our way down Mount Millicent alone. This suited me perfectly. Shouting "C'mon, Mom," I schussed down the mountain like my daddy used to do. Halfway to the bottom I caught an edge, corkscrewed one ski into the snow, and rode the rest of the way on a ski patrol toboggan. From the first aid station, the horn of the public address speaker started calling my father's name up through the pines. It took half an hour before he turned up, got me on my feet, and marched me to the car. When I did some whimpering on the drive down the canyon, he told me to stop malingering. My mother insisted on taking me to the hospital, where an x-ray showed a spiral fracture of the tibia. "Unusual," the doctor said. "How did that happen?"

I snuck a peek at my father, who looked stricken. It took only twenty minutes for the doctor to set the broken bone and wrap my leg in a warm plaster cast, but by then the more complex fracture between my father and me was beginning to show some very sharp edges. Seizing the advantage, I shook him down for a toy shooting gallery made of tin, with moving ducks and a gun that shot ball bearings. It cost twelve dollars, a full day's pay.

I hated it when he decided to move us out of the secure little world of Salt Lake City. In 1952, the blinkered smugness of the valley was lost on a small boy with a neighborhood gang who saw life as a boundless game of kick the can in the soft golden light of summer afternoons. But a story took my father over to Nevada and Bing Crosby's ranch outside Elko, where he did some drinking with the editor of the *San Francisco Chronicle*. This California sophisticate liked my dad's style and offered him a job. So when the *Tribune*'s editor ordered him to water down a review panning a local ballet company, he said the hell with it and quit. Piling his family into a station wagon, he took a bearing on the Golden Gate and drove west.

San Francisco in the postwar years had everything Salt Lake City lacked: novelists and poets, painters and sculptors, Jews, Negroes, homosexuals, transplanted Italians who fished for salmon and crabs and made the wine to go with them up in the Napa Valley. On a hillside in Sausalito, he transplanted us to an old Victorian house buried in nasturtiums. As a provider, he always delivered far more than the basics: not just the roof over the head and the tuna surprise on the table, but Val Bleecker, who showed the scorched asbestos pad from her woodstove in that summer's art show; Peggy Tolk Watkins, owner of the Tin Angel jazz club, whose drop-dead gorgeous lesbian girlfriends drove men in the Four Winds Bar to unrequited fantasies of rescue; George Draper, the New England aristocrat with a Locust Valley lockjaw accent who had flown with André Malraux in the Spanish Civil War; and, first among equals, Larry Doyle, owner of the liquor store, an honest bookie who honored all bets instantly. When he died, his funeral filled Star of the Sea Church.

As the 1950s unfolded, no one in San Francisco wanted to dwell on the war, least of all my father. But it was there, hidden behind the glamour of new maneuvers. The epicenter of his life was Hanno's on the Corner, a saloon on Fifth and Mission next to the *Chronicle,* where he killed time between assignments playing liars dice and poker with his friends. Along one wall was a steam table with a few limp hot dogs no one ever ate. The phone on the wall was a hot line to the city desk. When it rang, he would belt down one for the road and sprint for the Tenderloin or North Beach. He knew everyone, and everyone loved him. No one paid much attention to his drinking. Only my mother heard him sobbing the night he came home from San Quentin, where he had just reported the execution of Caryl Chessman, a death row star in the debate over capital punishment. He agreed to do the story only if the newspaper would let him cover the execution of an unknown inmate so everyone could read how lousy it was to kill any man, not just a celebrity. His crying jag lasted half the night. The next morning I snuck a look at his notes. Starting coolly, they began to unravel, then disintegrate into indecipherable spirals, the swirls foreshadowing his own future.

By the time he reached his middle thirties, newspaper work bored him. He said he wanted to make things happen, not just observe them—the professional witness being to history roughly what the professional hooker was to sex. He set up a small political consulting firm. His first contract was to promote a water bond issue that financed the diversion of northern California water to the thirsty maw of Los Angeles. This was a hard sell around San Francisco. He told friends he was thinking of printing a million bumper stickers that would say OUI OUI FOR WAWA. After the issue passed, he went on to promote Pat Brown's successful run for governor, a triumph that won him a reputation as a political gunslinger. In 1960, after John Kennedy squeaked past Richard

Nixon, he was leaning against the bar at the Alta Lodge next to Robert McNamara when the phone rang and the bartender announced that Washington was calling. "I'll take it," said McNamara, a lieutenant colonel during World War II up for secretary of defense by way of the Ford Motor Company. The bartender shook his head.

"It's for you, Tom."

Telling this story was as close as my father ever came to bragging. The call was from the president-elect's brother-in-law, Sargent Shriver, who needed someone to sell the new Peace Corps to a skeptical Washington press corps and a hostile Congress. Hanging up, he drove directly to the airport, and when he walked into the Peace Corps office seven hours later, he was still wearing his ski boots. Shriver took one look at him and said, "That's my man." In his new office he hung two pictures. The first was a portrait of his square-jawed boss, who signed it, "To my favorite Peace Corps poet." The second, a cartoon, showed him as a stubby, red-nosed operative in a black raincoat leading his staff: two equally louche ex-newsmen, one in a baseball cap, the other waving a tennis racket. The caption read, "Remember men. First impressions are important."

By then his drinking was beginning to scare his friends. One night he came staggering up the front walk just before dawn, too loaded to talk. My mother was frantic. Grinning blearily, he started reaching into his pockets. Out came wads of bills, tens, twenties, fifties, hundreds; he'd won the equivalent of six months' pay at poker. Then he collapsed. A year later his sense of irony, if little else, still intact, he checked himself into the veterans hospital in Salt Lake City, where a psychiatrist diagnosed him as an incurable alcoholic. On his first day in the dipsomaniac ward, he was sitting in his bathrobe gloomily considering the future when a fellow patient sidled up.

"Are you here to kill me?" said the loon.

"No," he replied. "Not if you behave yourself."

Confounding the shrinks, he reemerged in New York City with a new job polishing the image of Lincoln Center. At that point, something quite strange happened between us. As he regained altitude, I nosed over, lurching into a disastrous marriage and divorce followed by years of panic attacks, assorted fibrillations, and trips to hospital emergency rooms. Drinking to beat his record, I nearly ruined a second marriage to an outlaw Mennonite from Pinckney, Michigan, who saved me from the wreckage of the first. Now and then during those years, my father would wobble off the wagon. Each time I felt a sense of dread, as if, having no gyroscope of my own, I was doomed to topple after him into the stagy little melodrama he called The Curse of the Mathews Men.

In our Welsh genes, we may have shared an enraptured weakness for alcohol, but it was World War II that provided the chaser. He went into the war as an innocent, an idealist full of hope and energy; he came home an elusive shape-shifter. It was difficult for him show the simplest expression of fatherly affection. He saw poker and life as the same game: You had to sense weaknesses and exploit them, even if the other player happened now and then to be my brother or me. We never knew what he was thinking or what he would do next. He expected a commander's due: obedience and admiration. I experienced these as an annihilation.

To leave it at that would be to do him an injustice. Wasn't it possible that on coming out of Rattlesnake Canyon, I had told him I hated him simply because he had demanded a soldier's discipline from me only to fall on his snoot? How fair was that? I had fallen on my own. Was I whining because I hadn't outscored him as a man's man, a charmer, a lady-killer? For more than twenty years, like an obsessive out of a Woody Allen farce, I deliberated these questions with a psychologist. The therapist was a strong woman from Texas. She kept her own father's six-shooter in a drawer. One day when I had tested her patience beyond endurance, she pulled out the old Colt, slapped it on her desk, and said, "Tom, when are you going to get your daddy's dick out of your ass?"

I was so shocked it took me another year to work through her challenge, by which time she had died. She wasn't trying to unearth repressed trauma. There was no question of sexual abuse. After the war, my father's abhorrence for violence was so strong that even under provocation he never spanked me. What had happened between us was pure psywar: Better than rubber hoses—no visible marks or contusions. Everything hidden in the wetware of the brain. When I finally saw this much, I gave up drinking, too, and for a time the air seemed to clear. Over the next ten years, as I reached my forties and my father moved into his sixties, we settled on fly-fishing as the safest form of diplomatic relations. On the stream, he was an artist I could admire without reservation, the light flick of the rod, the line looping over the pocket water, the Royal Wulff floating to the rise. It once occurred to me that everything good between us could be told as a string of fishing stories.

That night when we stood shivering in Fruitland, I felt sure we were at least bumping toward peace in our time. Outside his new house in the mountains overlooking Park City, he had installed a hot tub, and we plunged in to soak away our hypothermia. I'd never felt closer to him. This was an illusion. The old poker player had dealt himself a fresh hand. Even naked, as we sat there in the swirling water, he managed to keep his new secret hidden.

My father was in love.

He was leading a double life. Back East he had a growing family, and its members didn't include my mother, my brother, my sister, or me. Each month he would spend three weeks in the mountains, then commute to Washington, where he was drumming up millions of dollars for political causes like the Sierra Club, the National Organization for Women, and gun control. Between flights, he had bumped into a younger woman named Ann Anderson, who had first caught his eye twenty years earlier during his time with the Peace Corps. She was now married and had two children. And when they met, he instantly sensed his old passion rekindle. Once again he felt like a troubadour.

The affair played out like one of my father's favorite movies from the 1950s—*The Captain's Paradise*. Guidebooks still list the film under the following categories: romantic betrayal, love triangles, bigamy. The hero was Alec Guinness, who plays the captain of a ferry between Gibraltar and North Africa, shuttling as wildly as my father was hustling between Utah and the Beltway. In one port the captain has a quiet, well-ordered domestic wife named Maud, in the other a flamethrower called Nita. The arrangement works perfectly until the mouse starts to roar and the hellcat decides to put on an apron.

Something like this happened to my father. Over the next ten years, for no reason I could see, he occasionally fell off the wagon. On his seventy-second birthday, he said he didn't want any parties. He thought he would just go into the woods for a few days to fish and be alone. The morning of the trip, my mother—she had picked up enough suspicious signals over the years to keep him under close surveillance—caught him at the supermarket pushing a shopping basket loaded with supplies, including a bottle of wine and a corkscrew. "Must be someone else's," he said vaguely. "I'm getting absentminded."

He went to look for another basket and my mother went home. But an hour later, her feminine intuition still clanging, she drove down the mountain to the airport, where the Delta flight from Washington arrived each morning. At the gate, she found my father reading a newspaper, waiting for Ann.

"Hello, Tom," said my mother.

"Uh," replied my father.

"Good-bye, Tom."

Ten years of suspicions and betrayals confirmed, she wheeled and ran out. He spent his birthday with his mistress. After eight days he phoned my sister so sodden with alcohol and guilt that he had to check into rehab. Over the next few years, he and my mother tried to repair the damage. He swore he'd broken off with the other woman, which, according to the rules of Courtly Love, is acceptable for any troubadour in a real jam. But he was in love and he didn't mean to let it die. In the end, he and my mother celebrated their Golden Wedding Anniversary with a divorce. During the proceedings, I came home one afternoon to find the red light flashing on my message machine. When I punched the button, I heard the voice of my father saying to the tape: "Ann and I are off to Italy tomorrow. Gotta go where the wild goose goes."

"The Cry of the Wild Goose" was a Frankie Laine ballad that

reached number one on the hit parade five years after my father returned from Italy. The song arrived two full years before the ordinary seven-year itch, but in his own mind, the lyrics had been playing for half a century. They dismissed the love of a woman who made the mistake of loving a foot-loose gander.

I played the message again. My father said, "Just wanted to tell you how much I love you." Then he rang off.

The divorce came through the following spring. When the old wild goose got remarried, I developed such a rage that I refused to talk to him for two years. One afternoon my sister called to tell me that he was hurt over my stony silence. I told her to tell him I thought stony silence was good. That now made two of us.

Fifty-four years after D-day, *Saving Private Ryan* played up the road from Sag Harbor, the village where I live. So far as I could see, everyone else came out of the theater with a lump in the throat, but after the movie I drove home wondering how so many heroes could return from whipping the Germans and then turn into such Huns as fathers. This line of speculation, based on a sample of one, was less than scientific. Obviously I was still seeing my father through the blood in my eye. Even so, I couldn't help feeling that when D-day celebrations rolled around and everyone was having warm feelings about the Last Good War, there was something darker going on below the heroic surface of the Greatest Generation.

By the civilian hourglass, the sand had run out on the war a long time ago. But were we missing something crucial when we saw World War II as simply history? If I was right and my father's war had never come to an end, was it possible that he shared this fate with others among the 16 million Americans who served in World War II? Could it be that among the veterans, men in their seventies, eighties, and nineties—now dying at a rate of more than a thousand a day—the war was still ticking as relentlessly as it had when they were young men wearing wristwatches with glow-in-the-dark dials, those timepieces you synchronized before moving out? And if the war was still seething somewhere inside them, how much collateral damage could be detected among their sons? Did a kinetic force from the war run through the GI Generation to the Boomers, and X-ers, and maybe even to the Next-ers, one generation after another of fathers and sons tuned by the war to the same pitch?

When I poked up an antenna to find out, the first signals were powerful. One day when I was trudging on the treadmill at the Personal Best Fitness Studio in Sag Harbor, the man sweating next to me said out of the blue that he had never had an open talk with his father about World War II. "Not once. Not one single time." On reflection, he added, they had never had an open talk about anything. Another time, on Memorial Day, I went into the hardware store to buy some batteries. On the counter next to the cash register was a snapshot of a young GI in a muddy trench during the Battle of the Bulge. I asked the owner of the store if he knew the GI's name, and he told me the young soldier was his father. Beyond that, the photo remained a mystery. "My old man wouldn't talk about the war. Ever." The picture came from an album his father had kept to himself for fifty years, taking it out of its hiding place only when he knew he was dying. Not long before he faded away, one of the last things he did was ask his son to make sure the album went to his grandson.

In spite of the outpouring of well-deserved tributes to the Greatest Generation in recent years, I started to wonder whether the Last Good War might be the Last Best Kept Secret. The more sons and fathers I talked to, the more I felt a small shock of recognition: Maybe this wasn't just about me. What would happen if I could find some way to rewind the tape?

As an experiment, I flew to Salt Lake City and drove back to the little house on Mill Creek, which I hadn't seen for fifty years. It was dusk when I arrived. Pulling up to the curb, I parked and walked around to the backyard. Even in the fading light, the silhouette of the roof to which I'd clung as a small boy was unmistakable. But I was not looking at a garage. In front of me, roughly at the level of my knees, stood a squat little doghouse.

A *doghouse?*

The discrepancy between the memory and the reality dumbfounded me. If anything marked the way I felt about my father, it was a certainty that I had sorted the past accurately, calculated all the angles, gotten him right. The truth was that I couldn't tell the difference between a place where you parked your car and a place where you parked your dog. The day he held his arms out to me, I was sure I would fall miles if I jumped and he blew the catch. Now, I saw that the plunge would have been something like three feet. You could measure it on any yardstick. On an impulse, I walked over to the house and stepped into the window well that had once swallowed me. The cement trim barely grazed my kneecap.

At that moment the lights in the house went on and a woman started yelling. She had seen my legs poking down in the darkness, trying to touch bottom, and her reaction matched mine toward the porcupine. This was not something I thought I could explain to her or the police. At her scream, I jumped from the window well, ran to the car, and burned rubber all the way down Twenty-third East.

A few days later I was muttering to myself on the treadmill back at Personal Best when Lester Ware, the owner, walked over to ask me how I was doing. I launched into an obsessive account of Doghouse Day. By this time I had polished the story so long and hard that it always reflected me at my personal best. But the look that Les shot me suggested that he wasn't anywhere near as impressed as I thought he should be. Les is an Olympics-class wrestler. He looks like Buddha and has otherworldly powers of concentration. He emanates the energy of a shaman operating from the fourth astral plane.

"What was your father thinking?" he asked me.

"Thinking? What do you mean, thinking?"

"When you wouldn't jump into his arms. What was he thinking?"

"He was thinking I was a little chickenshit. Worthless. No guts."

"I don't think so," Les said, shaking his head. "Try again."

"It won't work."

"Come on. Put yourself in his place."

"Nothing there," I said, finding it impossible to see anything at all from my father's point of view.

Les studied the ceiling for a moment. His voice fell a few decibels to the deep bass he reserves for hard cases.

"He was hurt."

"Hurt?" I said. "Are you kidding me? That guy was a killer."

"What are you, blind? Think about it. Your father's been away fighting in the war. He's had his ass shot off. He's seen his friends die. He makes it back alive, and on the day he gets home, his own son doesn't trust him. And you still don't see he was hurt? I'd say you're the one with the problem. What are you going to do about it?"

The first thing I did was cringe. Then I went home and took a shower. After that, I pulled out the record of my father's first Army physical. My sister Anne, keeper of the family records, had sent it to me. Stripped naked, he had weighed into the Army at 137 pounds. He stood five-six. That day at the doghouse, I had put him at about nine feet. When the doctors strapped the tape around him, his waist measured 30 inches—probably sucked in—and his chest went 35 inches, undoubtedly puffed out, but even so. As the next reality check, I stepped on the doctor's scale I keep outside my bathroom. Tommy Two now stood a touch under six feet and went 245 pounds. But inside this King Kong, who was struggling to get out? Pinocchio, trying to become a real boy? Couldn't I do better than that?

To advance any further, I needed someone who understood soldiers. So I enlisted the help of Col. David Hackworth, an old friend whose military career started in Italy near Trieste on the same ground and only a few months after my father left for home. Colonel Hackworth is a legend in the United States Army. He lied about his age to enter the Army at fifteen and went on over the next few wars to be awarded two Distinguished Service Crosses, ten Silver Stars, and eight Purple Hearts. He knows how to separate the men from the boys.

We got in his car and set off to buy a quart of ice cream.

"How's your old man?" he asked me.

"The guy dumped my mother," I said. "I'm gonna piss on his grave."

I stared out the window. Hack gave it some time, considering the way I was proposing to be mamma's little helper.

"You ought to cut your old man a little slack," he said.

"What the hell for?"

"He was with the 10th Mountain Division, right? Those men saw a lot of shit. They were fighting Hitler's best, not old men and boys. A lot of them got killed. When you see that, it does something to you. War changes you completely and for all time. No man comes home from war the same—not a single fucking guy."

Hack's lesson was too clear to miss: The real question for a son was not "What did you do in the war, Daddy?" It was, "What did the war do to you?" So, what if my father and I went back to Italy together? What if we recrossed the battlefields that changed him for all time before he returned to start overhauling me?

On my father's eighty-first birthday, I called him for the first time in twenty-four months. A woman picked up the phone. "This is Tom Mathews," I said. "The other one." The woman muffled the receiver with her hand. In the background I could hear my father's voice. "My God," he was saying. "Is that my son?" When he got on the line, I wished him happy birthday. Then I asked if he'd like to go back to Italy. Why didn't we climb Riva Ridge together, assault Mount Belvedere and Rocca Corneta? We could retake Torre Iussi, cross the Po River, storm Torbole and Garda.

"What a great fucking idea."

That was all he said the first call. A week or so later, I was sitting in my living room, poring over maps, when the new cordless phone at my elbow rang. I punched the talk button and heard a familiar voice:

"Tom Mathews?"

It was my voice. Me.

How weird, I thought. How could I be talking to myself over my own phone? I looked at the handset. Were they fitting them out now for karaoke?

"Hey, it's me. Your father. The old *paisano*."

His voice and mine were identical. I still couldn't tell us apart. Struggling out of *The Twilight Zone*, I started to tell him about dates, airlines, hotels, lines of march.

"You're in charge," he said. "You just say jump—I'll say 'How high?' "

Jump?

This time I was going to tell *him* to jump?

I started to laugh. When he asked why, all I could say was that we'd have a lot to talk about if we ever got to Italy. The minute he hung up, I felt a small stab of panic. The two of us weren't carrying just baggage from the past; we were carrying steamer trunks. I needed to lighten the load. Growing up in the shadow of the Greatest Generation meant a son also had to grow out of it, and, at a ridiculously old age, I still wasn't sure I knew how. Then, from somewhere beyond the range of logic, an idea occurred to me. One night, driving down the Long Island Expressway, I found myself humming "Give me some men . . . " an old Sigmund Romberg number recycled by romantics into a theme song for World War II. The lyrics went like this:

> *Give me some men who are stouthearted men*
> *Who will fight for the right they adore.*

The follow-through was that if you started with the right ten men, you'd soon see ten thousand more. There were other verses about getting guns for the sons of the ones who have won all our wars ("No more guns for you."); something else about men advancing shoulder to shoulder and bolder and bolder "as they grow and they go to the fore." Corny but rousing. Something still running on the electricity of a time before Hell No I Won't Go.

One of the reasons Hack and I got along was that he discovered I knew all the words. When I was little and playing soldier, I used to sing

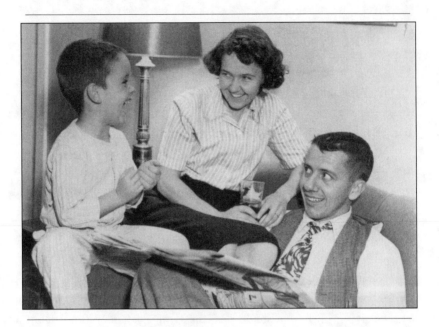

The Mathews family, an American Dream, 1948

the song at the top of my lungs. So did Hack, who then spent his life as the real thing. No one knew more about soldiers than soldiers; the same could be said of fathers and sons. All you had to do to see how World War II was still coursing through their lives was ask them. Why not recruit a squad to exchange stories, compare notes? No science. No sociology. No psychological drumrolls. Just ten fathers and ten sons including my old man and me. The mission would not be to question the nobility or sacrifice of the Greatest Generation, but to look for something hidden in the afterglow. The idea was quixotic, I admit. Basically, I was preparing to get closer to my father by staying as far away from him as possible. But why not? Get a horse, I told myself. Move out.

Chapter 2

Prisoner of War

Lt. Murray Greenberg, navigator,
U.S. Army Eighth Air Force,
England, 1943

Broken clouds over Leipzig. A green flare in Bedfordshire.

Go.

In the nose of a Flying Fortress poised on the runway at Thurleigh Airfield, Lt. Murray Greenberg leans over the small navigator's table tucked beneath a .50-caliber machine gun. In the cockpit just above him, the pilot is checking his instruments: superchargers pumped, fuel cells topped off, cowlings secure, props in good trim. Out on the wings, four 1,200-horsepower Wright Cyclone engines rumble to life, and the Fort, its bomb bay loaded with five-hundred-pounders, rolls down the airstrip. Lifting off, it rises though drizzle and ice to twenty-five thousand feet, where the sky is black with a thousand bombers heading for Germany. Outside, the temperature is sixty degrees below zero. During the climb, Lieutenant Greenberg reviews the odds on his life: five missions complete, twenty to go. Most men, he knows, never make it to fifteen.

Each of these heavy bombers of the United States Army's Eighth Air Force—the Mighty Eighth—has a crew of ten men: four officers and six enlisted men. On February 20, 1944, Lieutenant Greenberg was one of roughly ten thousand Allied fliers—pilots and copilots, navigators, radio operators, bombardiers, waist gunners, tail gunners, and ball turret gunners—approaching Leipzig. Through the Plexiglas as they looked to their future, all they could see were black puffs of flak.

Five time zones to the west, on St. Marks Avenue in Brooklyn, Shirley Greenberg, her belly swelling with a son, turned out the lights and slipped into bed. Soothed by her heartbeat, Harvey Joel Greenberg, four months to takeoff, settles in for the night, all systems go at 98.6 degrees.

BLAMMMMMNNNGGGG.

Steel rips through the fuselage. One of the waist gunners screams in agony. The bomber heaves like a huge, wounded beast. Smoke blinds the navigator. He hears the pilot's voice in the earphones. BAIL OUT! BAIL OUT! NOW!

Groping for the aft door, he jumps. Spinning in the prop wash, he sees the pilot leap, pinwheel against the falling bomber, and disappear in a red spray like a bug on a windshield. Then he hears the loud crack of his chute, and he is swinging back and forth, floating down to earth. A farmer takes him in and gives him food and coffee. Then the Germans find him and take him to a camp for fallen birdmen.

Sunup in Brooklyn. Shirley Greenberg opens the blackout curtains, and the light falls across the photograph of Lieutenant Greenberg she keeps on the dresser next to her bed. His letters begin "Dearest Shandel." His angel. But the mailman brings her nothing that day. Nothing the next day, nothing the next week. Then the telegram comes:

> The Secretary of War desires me to express his deep regret that your husband Second Lieutenant Murray S. Greenberg has been reported missing in action since twenty February in mission to Germany. Period. If further details or other information are received you will be promptly notified. Period.

Period.
For a month, she prays. Then a second telegram arrives:

> Report just received through the International Red Cross states that your husband Second Lieutenant Murray S. Breenberg is a prisoner of war of the German government. The Adjutant General.

Breenberg? Who is this Breenberg? Do they have the wrong man, the wrong wife? Please, God, no. But it is her husband, even if the War Department can't spell his name. The Germans have roughed up Lieutenant Greenberg and clapped him in Stalag Luft I with nearly nine thousand other Allied airmen. The camp's registrar, spotting the Star of David on his dog tags, has enrolled him as a Jew—POW 2817. Four months later, that is where he is still sitting when the International Red Cross in Geneva finally relays a message to him from back home:

> Lovely son Harvey Joel born seventeen June. Both very well.
> Love wife, Shirley Greenberg.

In the year that followed, POW 2817 survived on starvation rations in Stalag Luft I. After the Russians liberated the camp, he was deloused, put on milk and rice to soothe his ravaged innards, and sent home. The day he reached Brooklyn, his Angel showed him his son.

"Why is he so fat, Shirley?"

"He's a baby, Murray."

"Why did you call him Harvey?"

"I thought you'd like it."

"You should have called him Henry."

The first time I heard this story, I felt a sneaking sense of relief: Maybe it wasn't just my father and me. Outwardly, Lieutenants Greenberg and Mathews came from two entirely different worlds: the Mormon from Zion, the Jew from the Bronx; one an artillery officer, the other an airman. Lieutenant Greenberg played the violin. Lieutenant Mathews climbed rocks. But their first day back from the war, their first glimpse of their sons—Fatty and the Coward—made them a matched pair. Harvey Joel and I were born within a few weeks of each other; the two lieutenants might as well have returned on the same boat. The two reunions in the summer of 1945 were equally disastrous: the smoldering fathers, the cringing sons, the mystified wife-mothers struggling to put things right—nothing going according to plan.

Steven Greenberg, Harvey's younger brother, told me what happened. I met him a few years ago more or less by chance. His wife cuts my wife's hair. Her name is Deborah, and when Lucille told her that I had become obsessed with my father and World War II, she laughed and said, "You think *yours* is bad? You should talk to mine." I ran into Steven a few days later at Canio's Books on Main Street. He was ordering some Robert Bly translations of Pablo Neruda's poems and I was cruising for war stories. Steven is a landscape designer. He is a tall man, easy and athletic in his stance, with a soft voice, and, even at fifty, the eyes of a designated hitter. When I asked him about his father and brother, he looked, for just an instant, as if I had mugged him. Then he said, "Their lives were a constant battle zone."

Harvey was a plump little boy with a round moon face, good-natured and full of energy, the pride of his mother and aunts. Shirley nicknamed him Hank after Hank Greenberg, baseball's first Jewish superstar. Greenberg fought in the China-Burma-India theater of operations; he returned to Detroit and Briggs Stadium for the 1945 pennant race about the same time Murray got home. Shirley meant for the name to please her soldier, but it didn't work. Nothing about Harvey seemed to please Murray, who skipped all the basics of fatherhood with his first son: He didn't toss him up and down, he didn't haul him around on his back, he didn't buy him a bat and glove or take him fishing. "I can't remember my father ever playing with Harvey," Steve said. "Look in the family album, you see Dad holding Harvey, but there's no sign of affection. Ever. It was as if Dad never felt Harvey was his son."

The first thing Lieutenant Greenberg did after mustering out was to barrage Shirley with a campaign for a new child. The following year she gave birth to a daughter named Laura. Over the next ten years, to the astonishment of the Greenberg family, Murray ignored Harvey completely, concentrating on his daughter, turning her into his own Shirley Temple. He bought her corsages, squired her into Manhattan, took her to dinner and the theater. Since she was only six years old, this performance struck everyone as eccentric, but no one said anything about it. Eventually he closed the show, leaving Laura as bewildered as Harvey by his moods. When they joined forces in self-defense, Steven told me, Murray started lobbying for a replacement. "My father kept saying, 'Shirley, one more. One more. We'll have a son.' "

"Your father was talking as if Harvey didn't even exist," I said.

"That's right. For years he nudged my mother. She told him she was finished with children, but he kept at it until finally she said okay and I was born. I was the son he wanted, a second chance. What little love my father had to give, he gave to me. He didn't love Harvey, and both of them knew it."

From beginning to end, neither Murray nor Harvey Greenberg ever understood what had hit them: rotten karma, mutant genes, pick a demon any demon, nothing explained it. They fought each other all their lives, they both died young, and they both died disgusted with each other. From the sidelines, Steven asked his mother to explain what was happening to their family. "The war," she would begin, and then she would change the subject. That was the way things went for nearly fifty years. When she was in her late seventies and moving into an assisted-care apartment, she gave Steven and Laura a box that she had been hiding since 1945. She had never mentioned the box or its contents. When Steven and his sister opened it, they found all of their father's service records, his medals and battle ribbons, a set of handwritten journals, and more than one hundred love letters that he had written to his Shandel from Stalag Luft I. "The box came out of nowhere," Steven said quietly. "We were in tears when we opened it. It was like, why didn't we have this when we were kids? Why was this man's life so hidden from us?"

One morning a few days later, I heard thumping out on my front porch. Beyond the glass front door, Steven was stamping snow off his boots. Under his arm he was carrying a scuffed brown package tied with string. I let him in and pulled up two chairs. He put a large accordion file on the table between us. For a moment he studied the beat-up folder as if he might be making a mistake. Then he said, "Maybe this can help. Believe me, my father never talked about this stuff—ever."

Untying the string, he started pulling things out of the folder: a photograph of 2nd Lt. Murray Greenberg newly commissioned as a navigator; a thick sheaf of military records; a Caterpillar Club certificate from a New Jersey parachute company honoring downed fliers who had to hit the silk. After that, he drew out a Nazi armband, starched and neatly ironed. "Something Dad grabbed in the camp," he said, tossing it on the table next to a soiled German songbook.

He had assembled this sampling from the larger trove his mother had hidden away. Three years had passed since the material had come to light, but, as Steven talked, it became clear that the box had not yet given up its secrets. "I'm still piecing things together," he said, almost apologetically. The file folder he'd brought contained only a few letters. He told me he still found the others too painful to read. "I'm working through them very slowly. It's not a marathon—when I'm in the mood, a letter or two—I'm just letting it be." Feeling like a grave-robber, I asked if I could keep the folder for a while.

"I knew you were going to ask me," he said. "I just don't know how I feel about that. Usually, I'd say, 'Take it.' I'm not the sort of person who . . . but this stuff . . . even coming here . . . I thought . . . it'll be such a drag if I say no."

The words stumbled over the feelings, and for a moment both of us sat at the table paralyzed. Finally, because I couldn't think of anything to say, I went over to my desk and pulled out my picture of Lt. Tom Mathews. When I handed it to Steven, he reached over and picked up the photograph of his father, which he placed side by side with mine. "Look at those kids," he said. "Look at the smiles on their faces. They didn't know where they were going or what was going to happen to them. They didn't get it until they got their balls kicked in."

For a moment he studied the paired images. Then he shook his head.

"It's the same picture," he said. "They're the same guy."

On a snowy night a few days later, I went over to Steven's house, where I found him sitting next to the fireplace, mulling over our earlier conversation. In the firelight, what came back to him most vividly were his father's relentless drive and violent mood swings. "That's all I remember about him—his working. He was a workaholic, totally, always on edge. He had a very short fuse, and he'd just blow. Over anything—little things. He was free with his hands and he was free with the strap. He used it on Harvey, he used it on my sister, and he used it on me."

After the war, he told me, Murray Greenberg became a prosperous furrier in Manhattan's garment district. A shortage of funds didn't explain his frenzy. He could pay his bills, meet the $115 mortgage on a four-bedroom house with a large backyard in Freeport. Even so, he took a second job. Every night for three to four hours, he sat in an office behind a phone squeezing deadbeats for a bill collector. Each morning he got up at 5:00 A.M., grabbed breakfast, and hit the Long Island Rail

Road for Penn Station. At 6:00 each evening, he would come through the door, wolf down dinner, then go to the collection agency until 11:00 P.M. Sometimes on Saturday evenings, after Sabbath, he would take Shirley out dancing. On Sundays he would retreat to the backyard, collapse in a lawn chair, and pass out. "I go back to my early childhood, he wasn't there," Steve said, his voice in neutral. "He never took me anywhere. He never went to any of my basketball games. He never went to any of my baseball games—no, wait, he went to one Little League game and I hit a home run—but that was it. He was never home."

Then, with an abrupt lurch, Murray Greenberg would reverse into manic generosity. Once, when Steven was seven, his father came home unannounced and said "Come with me." When the little boy asked his father where they were going, his father told him, "Just come on." They drove to a sporting goods store in Rockville Centre. "Get what you want," Murray Greenberg said. "It was like a free-for-all," Steven remembered, smiling wistfully. "I bought a baseball glove, I bought a bat. I bought a five-speed bike. Everything I could lay my hands on. I came home with all this stuff, and that was it. Everything in one shot. Then nothing. That just about sums him up."

With Murray running hot and cold, Harvey took over as his younger brother's designated father. It was Harvey, not Murray, who taught Steven how to swing a bat and not throw a baseball like a girl. Out in the backyard, it was Harvey who showed him how you knit your fingers around the laces of the football to give your passes a better spiral. On the basketball court, it was Harvey who taught him how to set a pick. Harvey never ran out on him. He came home and coached his brother every day.

But by the time Harvey reached his teens, he could be just as explosive as their father. "Oh yeah. He beat me up all the time," Steven said. To survive in the no-man's-land between his father and brother, Steven had to develop protective armor, the quick feint, the timely white lie. Even though his father favored him, he told me, he knew he couldn't trust him. And like me, he was afraid. "I didn't want his wrath, I didn't want to get what my brother got." So as life gyrated forward, he improvised, the same way I had always vamped, tiptoeing around his father, bunkering his feelings, sealing off openings.

When Harvey went to college, his father insisted that he live at home: It was cheaper than a dorm at Hofstra or a separate apartment. Beyond that, Murray Greenberg was convinced that if he let Harvey out of his sight, his son would only screw up. One night his fuse popped over Harvey's latest infraction. Steven saw his father barrel down the upstairs hallway toward his brother, steaming in rage. But Harvey had filled out over the years, and on that particular night he held his ground. Lifting Murray Greenberg, he turned him around and pinned him hard against the wall. "Never again," son warned father. "Don't touch me ever again. If you come at me again, I'm going to lay you out."

Steven, nine years old, watched as his older brother lowered their father to the floor. Then Harvey went into the bedroom and closed the door. "I was screaming and crying," Steven told me. "My mother, as usual, was trying to make it okay—she was always trying to keep the peace. I watched my father and mother go down the stairs and into the living room. She sat in her chair and started to cry, and he got on his hands and knees in front of her, and I heard him saying, "What is wrong with me?" Over and over. "My God, what is wrong with me?"

No one ever found out what was wrong with Murray Greenberg. Shirley Greenberg had her own theory. "The war killed him," she told her children. "He was never the same man." For twenty-five years, she had been telling herself that something terrible in her husband's body explained what was wrong in his soul. Sometimes in bed at night, he would groan and reach for his leg, and when they turned back the covers, he would be bleeding: a tiny point of steel was working its way out of his flesh. The war explained everything, she told Steven. She took his father to a doctor who thought that a needle of flak no one had caught might be causing his misery.

There was no way to be sure. At that time they didn't have MRI machines, they couldn't do CAT scans. All they knew was that the patient was getting worse. As the sixties petered out into the seventies, he began to have trouble walking; his arms and legs would cramp, he'd suddenly twitch, lurch, and fall. Some days he found it difficult to swallow, then to breathe. Eventually, in the late 1960s, Shirley took him to a Veterans Administration hospital, where an alert doctor detected the symptoms of amyotrophic lateral sclerosis—Lou Gehrig's disease. The diagnosis explained part of Murray Greenberg's odd behavior—the twitches that convulsed his limbs—but not much more. In men, ALS develops with middle age, so it didn't explain the frenzy of his life from the middle 1940s through the middle 1960s. All ALS really did was finish him off.

By the time he reached forty-nine, he could no longer walk. He could barely talk. His fur business went under, leaving Shirley with only five thousand dollars. She took a day job. In the mornings and after school, Steven, fifteen, encased in rage—at the doctors, at his old man, at himself—dressed, bathed, and watched over his father. Just before the end, they took Murray Greenberg back to the VA hospital. For a brief moment he went into a remission that gave him back his power of speech. When the doctors called with the good news, Steve rushed to the hospital, where he leaned over his father's wheelchair, hoping for a reconciliation. Looking up at the son, the dying father said, "Get a haircut."

Steve stared into the fire. "Those were the last words my father spoke. No 'I love you.' No 'I love your mother.' Just, 'Get a haircut.' It blew my circuits. At his funeral there were no tears."

On the day of the funeral, Harvey was twenty-six, Steve was seventeen. What Steve felt initially was an enormous sense of "My father wasn't around anymore—he'd set me free." But it wasn't going to be as easy as that. In the years that followed, whatever corrosion was eating at the father kept working on the sons. Steve told me he knew that was true thirty years ago, and he still feels it today. "I don't think I've ever gotten to the depth of my dad," he said, his voice falling so low you could barely hear it, and then rising to a confession: "I gotta tell you, I'm still seventeen with my dad. That's where I am—stuck."

Murray Greenberg was not a father you could shed like a worn-out coat. Long after his death, he haunted both of his sons. "What was I going to do?" Steven said bleakly. "I pretended to be someone I really wasn't. That was the safe bet. I just didn't want to get the strap. It was a matter of survival—I've carried it with me my whole life." What about Harvey, I asked him. "Harvey got to do battle with our father. Almost to be victorious. Physically, the old man couldn't overpower him. So Harvey got to dispel him, cast him aside. I never had any kind of relationship with the guy. Maybe my brother was better off in some way. I think he was at peace. My father had died, he hated him. That was it."

After his father's funeral, Steven went to San Francisco to check out Haight-Ashbury. Toward the end of the Vietnam War, his draft board ordered him to report for classification. Scamming the Selective Service System in a way his father would never have done during World War II, he kept moving, shifting addresses. Each hop got him a three-month delay, until General Hershey finally threatened to arrest him. At that point, he went to Canada. "I was over the border. I was gone. My mother told me to do it. Only time in her life she was proactive. She wasn't going to let what happened to her husband happen to her son. She said to me, 'No way is it gonna happen to you. No way are you going to war.' She knew. In her naive way, she knew." With thirty-five hundred dollars in his pocket, he kept driving north until his stash was enough to buy him a 160-acre farm. A week later Richard Nixon unplugged the draft. So, Steven could come home. But he still owns the farm today. Although he hasn't seen it in eighteen years, he refuses to sell it. Deb thinks he is crazy. He says he's only taking the normal precautions.

After slipping and sliding for ten years, he came to see that the one person over thirty he really couldn't trust was himself. "I led a life of trying to have the least possible responsibility," he reflected. "I grew physically, but not emotionally. Whenever I got close to someone, I'd make sure it would blow apart." At that point he met Deb Rossow. His equilibrium improving, he dragged a local judge to a bird sanctuary on the edge of Long Island Sound and they got married. "Something said to me, you can't run. You have to make your stand." If he saw the irony in what he had just said, he kept it to himself: The metaphor he used for pulling himself together was military.

While Steven was struggling to reassemble the fragments of his life, Harvey was flying apart. First his health collapsed. He developed agonizing stabs in the gut that his doctors attributed to stress. When he reached his thirties, he developed Crohn's disease, a life-threatening knotting of the intestines. By thirty-one he was wearing a colostomy bag under his shirt. In his forties he developed throat cancer, possibly because of the steroids used to treat his plumbing. After surgeons removed his larynx, he had to speak with a device pressed to his throat. He sounded like a robot and sometimes behaved like one. Harvey had a son, but as a father he was often remote. "It was awful," Steve said. "I'd tell him, 'You're just like our old man.' "

The boy who was too chubby the day his father got home from the war died when he was fifty-seven. He went fishing one morning off Seaford, on the South Shore of Long Island. It was a nice day and he had a few beers and fell off the stern. It took only ten minutes to fish him out, but by then, seawater had flooded the tracheal hole in his throat and he was gone. The day Harvey drowned, he couldn't even shout for help.

The fire had burned down on the hearth. Steve finished the story and rose, offering to heat another cup of herb tea. But both of us had had enough for one night. At the door, we shook hands. It was still snowing in the village. Peering down Main Street, he warned me to watch out for the ice.

Was Shirley Greenberg right? Had the war killed her husband? Did he live out the rest of his life as an otherwise undiagnosed zombie? Weren't fathers supposed to be ecstatic over their first son? What had made him turn away from Harvey? Perhaps some answers could be extracted from Shandel's archive. When I proposed this to Steven a few days later, he agreed to let me spend some more time with the trove if I didn't mind shifting operations to his kitchen.

The next morning, I turned up at the Greenberg house early. After clearing the kitchen table, Deb gave me a hot cup of tea and told me I could stay as long as it took. Then she went out and came back a few minutes later with a narrow box and a small straw basket. Putting them on the table next to Steven's folder, she left for work. "Clueless men," she said, breezing out the door. "What would you do without women?"

I spilled the contents of the little basket on the table. Out fell a bronze medal with a screaming eagle, thunderbolts clutched in its talons; a set of sterling silver wings; a Purple Heart. Inside the box I found a tangle of buttons and pins that turned out to be two complete sets of insignia from the U.S. Army Air Corps, plus a second lieutenant's bars and a navigator's winged propellers; and five strips of campaign ribbons in blue and orange, brown, red and green. Lieutenant Greenberg had been awarded two Bronze Stars for valor.

The smallest item, not much bigger than a tie tack, I almost missed. It was a pale gold pin with a blue enamel field. On the field was a Star of David. The largest was a rectangle of gray metal, heavy, and about the size of a credit card. When I flipped it over in my hand, I saw the words Stalag Luft I. Above the name of the prison camp, someone with a hammer and steel punch had pounded in the number 2817. What I had in my hand was Lieutenant Greenberg's POW tag.

The pieces were all there in the box, jumbled but at hand if I could complete the puzzle. Rummaging in Steve's accordion file, I found the picture of Lieutenant Greenberg and propped it open on the table like the picture on the box top of a conventional jigsaw puzzle. Below the face, I organized the insignia, medals, and ribbons, arranging them in front of the picture as if they were pinned to his uniform. The exercise was whimsical, but it produced immediate results. Steven was right about the similarity between the photograph of his father and my father. This one, like mine, had clearly been shot before Murray Greenberg left for the war. On his uniform he was wearing only basic insignia, not the items I had spilled from the basket. They had come later. What I had arranged on the table in front of me were the medals on a dead man's chest.

Fascinated, I arranged the swastika armband, the small Wehrmacht songbook *(mit melodien),* and a pair of Luftwaffe pilot scarves off to one side. The tabletop was beginning to take on the look of one of those introductory panoramas on *Masterpiece Theatre.* I became so absorbed in it that I didn't hear Steven come into the kitchen.

"I've never seen it like that," he said, looking over my shoulder at the expanding montage. "I've never seen it all come together."

"What happened to his uniform?" I asked him.

"Harvey kept it."

"Harvey? Harvey who hated him?"

"Yeah, that's right. Weird, isn't it?"

The same Harvey who was supposed to have died cursing his old man had kept his uniform. The connection between them, bent in ten different directions, had remained intact. The thought prompted Steven to remember that he still had his old man's footlocker out in the barn. He'd taken it with him wherever he went until the metal bottom finally rusted and fell out. Steven's footlocker reminded me of my father's Army parka. I had worn it until its fine white down stuffing started leaking so badly from the seams that even slobs wouldn't sit next to me. Why would a son do that if he really hated his father's guts?

The next item from Steven's folder was an old envelope, Post Office tan, containing a U.S. Savings Bond wrapper (empty), Western Union Money in a Hurrygram (also empty), and a small postcard from Local Board 112 in the Bronx:

Official Business

Notice of Classification

1-A

(until____, 19____)

The classification, Murray Greenberg's ticket to World War II, was blank, valid from here to eternity, an open-ended invitation to be killed. The Tremont Station had postmarked the card 2 P.M., February 9, 1942. I turned it over in my hand, trying to grasp what he had felt the day it arrived at his parents' apartment on Morris Avenue. Who was this young man Uncle Sam wanted so badly and for such a long time?

The basics were on a brittle sheet of paper: Army Air Force Form No. 5.

Serial Number 0-688432

2nd Lt. Murray S. Greenberg

Born: 18 September 1919 in New York

Commissioned: 5 Aug. 1943, in San Marcos, Texas

Height: 5' 10" Weight 150, hair, black, eyes, brown

Parents: Naturalized, from Russia

Wife's Address: 1466 St. Marks Avenue, Brooklyn, NY.

Says he has 3 years college, says major was Public Speaking, fin-
    ished in 1939.

The Army didn't need any more than that. The form made me re-member something Steve had told me that first night by the fire. He had taken his own son and daughter to Ellis Island to trace their Green-berg ancestors. During the great wave of immigration that came just before World War I, his grandfather and grandmother had left villages fifteen miles apart in the Pale of Settlement for the United States. Their son, Murray Greenberg, was born just after Woodrow Wilson's war to end all wars, which made him a prime recruit for the next one, even though violence was never part of his nature. He'd grown up within egg cream range of the Grand Concourse, speaking Yiddish, a free spirit who broke with the Orthodox Judaism of his father.

His reaction to the draft notice was galvanic: He asked Shirley to marry him. In her box, she had kept a wedding picture showing him in his tux, eyes twinkling, a Morris Avenue David Niven with a pencil mustache, the three sharp points of his handkerchief poking up from his pocket, knife-edge creases in his trousers, looking into the camera as if youth and goodness alone could defeat Adolf Hitler. A second picture, this one of Shirley, shows a heartbreaker with black hair done in a tight finger wave, her eyebrows wickedly plucked, her lipstick precise; she's elegant, sexy, irresistible—the knockout who became his angel.

Poking around the folder, I pulled out a huge, crumbling envelope marked: Full Service Records of Greenberg, Murray S. 0688432. Ten copies of everything. He had enlisted in June 1942, doing his basic training that summer, making private first class, then going on to radar school, where he made corporal. At that point, the Army, certain beyond dispute that all bright Jewish boys were wizards at math, made him an aviation cadet and sent him to navigator's school. He did his preflight training at Eglington Field, then qualified as a navigator in San Marcos, Texas. In August 1943 the Army commissioned him as a second lieutenant, issued him a .45 sidearm, and sent him to Geiger Field in Washington to learn the ways of the Flying Fortress. No one had told him that while the Army trusted his brains, a lot of pilots, mostly Southern, didn't like Jews.

About that time, Harvey was conceived. In the middle of November 1943, Murray shipped out for England, not knowing that Shirley was pregnant. He was assigned to the 306th Bomber Group (Heavy), known around Thurleigh Airfield in Bedfordshire as "The Reich Wreckers." When he arrived, it was not entirely clear who was wrecking whom. In the Mighty Eighth, losses were so high that it had become almost statistically impossible to complete the twenty-five missions required to go home. Before the war was over, 30,000 airmen from the outfit were dead or missing and another 30,000 were scattered across German prison camps. Like Yossarian in *Catch-22*, Lieutenant Greenberg was left to ponder just who, exactly, was trying hardest to kill him.

Within his Records Jacket, I found the following box score:

Combat Record:

1944

Jan. 14 . . . first combat mission, 4:30 hours

Jan. 21 . . . second combat mission, 5 hours

Jan. 29 . . . third combat mission . . . 7:30 hours

Jan. 30 . . . fourth combat mission . . . 7:05 hours

Feb. 1 . . . fifth combat mission . . . 8:15 hours

Feb. 20 . . . MISSING IN ACTION

Missing in action. Over and out. Where was the rest of him?

Upending the folder in a puff of dust, I spilled out all that was left. What I saw on the table was the beginning of a paper trail leading directly into the missing sixteen months of Murray Greenberg's life: a few yellowing newspaper clippings, a handful of letters, and two small composition books with faded blue covers, the kind European children use in school (Printed in Sweden, *Kriegesgef. Hilfe*—Y.M.C.A. War Prisoner's Aid Program). The longest of the news clippings carried the byline of Sgt. Andy Rooney, a *Stars and Stripes* reporter starting out on the career that took him to the top of CBS and *60 Minutes*. ("The greatest collection of American air aces ever assembled sat, some of them a year and a half, in Stalag Luft I, the German prison camp at Barth on the Baltic, before they were freed.") Those aces included Col. Hubert "Hub" Zemke, commander of the 56th Fighter Group, "The Wolfpack," a P-51 Mustang jockey with nineteen kills, and Lt. Col. Francis "Gabby" Gabreski, also of the 56FG, who flew P-47 Thunderbolts, outscoring everyone else in the Eighth with twenty-eight to his credit. The Germans had jammed nine thousand Allied prisoners into the camp's wooden barracks; daily rations were a loaf of bread for seven men and a bowl of turnip potato stew. "A good mess manager would tell you there were worms in the food. A bad mess manager wouldn't tell you."

Lieutenant Greenberg had also saved a clip reporting that Col. Henry Spicer, who arrived three months after he did, was sentenced to death and placed in solitary confinement, where he was awaiting execution "for giving a pep talk to the prisoners." The smallest of the clippings, wrinkled, slowly disintegrating, said this:

> The Swiss Radio confirmed yesterday reports out in the last days of the war that Adolf Hitler ordered all Allied prisoners to be shot. The President of the International Red Cross says the Wehrmacht refused to carry out the order after Dr. Burkhardt of the International Red Cross met Himmler and got permission for the Red Cross to enter POW camps to prevent any last-minute executions.

Dr. Burkhardt had made his trip in March 1945. For sixteen months, Lieutenant Greenberg and the other men in the camp had gotten out of the sack each morning not knowing whether or not today would be the day the Germans meant to shoot them—Jews like Lieutenant Greenberg most likely at the head of the line.

On the cover of the first composition book, he had written "Books Read as a 'Kriege.' (Listed Alphabetically by Author)." Inside, he had compiled an astounding bibliography. Instead of scratching days on the wall to keep track of time, he obsessively listed the books he read, hundreds of them, putting a small star after his favorites. The collection ran from Jane Austen to Voltaire. He'd started with classics: *Bulfinch's Mythology* and Dante's *Inferno*, Samuel Pepys's *Diary* and Stephen Crane's *Red Badge of Courage*, Lytton Strachey's *Eminent Victorians* and Herman Melville's *Moby-Dick*. He'd stuffed himself on Charles Dickens and Anatole France, Mark Twain and Rudyard Kipling, John Steinbeck and Robert Louis Stevenson. At odd hours, he'd dip into *Skiing for Beginners and Mountaineers*. One of the entries went beyond irony: He had, for a time, lost himself in Frank Graham's *Lou Gehrig: A Quiet Hero*.

The reading list represented the state of Lieutenant Greenberg's soul. The state of his body he entrusted to a second, much shorter list: German Rations Per Week. On it, gram by gram, he recorded what he ate—a near-starvation diet of black bread, potatoes, and turnips, with an occasional scrap of horse meat or wurst. Behind the weekly menu, he drew up a list called the "POW's Ideal Red Cross Parcel." The parcels kept the men in the camp from going under: Canada sent the best butter, jam, and corned beef; the British forwarded the finest tea, cocoa, bacon, pudding, and oatmeal; the U.S. the best roast beef, tinned salmon, Spam, sugar, chocolate, and cigarettes.

The final entry in Lieutenant Greenberg's book of lists was a two-page address book: thirty-one names, those on the first page mostly Jewish, those on the second a hodgepodge. Eleven of these fellow prisoners came from Brooklyn, Long Island, and Chicago, the rest from all over the United States—Valparaiso, Indiana, and Toledo, Ohio; Winthrop, Maine, and Middletown, Connecticut; Algonac, Michigan; Mesa, Arizona; Verona, Illinois; Hoboken, New Jersey. Everywhere. These were the men he didn't want to lose. If you made Greenberg's List, it wasn't a matter of when you got home, but if you got home.

You couldn't go through these documents without sensing the man who had accumulated them. For the first time, it struck me that the character I was identifying with in this story was Lieutenant Greenberg, not Steven; the father, not the son. As I was mulling this over, Steven came into the kitchen.

"Look at that," he said, sizing up the pile on the tabletop. "It's coming together. How do you do that?"

What was it that Les Ware had said about me and my father? Try to put yourself in his place?

"I couldn't do it if it was my old man," I said to Steven. "It's a hell of a lot easier with yours."

Picking up a sandwich, he paused in the doorway before heading back to work.

"Don't stop," he said.

Among the papers that first day, I found the rumpled three-day pass that Lieutenant Greenberg had stuffed in his pocket and carried to

Paris. There was also an odd telegram to his wife saying that he had landed in New Jersey, but not to try to contact him. Why? That evening I phoned Steve's sister, who said that Murray had come out of the camp ridden with lice, that he had severe ulcers, and that it had taken six weeks on a rice and cream diet to get him in good enough shape to send back to Brooklyn. After that, she said, the lieutenant, his angel, and then their children were left to sort out the rest of the damage.

"How could it happen to such a loving family?" she asked. "It wasn't his fault. Those poor guys. All those good men. It was never their fault." Over the phone, I could hear her crying. "I know this now and I can't even talk to him. So much remains. Why, when, how could we do this, what could we have done differently? Questions—so many questions."

The next day I sat down and started to read the letters. They were short, written on Form No. 111 from the War Department Post Master General ("Important: don't get your man's Army serial number mixed up with his POW number"—folded three times and unsealed—"Write clearly, within the lines—type or pencil in block capitals to expedite censorship"). Down in the lower left corner of each letter, you could see the fading stamp of U.S. Censor 11038. Scribbled in the margins, notes in Lieutenant Greenberg's handwriting recorded when he had received each letter from his wife. The *Kriegefangenengpost* had been in no hurry to put through the mail. For the first six months after he was shot down, he heard nothing from home.

The first newsflash on Harvey didn't come from Shirley; it came from his sister Roslyn. "Dearest Murray," it began. "Well how is our proud Daddy today?" I winced. *Just great, Ros. Worms in the stew. Wish you were here.* After watching Harvey fall asleep, she told her brother, she and Shirley had gone "out." First they went to the movies, then they stopped for ice cream sodas, Shirley looking "lovely in her summer cotton dress," not at all like a new mother. *Swell. Who tried to pick them up?* "Murray, I don't want you to worry about things at home at all.

Shirley has all the money she needs and everything she needs and wants in material things." So did Harvey: a baby carriage, a "lovely pair of rompers," and "When Mom comes home from the farm she's going to bring him your old boxing gloves." *Hey, Ros, you really know how to cheer up a starving man.*

Roslyn was only trying her hardest to ease his mind, and for all I knew, her message made him feel wonderful. But then again, maybe it didn't.

Shirley's first letter, written nine days after Harvey was born, didn't arrive in Barth on the Baltic until well into August. His angel said all the right things.

> My Dearest Darling
>
> I love you!
>
> Your wish has come true, dear, and you are now the proud daddy to the most handsome son ever. He is really a beauty and is the perfect image of you. He weighs 8 pounds 10 ounces, your laughing eyes, the tiniest nose ever, a small bud-like mouth and the chubbiest cheeks. He even has your hair, Darling. When I look at our son, Harvey Joel, I see you precious. The folks are simply wild over him.
>
> All is fine here and your Shandel is feeling great.
>
> My darling, I was so glad to hear of your well-being. I love you so very much, dearest, forever and always.
>
> Today your mom and Molly Sorger shall pay your son a personal visit. Your son certainly has a way with women—takes after his dad even in this respect. He's really a fine boy and good, too. I shall take good care of him for you, precious, and I know that he shall love his daddy just as much as I do—and that's so very much. Your picture is there right beside his crib.
>
> God bless you, my darling, and may he keep you well and safe always. A million kisses to you from the baby and your wife plus from the rest of the family.
>
> I love you. Shandel.

One image jumped from the page: that photo next to Harvey's crib. It had to be the photo Steven and I had set side by side with my father's. The same face that had looked over Harvey's crib was now studying me across the kitchen table, smiling enigmatically. In October, Shirley Greenberg wrote again.

Darling Murray:

Hope all is well with you, dear. Things are running along most smoothly here at home, and I needed to tell you how joyful your son has made it for us. He certainly is the prize baby in the neighborhood. Darling, we have a son that comes only once in a lifetime for two people like us. For instance, and I doubt very much if there is another to be compared with our Harvey. At present, he's playing with his toy doll Suzie, and from the conversation he's having with her it looks as though she is in for a fierce argument . . . His wardrobe is even more elaborate than mine, darling, and his toys are seen everywhere. Abie has ordered a big Teddy bear for him. So, precious, you needn't worry about your precious son, we're taking good care of him for you. I hope and pray that my prayers shall be answered soon. Take good care of yourself, my dearest husband, and God Bless You! With all our love and kisses and my best regards to the boys. Love.

Shandel.

His toy doll Suzie? Was that what our fathers were fighting for? Mercifully I had forgotten my first doll, but three years after the war I was there in that closet with my father's Army equipment talking to a cricket. Was it really so surprising that they thought their sons were missing a piece or two from the total complement of manliness? On the other hand, what else were mothers supposed to do: take up chewing tobacco? In between the lines of Shirley's next letter, dated November 17, 1944, the first anniversary of Lieutenant Greenberg's departure for the war, you could see how her brave front was under assault.

My Darling,

Hope you are well and in good spirits. Haven't heard from you in over two months already. However, I'm learning to be patient, and so I'm sitting tightly. We are all fine here at home, and your precious son is just blooming away. God Bless him! He's really quite an active boy, dear, and so we're all kept on the go, most always. He should be sitting up by himself, most any day now. Darling, he's all you! My dearest it is just a year that you left me to do your share, and it seems like a million years have passed. I do miss you so, my darling. But I'm quite confident in believing that I shan't have to wait another million years. For that day when I shall see you again, I love you with all my heart.

Shandel.

In that "already," wasn't there a jab of the guilt needle: It's not like you have anything else to do, Murray, so why don't you write your wife? And wasn't there something off-key in that phrase "left me," pulsing with its note of abandonment, as if the war were a mistress? Lieutenant Greenberg hadn't left her. He'd done his duty. What to make of that "I shan't have to wait another million years," with its ultra-proper diction? Here were a man and a woman with an infant son between them going through an agony of separation. But POW 2817 was the one doing the true hard time.

I'd set aside the second composition book for last. On the third morning in Deb's kitchen, when I finally opened it, what I saw was a scrapbook. In it, scattered among long, handwritten stanzas of poetry, Lieutenant Greenberg had pasted everything he could find to shore himself up: letters, snapshots, a telegram reporting Harvey's birth, a Jewish New Year's card, and a two-page program for a concert by the Stalag Luft I orchestra on April 10, 1945, three weeks before the Russians liberated the camp. Among the first violins playing Haydn, Grieg, and Tchaikovsky at 1700 hours, I found M. S. Greenberg.

Unlike the book of lists, the scrapbook had no title on the cover; but inside, on the first page, the prisoner had dedicated what he had saved "To Shirley." He had printed her name in large block letters unlike his tidy cursive script, turning the h behind the S into a wide, calligraphic hug. Having zero to call his own, he had dressed up her name, the only gift he had to offer his angel.

In the middle of the book, he had written out a prose poem called *Parable of the Birdmen*. The poem was a dark satire after the King James Bible in the cadences of H. L. Mencken, an evocation of what it had felt like to get shot out of the sky:

"One morning as the sun first shineth on the hut of the sleeping birdmen, the C.O. entereth therein and he sayeth, 'Arise, for the time of briefing is at hand!' After listening to the riddles" of the intelligence officers on wind and clouds and the ways of the enemy, the birdmen "entangled themselves with many hooks and straps after a confusing manner," then they "breaketh the bond of the earth," and, "their fuel dribbling fast," they "drew nigh unto the target, where they beholdeth many and numerous flashes among them and they weaveth and swoopeth to escape the flak." "Red I, calleth the Great Grey Owl, whither shall we turn, canst thou not lead us out?" "And great cults of enemy birdmen descendeth, and Red I called to Red II saying, 'Wherefor art thou?' And Red II answereth saying, 'Lo and behind, I spinneth out and am lost unto thee!' Then they sayeth one unto the other, 'Hitteth the silk!' And the white parasols fluttered earthward. Finis."

The final entry in the book was a longer poem about another bombing run over Germany. The anonymous writer titled his quatrains *Combat*.

> *The stuff is still bursting big and black,*
> *And you curse the guy that invented flak*
> *It pounds on the ship like an angry surf,*
> *You're scared as hell but you keep your nerve.*

You feel her lurch and start to drop,
And over the phone comes 'feather the prop.'
And smoke streams from Number Two,
But your pilot's quick and he pulls her through.

The group behind is in the flak now,
And catching hell from stem to bow,
You watch two ships go falling down,
They both blow up when they hit the ground.

Shirley Greenberg's letters were written on the standard letter form used to send mail to POWs. A little further on, Murray had opened up a blank form, round above the first fold and square at the bottom, and pasted it into his book. The shape reminded me of something, but at first I couldn't place it. Then I noticed something strange. The acid in the form's cheap paper had broken down, leaving the outline of a tombstone in sepia on the facing page, just like the shadow left in an old volume by a forgotten news clipping or bookmark. Next to this ghostly tombstone and shadow, the prisoner of war had written out a couplet from John Dryden's *Epitaph Intended for His Wife*: "Here lies my wife: here let her lie! Now she's at rest, and so am I."

Why would Murray Greenberg make such a black joke? Remembering his book of lists, I grabbed the letters from home and started tearing through them again. The letters were also lists, endless lists of the love and symbols of love showered on Harvey: the baby carriage, the rompers, the four pairs of pajamas, the lovely blue snowsuit. While Murray was starving, dreaming of the ideal Red Cross parcel, Harvey was gaining five pounds every time someone dropped by with another load of goodies. Those milk-fed, chubby cheeks. Jesus, that Suzie doll? Suddenly I found myself thinking: The hell with the little sissy. The identification was unnerving. Wasn't this precisely what my father had been thinking about me when he walked away from the doghouse?

Was it possible that everything Shandel tried to do to ease her lieutenant's pain had tragically misfired in Stalag Luft I? The content of these love letters ran at roughly one page about Murray to three about Harvey. Over and over, trying to buck Murray up, Shirley identified the son with the father: "Darling, now that I have our son to love all day, I see your vision in front of me constantly, because our son is you." Here was Harvey, the ultimate replacement, upstaging his father. "Harvey knows you quite well now! All I have to say is 'Harvey, where is Daddy?' and he looks at your picture on his bureau and beams from all sides." But daddy wasn't on the bureau. Daddy was POW 2817, who had to be deloused, dewormed, and fed that rice diet before he could keep anything stronger in his own stomach. Was it any wonder that when he saw those chubby cheeks on his son, he didn't beam?

It was getting late, the sun was no longer shining through the skylight over the table, the kitchen was cold. When Steve came in from work, I showed him the letters and the two composition books, his father's lists, the brown shadow of the tombstone. "I don't want to sound like a bastard," I said. "But is it possible that all your father wanted after the Germans shot him down was to hear his angel whispering love to him. Instead, he got way too much of Harvey?"

Steve studied the scrapbook and nodded. And then a stricken look crossed his face. He pointed to the letter and the passage where his mother had gently groused about not hearing from his father for two months. "That gap she's talking about had to be when he was in solitary confinement. He only told two stories, and I never knew where they fit in until now. The first was about someone killing a German guard with a fork from the mess hall. The other one was about trying to escape. They tunneled under the wire but when they came up out of the ground, the Germans were waiting for them. That's why he was in solitary confinement. There was no way for my mother to know that when she wrote the letter."

Steve suddenly looked ashen. He leaned against the kitchen wall, as if to brace himself, and recognition arrived like a convulsion. "I laced into my father," he said, so softly you could hardly hear him. "When he was sick, I did that. We didn't know what Lou Gehrig's disease was, and I thought he was a vegetable. I thought he couldn't hear, so I said, 'I hate you. You've ruined my life.' For a whole year I laced him, and then I found out that even when ALS gets bad, the patient's brain still works. He could hear everything I said. He understood everything. Every word."

Steve's voice sounded strangled. "Every day is an exorcism," he said. "It never stops. We don't know what we do to each other. We never know until it's too late."

Chapter 3

BAR Code

Sgt. Edgar Persan, BAR man,
100th Infantry Division, France,
1945

The GI next to the cash register at Henry Persan & Sons Hardware had an M-1 fitted out as a grenade launcher near his right hand. The butt of a sniper's rifle was planted at his foot, and he was shooting me an unnerving thousand-yard stare. It was Memorial Day, and I was looking at a photograph of a mud-caked soldier leaning against the side of a deep foxhole during the Battle of the Bulge. Poking out from his position, a Browning Automatic Rifle commanded a field of fire through a forest of bare, wintry trees. The foxhole couldn't have been more desolate, but oddly enough, it gave the impression of a taut, well-run hardware store. Wedged into the dirt walls were shelves made of empty C-ration crates. On the shelves, the BAR man had neatly arranged stacks of fragmentation grenades and magazines of .30-caliber ammo. Somewhere on the far side of the trees, the Germans were on the way, and this guy was open for business.

The soldier appeared to be about twenty years old going on one hundred. On the butt of the grenade launcher, he had carved the initials E.P. I looked at the face more closely. From under the steel helmet, the look in his eyes powered out a signal to all clueless civilians and rear echelon motherfuckers: Where are you knuckleheads? Who was this unknown soldier? Standing next to the cash register, Bob Persan picked up the picture and handed it to me. Bob is a tall man, circling fifty but still lean and muscular, with short blond hair and a neatly trimmed mustache. In one ear he wears a small gold loop, the kind divers in Tobago award for valor. Clearing his throat to keep any loose bubble of emotion from his voice, he said, "That's my dad."

The initials on the grenade launcher stood for Edgar Persan, at the time a private first class with the 100th Infantry Division somewhere in France. He was also the oldest son of Henry Persan, founding father of the hardware emporium that Bob now owned. The wooden counter under the cash register, worn smooth by three generations of Persans, covered a set of nail bins that went back to his grandfather's original store. On Memorial Day and Veterans Day, Bob told me, he liked to display the picture. Old vets coming in to buy tools, or marine hardware, or light bulbs would look at it and nod, exchanging a silent password with his old man. The local beer distributor liked the picture so much he always nudged it from its position near the Snickers box to a better spot on the counter. A collector of World War II memorabilia who came in one day told Bob it was the best picture he had ever seen of an American GI in France ("And believe me, I've seen thousands"). Another time, the owner of the Sag Harbor Yacht Yard handed Bob a small metal box, angled on the top and about the size of a cigarette pack. "Thought your old man might like this BAR mag," he said. Bob mailed the box to his father. About a week later the phone rang. Ed Persan was calling from Florida. He started to say something, and then Bob heard his voice get hoarse.

"The hell you get that BAR mag?"

"From Lou Grignon at the yacht yard."

To Bob's astonishment, it sounded as if Ed Persan was choking up on the far side of the line so he just kept talking. "Lou said he and his brother were collectors. Thought you'd like to see it. I had it next to your picture here." The old BAR man coughed. "Jesus, this brings back memories," he said. "You're supposed to put eighteen rounds in the mag. You can actually put nineteen in, but you never put in more than seventeen or it'll jam on you. The last thing you want is that sonuvabitch to jam on you." But then, his voice catching again, he thanked his son and abruptly rang off. As Bob told the story—fondly, a son who loved his father where I was still nursing a grudge—I began to wonder whether Ed Persan and my old man shared the same code: For both of them after the war, some sense of honor that I had never understood seemed to demand silence. Now and then back in the 1960s, Bob told me, his father might spend an evening in front of the TV watching *Combat*, correcting dumb mistakes for Bob and his older brother Gary. "Throw a grenade that way, get you killed. They'd roll it right back. The right way's to yank off the teaspoon and pull out the pin, let the fuse burn some. *Then* you toss the sonuvabitch. Works— unless the fuse is screwed up."

"What happens then, Dad?"

"What happens then is *you* get blown to hell."

After that, Ed Persan, like my father, would shut down. Always. When the Veterans of Foreign Wars set up a post across the street from the hardware store they ran up-island before moving to Sag Harbor, Bob asked him why he didn't sign up.

"You see that VFW guy comes in here?" Ed said. "The one with the cervical collar around his neck?"

"Yeah, I know him, the guy always talking about the war?"

"Right. Him."

"The one who got shot ..."

"Bullshit on him. Only injuries that guy ever sustained he got falling off a bar stool. He makes believe he was in the war. Those guys over there, they never saw any action."

No bar stools, no bullshit. No war stories. Those were the rules for nearly fifty years. But then, during the last summer of Ed Persan's life, Bob went out to the family's summer place in Montauk one afternoon and found his father slowly turning the pages of a large, black photo album, the dark leatherette cracked and peeling at the spine. Leaning over his father's shoulder, Bob saw that he had stopped at a page with nine snapshots pasted neatly in three rows: a wide field, some trees, a ditch, and a dirt road curving off toward the horizon, where a church tower rose above the rooftops of a small village. The field was empty, as if ready for spring plowing. "Hey, look at that, Dad," Bob said. "Nice field. Why don't you take Mom and go to France? You're retired. You've got nothing else going on. Why not go back?"

His father stared at the pictures tombstoned across the black page. After a long time, he pointed to the ditch running along the tree line. "We were dug in here," he said. "They were all over us. Kraut 88s. We were getting hit pretty heavy and we had to trench in, get cover ..."

Suddenly his voice broke.

"We lost sixteen men in that field."

And for the first time in his life, Bob saw his father cry.

It was a very cold day in the coldest winter anyone in France could remember, when Rum Nose Barada pointed his Kodak Brownie at PFC Persan and yelled, "Hey, Ed, smile." The beak on Rum Nose, a private from the Bronx, was glowing like an electric cherry, and Persan, a fellow shutterbug, managed a faint grin. On that freezing day in 1945, he and Rum Nose had been fighting their way toward Germany for three months. Ninety straight days of combat had cost them whatever basic training had left of their youth. When they shipped aboard the U.S. transport *George Washington* the previous October, they were still carrying the horseshoe bedrolls doughboys hung around their necks as they set off for World War I. Scrambling down a cargo net into a landing craft, they had started the war near Marseilles. At the staging area someone turned on the radio in a staff car, and American dance music floated through the darkness. Just as everyone was beginning to feel nostalgic, Axis Sally broke into the broadcast. Welcome to France, she told the 100th Infantry Division. Move on up, boys. The German 708th Volksgrenadier Division is waiting in the High Vosges to cut off your nuts.

No one in the entire history of war—not the Romans or the Huns, the Burgundians or the Swedes, not the Austrians, Bavarians, Germans, or French—had ever succeeded in dislodging an entrenched army from the mountains of the Vosges. Rum Nose and Ed moved forward and pasted the 708th Volksgrenadiers. Then they chased the German First Army all the way to the Maginot Line, holding firm during the Battle of the Bulge, and surging forward to Mannheim. Eventually, after 185 days of continuous combat, they rolled to a stop. From Marseilles, they had advanced 186 miles. Along the line of that advance, their casualties were 3,656 men wounded, 180 missing in action, and 916 killed.

The details of this march were so excruciating, Ed Persan never told his sons about them. But like Rum Nose, he had carried a Kodak as well as a rifle and preserved the snapshots in his secret album. You had to go to history to link illustrations to text. On the Internet, I found an after-action report from the 100th Division posted by a reunion group of survivors. One of these soldiers, a man named William C. Watson Jr., had written an account called *First Class Privates*. In March 1945, Watson reported, the weather was so bad that only one out of four rifles would shoot. Mud jammed the others. The soldiers, ordered to move forward, pack, and police their weapons, had to work across the bodies of dead Germans lying in a trench, their boots sinking into flesh and mud, a "stew of death." Someone ordered them to take ten. They moved up a hill and into some trees, thinking, wrongly, that they would escape the observation of live Germans. From what happened next, apparently Watson was within earshot of Bob's father.

> We had barely settled down—a few had lit cigarettes—when it happened. A salvo of 88mm shells came in directly on top of us. There was no mistaking the high-pitched screech of an incoming 88 and nothing more frightening. They burst in the treetops above us, ripping off the tops and spraying the ground with shrapnel and wood fragments. It was over in seconds, just a half dozen rounds, or maybe fewer. Nobody counts accurately at such a time. But the nightmarish result will never be over for me. I had dropped flat, face down at the sound of the incoming barrage. My closest friend and fellow mortarman, Edwin Tarter, had dropped beside me. He groaned once, and I looked over to see that he had been cut almost in half at the waist. There were the terrible and unmistakable screams of the wounded but they were not from Tarter. He died instantly without making another sound.

Multiply that by sixteen, I told myself, and you approach the sum of what Private First Class Persan would never be able to tell his sons.

Persan's Hardware is just up the block from my house. A few days later, I heard a knock at the door. Bob was standing out front. Under his arm he was carrying his father's photo album. We went into the dining room and put the record of Ed Persan's secret war on the table in front of us. The old soldier would probably have told us to keep our noses out of his business, but the album is mesmerizing. What's in there that Ed wanted to preserve? Why did he hide it away for so many years? Why did he dig it out that last full summer of his life, and then, once it was back in the light, why couldn't he talk about it? Bob was still sorting through the puzzle. "All I know is that every time I went out there, which was about once a week, he had that book out. He'd start looking at it, he'd start to explain, and then he'd choke up."

Ed Persan had his own explanation.

"Hormones. Those fucking female hormones."

For eight years he had been fighting off cancer, always beating the odds. But by that last summer, he knew he was dying, even though the wizards of oncology were giving him the works. Now and then, leaning against the counter in the store, he'd joke about their latest protocols. "They got me on these female hormones. You believe that? My tits are growing and I got to tie a string around my pecker so I can find it to pee." He would laugh and his friends would laugh with him, shaking their heads in admiration as he headed out the door for his car. Then he'd go back to Montauk and pull out the album. He worried about what would happen to it after he was gone. Before he died, he asked Bob to make sure that it went to his youngest grandson, John. Now, looking at it on the table, Bob and I are thinking the same thing. Why skip a generation? Why didn't he give it to his son?

We opened the book.

The inside cover, where Ed Persan had attached his ribbons and medals, was lined in purple satin. In the place of honor at the top he put an olive drab patch with a musket—his Combat Infantryman Badge. The CIB is the Army's award for "exemplary conduct in action against the enemy." Action was the word that counted. You didn't get the CIB for typing up morning reports. You got it for killing the other side before it killed you; for doing the job well, the Army added ten dollars a month to your pay. Below the CIB patch, Persan had arranged his campaign ribbons, red and white, green, brown, and rainbow. On the top right corner of the page he had glued his Bronze Star.

The medal had darkened with age, but the red ribbon with the narrow blue was still bright, sharp enough to pass any inspection.

"What was that for?" I asked Bob.

"You couldn't get it out of him. Something about a machine gun nest."

Like Rum Nose, Ed Persan took his pictures seriously. The images in the album were arranged chronologically: We were looking at a documentary, starting with basic training at Fort Jackson, South Carolina. The first shot showed Persan sitting in the open door of his barracks, the sun beating down on him, not quite erasing the what-am-I-doing-here look from his lean young face. In the next picture, bare-chested, bare-legged, grinning into the camera, he was holding a full washtub of dirty fatigues. The camera, swinging right, to the top corner of the page, showed him kneeling in the same doorway, this time with his M-1, peering out from under his steel helmet.

He devoted the next seven pages to capturing the rough, jostling, masculine humdrum of training: young men, most in their late teens, washing up in a long, open trough behind the barracks, mustering for roll call, sweating through rifle drill; young men with open, innocent faces, draftees and volunteers, GIs not officers, no West Pointers, no Virginia horse country aristocrats like George Patton. Face after face. The little dark kid, maybe five-foot-five in his combat boots, next to a giant with an Irishman's smashed nose; the guy with the well-greased hair and the Sicilian eyes, his Little Italy class lost in a uniform three sizes too big; the youngest—could he be any more than fifteen?—turning from mail call to stare into Persan's camera; the joker in the floppy fatigue cap, lowering his head and charging at the photographer; young soldiers, arms draped around each other, shoulder to shoulder in the hot, white light of the overexposed frames. Toward the end, Persan handed his camera to someone who took a picture of him standing next to a friend in a matching uniform: dark shirt and pants, boots, and puttees. Boy Scout summer camp until you look closer and see the bayonet hanging from Private Persan's web belt.

Flipping the heavy, black page, we turned up the first small surprise: a huge picture, twice the size of the snapshots, of a pretty brunette with finely permed curls, Ipana-white teeth, serious lipstick, and kiss-me-soldier eyes. "Not Mom," Bob said thoughtfully. His parents had met before the war, but they didn't get married until after Ed returned. What followed were three pages from a three-day pass in 1944: Ed and the pretty girl sitting near a fallen cedar, riding in a one-horse surrey with a fringe on the top, looking into the moat of an old stone fort, cruising past palm trees in a Ford roadster. It looked about as sinful as an Andy Hardy movie.

Jump cut.

Bob turned the page and the two of us were in the Battle of the Bulge. The first shot showed a small guy standing in a trench much like Private Persan's own, except that this soldier has a red cross painted on his helmet. Where Rum Nose Barada had caught Persan working out of a small muddy arsenal, this man has a canopy over his hole, and no weapons. Next to him lies an empty helmet and a ripped-open box of field dressings. The photographer has written a caption in ink.

"Medic" Huston.

I wondered about the quotation marks, and then I got it: Bob and I were looking at a picture of a shout. To identify Huston, his father had used a wounded infantryman's cry of pain.

Next to the medic, two GIs hunker down in a blasted wood. Above them, Persan wrote Pappy and Fred. Below, he wrote Sandwich Hill. Bob says, "I asked him about that. He told me they were surrounded for days, they ran out of rations, men were going down right and left, and then a plane flew over and dropped them sandwiches."

The final picture in this triptych was a bullet-splattered concrete emplacement dug into a hillside at the top of a narrow dirt path. Underneath, Bob's father had written March 16, 1945.

"What's that?" I asked.

"Don't know."

The answer turned up on the next page: a yellowing newspaper clip from the *New York World Telegram*, Monday, June 25, 1945 (55 from This Area Decorated in Ceremonies Honoring 100th Infantry Division). Under the list for Bronze Star, a large block of names printed in tiny agate type, one name had been circled with a soft lead pencil: PFC Edgar R. Persan, 1200 Rogers Ave., Brooklyn. Underneath the clipping, Persan had hidden a photo of himself standing at attention. On his shoulder is the 100th Division patch he later glued to the front cover of the album. A one-star general with a showy .45 on his hip is pinning the medal to Persan's chest. Scotch-taped to the same page, lower down, is a copy of a citation for valor award.

> While the second platoon of this company was detailed to pro-
> tect the right flank of Fox Company in an attack toward Rey-
> ersvillers, these men at the risk of their lives under small arms fire
> and heavy mortar barrage, worked their way through an enemy
> mine field in the open to successfully attack and eliminate a Ger-
> man machine gun nest whose fire was holding down the rifle pla-
> toon. Their action resulted in killing the enemy gunner and the
> capture of three others. Sgt. Krokum acted on his own initiative.
> The others volunteered to accompany him.

We have found the rest of the war story Ed Persan couldn't tell his son. When he turns the page, we are looking at a shot of a rifle platoon. The picture was taken after the assault on the German machine gun, and the platoon, which should have had thirty to forty men, is short: Only nineteen men are looking into the camera. On the facing page is the picture of the field that Bob's father was staring at the day he broke down—the one where the German 88s came screaming down and sixteen infantrymen died.

In gold letters on a green field, the sign in front of Bob's place says Henry F. Persan & Sons Hardware Est. 1915. Bob's grandfather founded the business in the German section of Flatbush during World War I. After World War II, Bob's father moved the store to Uniondale, Long Island, and fifty years later, when Bob took over, he shifted operations to Sag Harbor. Today the store is open seven days a week, a work-ethic rebuke to the derelict Bulova watch case factory up the way on Division Street and Murph's Tavern just across the road. Depending on the season, Persan's is the place you go to find a hoe, a rake, a snowblower, or a twelve-inch galvanized spike to stabilize the arthritic joists under your garden shed. "Everyone comes in here," Bob told me one day when I stopped in to pick up a pair of oars. "Sixteen-year-old druggies off the street, guys off the yachts, everyone in between. I love this business. Sell a fifteen-cent washer, you improve someone's life."

Bob must be the only man in the world who believes that a window display with an eighty-year-old box marked Carborundum Powder will boost sales. Standing in front of the window, he said fondly, "Look at those dovetail corners. That's my grandfather's handwriting." I followed his gaze to the little box, where the ancient carborundum powder has caked to the bottom like mummy goop. Near the box, his grandfather's black safety glasses, missing one temple, occupy pride of place next to an array of wood-handle screwdrivers, pliers, wrenches, and calipers. In the same window, Bob keeps on display the iron claw that three generations of Persans, fathers and sons, have used to grab common nails for weighing and bagging. As I look at all this, he senses my hesitation. "Yeah, yeah, I know what you're thinking. Women look in this window, they yawn, but guys—I'm telling you—they really get into it. Come on inside—there's something else you gotta see."

To step through the door of Persan & Sons is to feel something enormously reassuring: The same world that tears itself to pieces in war pulls itself together with hardware. To the minds of three generations of Persans, a man is only as good as his stock. From a drawer in the office behind the nail bin, Bob pulled out a strange object that looks like a whimsy of Dr. Seuss: two long legs made of rods that look suspiciously like oil dipsticks, one brass knee joint connecting them, a small wooden handle up top. "Look at this. You drill a hole in the ice on the pond, right? You stick the tips down into the hole. You pull the handle and one leg comes up at right angles under the ice. See that mark there?" He pointed to a golden scratch on the longer leg. "That's four inches. If it measures four inches, it's okay to skate. Anything less, you're on thin ice and you gotta come home." Winters when Bob's dad was a kid, he carried the ice tool. The rest of the time he worked in the Flatbush store, doing repair jobs. The reputation of the first store was so good that Harry Houdini, a Brooklyn boy, called all the way from 113th Street in

Manhattan when he needed some windows reglazed. What Ed remembered most was the double HH monogram on the magician's custommade tiles. During the Depression, Bob's father took over as head of the family even before he had created one of his own. In 1939, Henry Persan developed severe diverticulitis, and his doctor told him he needed an operation. The night before the surgery, he had a premonition and called his son to his bedside. "Ed, take care of the family," he said. The next morning he went under the ether and died under the knife. At nineteen, Ed took over the Persans along with the store. He ran the business until he was drafted in 1943, then closed for the duration. When he got back from Europe, he spent the rest of his life keeping the promise he had made to his father. He knew his business, which was hardware, and he knew his larger purpose—his family.

Before shipping overseas, he had fallen in love with a high-spirited, beach-loving brunette from Forest Hills who went to college at Adelphi. Her name was Florence Elizabeth Sanders, Betty to her friends. Despite the spectacular figure she cut in a bathing suit, she was a strict Catholic. Ed was a Lutheran himself, but religion didn't make any difference to him because after the war he stopped going to church. The one thing that bothered him about Betty was that she smoked cigarettes. "He scoffed at weaknesses or stupidity," Bob told me. "He told me, 'I come back from the war, your mother was smoking, so I said, "I'll never marry you as long as you're smoking." ' " She crumpled her last pack and they stayed married for the next fifty-three years.

For a short time, Ed tried working in a bank, but he didn't like bankers, so he reopened the hardware store. A photograph from 1946 shows him back behind the counter, a 100-watt smile on his face, his sleeves rolled up, his gut as flat as the day he came out of basic training. About this time a social-climbing neighbor who came into the store made the mistake of saying to him, "My son's still at the bank." "Yep," Ed shot back. "But I've got a brand-new car." He paid for it with long hours and an eye for new possibilities in hardware after the war. In the photograph, the nuts and bolts, hacksaws and key blanks, electrical testers and paintbrushes recede into the background, upstaged by a shiny array of kitchenware: aluminum pots, pans, and double boilers, and no less than four glistening varieties of teakettles.

His business and family expanded side by side, rising on the great swell of suburbanization that followed the war and the Levittown boom out on Long Island. He moved to Uniondale near Massapequa, where Betty had a baby in 1949, a boy they named Gary; Bob weighed in four years later, then Brian in 1957. A new generation for Persan & Sons, and Ed, in his son's view, was a father obsessed. "It was the combination of the war and what his own father said to him the night before he died. It's hard to explain. But I think when he was over there and thought he might not make it back, he told himself that if he did get out alive, the thing to do was go home and be a good father."

If ever the war spared a man to take on such a job, it was Ed Persan. Six feet tall, steady in the wheelhouse, scanning the water for signs of bluefish and striped bass, he was straight as any carpenter's rule back at his store. He didn't brood, he wasn't a lush, he didn't cheat on his wife, and he didn't whack his sons. At the same time, he was salty, sometimes profane, and he was tough, very, very tough. "Let's put it this way," Bob said, "my dad didn't cry at the movies."

If you asked him, he'd tell you he had learned only one thing from the war: If he lived to a hundred, he would never again eat green beans. The rest of Army chow he could take, but all those overcooked green beans, the hell with them. So far as Bob could see, nothing else seemed to faze him. "I always thought it was from surviving in the field. You come back, you have already made it. After that, what do you have to fear?" When Bob was a little boy, his father ordered a hull for a Jersey sea skiff, a twenty-six-foot wooden boat. He finished it himself, putting on the decks, building the wheelhouse, dropping in the engine, fine-tuning the single propeller. Then, with Bob in the stern, eyes peeled for sea turtles—to a boy five years old they looked as big as dining tables— Ed put to sea. "Today everyone's got two engines, two screws. Not my dad. We'd be out there fishing forty to sixty miles offshore with that single screw inboard. He'd lift up the engine cover, tinker with it, fix this, fix that. And I'd say, 'Dad, what if the engine conks out?' "

" 'Ah, that'll never happen. You don't have to worry about it.' "

Thursday was Ed's day off from the store, and when Thanksgiving arrived each year, no matter how cold the weather, he made a tradition of going out for cod. He'd invite men from the store, a few friends; he'd fill up a big thermos of hot coffee; he'd stow a small mountain of sandwiches next to his middle son; and he'd set a course through Jones Inlet for the Atlantic. In the fall, the inlet was always rough. The swells would roll in, the boat would start heaving, and so would Bob. "As much as I hated to go out there and get seasick, as shitty as I felt, I always went with him. Shucking clams. We'd open them, pull out the stinking clam bellies, bait the hooks. He'd bring galvanized tubs, and when we came bucketing back through the chop, they were always filled with codfish. In the summer months we'd go floundering, fishing in the bays or going farther after stripers. I remember guys fifty years old out there, never caught a striped bass surf casting all their lives. Since I was ten years old I've been bailing them off the back of the boat. It was great. You felt you had a leg up, an advantage."

From the skiff, his father moved up to a thirty-two-foot Pacemaker. Winters, he kept it in his sister's backyard near the Schmidt Canal; summers, he launched it and headed east. At ten, Bob was taking the boat to Montauk single-handed. "My father always insisted I do it myself. I took it out, docked it wherever we spent the night, took it through the locks and up through the Peconic and Great South Bay. My father would sleep down below. We had a buzzer, a doorbell, so when he was down below with the engine running and I needed him, all I had to do was just hit the buzzer. He'd stick his head up and I'd say, 'What about this, or what about that?' And he'd explain, he was always explaining. I knew navigation by the time I was ten. He showed you how—he trusted you."

With trust went responsibility, but not in the Scouting way of Baden-Powell or *Boys' Life*. Ed was just being practical. His old man had died young, he knew from the war the contingency of his own life, and he wanted his sons to have enough experience to take care of themselves sooner, not later. A few days after Bob's sixteenth birthday, as soon as he got his driver's license, Ed gave him a check for thirteen thousand dollars. "He said to me, 'Go down to Bass Chevrolet and order your uncle and me two cars.'" He pointed to the paint chart. "'I want that blue, your uncle wants that brown. No air-conditioning. Nothing. Just order me a couple of cars.' When I walked in, they couldn't believe this kid with thirteen thousand bucks in his hand. Then someone said 'That's Ed's boy,' and I got the cars."

As a soldier turned father, Ed Person had endured Army chickenshit on two continents; he chose not to inflict it on his sons. Partly this was because with Bob, although not with Gary, he didn't have to issue orders. "I didn't argue with him. I'd be afraid to. If he said, 'You come home at 11:00,' that was it. If I forgot and turned up at 11:15, godawmighty, your tail was on fire." Mostly Ed left discipline to Betty, who imposed it with wooden spoons, escalating to wooden brushes, then to metal spoons and, if all else failed, to the ultimate threat: "WAIT UNTIL YOUR FATHER GETS HOME." But when her enforcer got back from the store, he seldom used muscle. "Oh, maybe now and then, if you did something stupid, he might chase after you and smack you on the back of the head. But I don't think that's a hit."

Ed hit Bob only once.

Bob was seventeen, and he came home one time redolent of tobacco.

"You been smoking?"

"No."

BAM. Ed slapped him across the face.

"I went, 'Holy shit,' I was so startled. He was upset with himself. He said, 'I hit you because you lied to me, not because you were smoking.' Then he apologized and he never hit me again."

Ed could be tightfisted over spending money on himself, but he was generous to his family. When Bob finished high school, Ed asked him what he wanted for graduation. That particular June, Bob and a few friends wanted to go down to Mexico to surf.

"Know what I want," he said. "A Volkswagen van. Like a camper. For the surfboards. Mexico. I want to go surfing."

"That's all? Forget it. I'm not buying you a van. What else do you want?"

"That's it."

The memory still makes Bob laugh. "You know what I got for my graduation? A Volkswagen van. A toy one. Matchbox."

Ed said, "The doors open."

Bob opened the door and found a fifty-dollar bill folded and crunched under the toy dinette.

Ed said, "Save your money. Buy a van."

So Bob started banking what he earned at the store, confident that when his father sat him down that way, he was always working on a deal for him. A year passed. Bob still wanted the van. So Ed said, "Why not take my station wagon? I need to trade it in. I own the business, I don't have to answer to anybody, if I want to get rid of my car for nothing, I can do it. I'll sell it to you for two hundred bucks." That's how Bob wound up with a 1967 Impala station wagon with an electric rear window for the price of a good racing bicycle. "And, man, I turned that Impala into THE surf vehicle. I put in an eight-track tape deck. I put in extra speakers. I remember my father hanging out, looking in the car door, and he was like, 'Wow. Hey Marvin, come over here and look at this car. Listen to that music.' "

To cover up the electric window, Bob went to the yardage store and came home with an armload of curtain material in a wild Hawaiian pattern. The idea was that no one could look in while he was sleeping on surf trips, solo or whatever. There was a problem: Bob didn't know how to make curtains. His father sat him down in front of the sewing machine.

"I said, 'Dad, how do you know how to sew?' "

Ed said, "The hell you think taught your mom to sew?"

Tape deck cranked to total bliss, rear window wildly signaling "Aloha," Bob ripped down to catch waves in North Carolina twice a year; three or four times a summer you'd see his Hang Ten Impala burning up the dunes in Rhode Island.

Bob didn't go to college; three seasons of the year he worked, over the winters he surfed. He started in Puerto Rico the first winter after he finished high school. As December approached that year, his father worried about him. They went fishing for stripers just off the light-house at Montauk, fifteen to eighteen feet of water, a very cold day. "We were trolling bucktails for bass and I got a hit—you can tell the difference between a bass and a bluefish—just as my father was saying, 'You know, Bobby, why don't you stay here for the winter instead of go-ing to Puerto Rico? I'll tell you what. I'll leave the house open. I'll pay for the heat. Just stay on. You'll have the whole house to yourself.' " Bob was leaning back on his rod, reeling like a madman, and when the fish came up out of the water, it was a deepwater cod. "I remember it was so cold that day my hands were freezing. And I said, 'Dad, when I'm catching codfish in fifteen feet of water, I'm out of here. It's time to go.' " Ed Persan accepted this declaration of independence. "He just laughed and we finished fishing and that was it—I hightailed it to Puerto Rico."

Father and son played it that way through most of the 1970s. For the first three years, Bob went to the Caribbean with friends, then he started going to Tobago by himself. He surfed big waves, hung out with Tobagan divers. One night he and the divers got smashed and they ini-tiated him as a beach outlaw. Using bush rum for an antiseptic, they drilled him an earring. I once asked Bob what his old man said the first time he saw that little band of gold.

"He said, 'The hell is that?'

"Come on, Dad. You gotta give customers something they can find fault with. Better for them to be looking at you thinking 'This guy's got a hole in his ear' than thinking that you run a lousy store.

"Ed said, 'Maybe you got a point.' "

Self-reliance was what counted with Ed Persan, nerve; but he also believed in priming the pump. He gave Bob's aunt a small house, then, years later, bought it back from her for $37,000 and bestowed it on Bob. Three years later Bob sold it for $70,000 and had the grubstake to get a bigger place. When he went to the bank for a mortgage, he had no credit and the bank stalled. "Bullshit on them," Ed said. "I'll loan it to you. How much?" Moving from the 1970s into the 1980s, Bob got married and needed more space, so he bought a new house near the beach and started to rebuild it. The house was modern, airy, the first he'd ever built, solid clear through. Its centerpiece was a new staircase. From a millwright, he bought some oak stringers. An old-timer who worked for his father taught him how to lay out the treads. He completed the job with trim balusters and a brass rail, then invited Ed over to the house. "My old man never got excited about anything, but he was very pleased with that staircase. He wasn't a soft guy. He just about got out, 'I'm very proud of you,' but it was hard for him to say. He almost choked on the words. It came out like, 'Ummmmm. Proud of you. Uhhhh. Good job.' "

They shook hands.

While Bob took to Ed's benign authority and flourished, his older brother Gary kicked hard against the traces. It mystified Bob. But when they were kids, Gary was the cool brother. During Vietnam, Ed did everything he could think of to keep Gary in college, not for political reasons but for a practical necessity. "I guess my father could see that he was a knucklehead. He knew he wouldn't make it back." Every time Ed had to cut his oldest son slack, he came down harder on the younger brother. "He'd say, 'Goddammit, you're not going to go that way,' and I'd say, 'Hey, Dad, I'm only gonna hang out with Catholics,' but he'd blast me, set curfews, check things out. You wouldn't cross him."

Over the next twenty-five years, the prize and the prodigal set off in separate directions, Bob into hardware, Gary into commercial fishing. The older brother became High Hook: the best bass fisherman in Montauk. Fishing with a bucktail, only Johnny de Mayo could compete with him. But then the state took away the striped bass industry and Gary hit hard times. For a while he switched to tuna. He bought a bigger boat, installed big brine tanks. The Japanese knew he did a kosher kill, floated the carcasses in the right brine. They would buy Gary's tuna over the catch of other fishermen, who raced into Montauk with fast boats but paid less attention to the fish.

The arrangement worked well until Gary developed Lyme disease and started returning from ten-day fishing trips with his knees swollen like melons. Arthritis ate away the joints and he moved to Florida. Ed bought him a house. "You'd see my father down there on his hands and knees, ripping up the carpets, nailing the floors, just to save Gary money." To say there is a distance between the two brothers is only to recognize the facts. Gary still mystifies Bob. "He would come home at all hours and not worry about anything. I wouldn't come home with my hair out of place. Maybe I didn't want to disappoint my father, I don't know. I certainly wasn't afraid of any lectures. So why would one brother be that way while the other brother would do whatever he wanted?" The question jarred me. The answer, all too clearly, was that a father doesn't hold all the cards, no matter how it may look to a son early on—or forever if he refuses to see it. So why was I insisting on forever?

Three wood pilings by the side of Old Westwood Road marked the turn into a sandy drive that burrowed through the beach plums to Ed Persan's summerhouse at Montauk. I drove over a few days later. Out beyond the dock, a stiff wind was blowing up whitecaps on Lake Montauk. The halyard on the flagpole next to the dock was straining at its cleat. Ed Persan was not a superpatriot and he was not a sentimentalist, but out at Montauk, he flew the flag all summer long, not just on the Fourth of July. He taught his grandson how to run the Stars and Stripes up the pole, the right way to take the flag down, how to fold it into a triangle, stars out, for the night.

Steadiness, endurance, gruff good humor—he relied on inner virtues that he maintained the same way he took care of his tools. They were always near to hand, clean, sharp, reliable. The thought of retiring was a nonstarter, as foreign to him as the ugly McMansions that eventually advanced up the south side of Route 27 toward his castle at Montauk. He was a bull. "My dad was never sick. He didn't believe in it," Bob had told me. "I can't remember a single day when he stayed in bed." Mind over migraine kept him going, and he demanded the same from his sons. For a time when Bob was a boy, he had a mysterious allergy, and after school he saw an allergist who gave him shots. Ed Persan indulged the allergist for a while, but finally one day he said to his sneezy son, "Bullshit. Old Doc White says you got a pinched nerve, probably when we dropped you off the bassinet when you were a little kid. You go see him." Doc White, the local chiropractor, had an office a few blocks up the street from the hardware store. The following afternoon, Bob went in to get his backbone cracked. "You know what? My allergies disappeared." I laughed. My father had cured me of asthma the same way. It had been a long time since I'd given him credit for anything.

When the time came, Bob had to gentle the bull out into the pasture. A doctor told Ed to take it easy, so he knocked off for three weeks, then went back to the store. "I'm fine." "Look, Ed," the doctor told him. "The only way you're going to get better is to get away from the store. Go down to Florida." So Ed took his own temperature and accepted the advice. He liked Florida. He rented a small aluminum rowboat, fitted out the stern with a six-horsepower outboard, stuck a Calcutta bamboo pole with a special rig in the bow, and went out after sharks. Huge sharks. Sharks the size of small whales. Some days you'd see him, his little boat offshore, leaning back against his bowed bamboo and sizzling line, slashing through the blue water on a Nantucket sleigh ride behind Moby-Jaws.

After five months, the old man came back from the sea and walked into his store.

"Well, Bob, the doctor gave me a clear bill of health and I'm ready to come back to work."

At this point, Bob thought *he* was the one who was going to have the coronary. He said, "Dad, you're past fifty-five. You know you're gonna want to retire in a couple of years or you'll never be able to get out of this place. You know if you come back now, you're going to be locked in again. You need to retire." To his surprise, there was no eruption.

"You're right," he said. "Why not? I'll try it."

Stepping into the boss's job had a profound effect on Bob: He felt much the same way he'd felt as a boy, bobbing thirty miles offshore in a one-screw wooden boat. He said, "Dad, this makes me nervous. I'm not sure I can do it."

"Ah, don't be ridiculous," his father told him. "Of course you can do it."

So Bob took over, running the place in Uniondale until the neighborhood turned so bad he had to pack a gun to the deli as well as the bank. At that point he moved the business to Sag Harbor, within easy reach of Montauk. Ed moved to Florida, spent summers in Montauk, kept his eye on things. "We always talked. All the time. Always matters of fact: business problems, problems with my finances. The weather. Advice on building stuff. Everything. But he never got mushy."

So the father retired to Florida and his sons grew to be men, and every summer when their old man came barreling north, they'd get on the phone and yell "Edgar alert!" Before he hit the Long Island Expressway, they'd be out there polishing the windows, cleaning the gutters, hanging pots of red flowers under the eaves. Then they'd waterproof the deck and paint the garage. After that they'd prune the shrubbery, limb up the trees, mow the lawn, and then collapse into the scrubbed chairs on the deck, waiting for him to pull up the drive. All summer he'd preside over new projects. Everyone respected him. Robby Rosen, the ferry captain, the guy who built 130-foot, $16-million boats, a genuine hands-on guy, would bring huge electric motors to Persan's workshop. "Hey, Ed. What's the matter with this thing?" And Ed would grab a screwdriver and go to work.

Brian Persan, the youngest of Ed's boys, watched his old man and absorbed lessons lost on wilder sons around Montauk. He was quiet, introspective, a work ethic loner so intent on perfection as a builder that he would still be ripping out and redoing jobs when others had already sent their bills. Winters he fed the feral cats who took shelter around his father's house.

The house next door was owned by Maxwell Desser, a painter of seascapes and boats, big in the American Watercolor Society, not so good around tools. Ed took care of him. "Max was a painter, so he didn't know much. My father would always be over there doing his work. You'd hear him yell, 'Don't worry, Max. Come on, Bobby, we're gonna rip out Max's fascia and put in a new one.' " Desser reciprocated with paintings. Ed's favorite was a large picture of Nick's Fishing Station in Shinnecock. "Big bunch of boats sticking out," Bob said. "Kind of abstract—but nice." His father liked the picture so much, he started taking it with him to Florida for the winter. When Desser found out, he painted a copy, exact except for one detail: He changed the boat trim from wood to chromium to make it look better in Florida waters.

A lot of good years passed that way until Ed neared seventy and his prostate attacked him. When the cancer metastasized, appearing in his neck, his bones, then his colon, Ed was stoical. Then one day he came home from the doctor and sat down with Bob. "They said I got about a year or two to live." Bob's mother said, "Bobby, I was there. The doctor said, 'You've got six months, *maybe* a year to live.' " Eight years later, Ed was still on his feet. One summer he spent hauling hundred-pound fish boxes on Gary's boat. Another of the neighbors was Dr. Marvin Kusher, dean of the medical school at Stony Brook University. He steered Ed to specialists who knew their business. But eventually Dr. Kusher took Bob aside and said, "Bob, you've got to watch your father. He's such a good specimen, even though he's got cancer, to be his age and healthy as he is, they'll try things on him. Don't let them make him a guinea pig."

Right up to the last summer Ed put up with everything—even those female hormones. That October, Bob drove him to the airport. One evening in early November, Ed called and said, "I feel like I've been shot at and missed and shit at and hit."

Ed Persan never complained. The old Army expression alarmed Bob. He called his father the next day.

"How you doing?"

"Better."

Bob let twenty-four hours go by, then he put in a second call.

"How you doing today?"

"Lot better."

That Friday he was feeling so good that Gary drove down from Melbourne and they went out to dinner. But by the time they were clearing the table and going for the coffee, Ed began feeling antsy. "All right, come on," Gary said. "Let's go back to the car." Ed missed the handrail, fell, and broke his collarbone.

On Tuesday, Bob got a call from his mother.

"I don't know, Bobby. Your father's not doing well." Bob heard her calling over to the hospital bed. "Ed, you want to talk to Bobby? He's on the phone."

His father, too drugged to talk, was saying "Hnnnn."

The next morning, Bob's Aunt Doris called. She was the baby in the family, the one who loved Ed the most. She said, "Bobby, you've got to get down here."

"How bad is it?"

"I don't know. I just don't want to think about it."

Bob caught the next plane and drove straight from the airport in West Palm to the hospital. "I guess I got there at 7:30 that night. Uncle Herb and Aunt Doris were sitting outside the room and I asked how they were. Uncle Herb said, 'I just want to warn you, Bobby. Your father's pretty sick. He doesn't look like you expect him to look.' " The three of them went into Ed Persan's room. "He must have heard us talking outside, because his head popped up. I thought he looked all right, considering. Aunt Doris is like, 'Edgar, Edgar . . . Bobby's here.' "

Bob stayed through most of that first night, taking his mother home at one point, then returning at six the next morning. "I couldn't leave him, couldn't leave him. I just felt I should be there. After a while, I said, 'Dad, it's okay to let go. You don't have to . . . everything's fine. Mom's taken care of. Everything's fine.' He knew he wasn't gonna recuperate. He just lay back. I swear it was knowing that he couldn't fight anymore."

Ed Persan died the next day. Bob took his mother home from the hospital. In his father's bedroom, an item on the dresser caught Bob's eye. It was something the soldier in Ed Persan wanted next to him until they took him away.

The BAR mag from his son.

Chapter 4

Double Jeopardy

"Sgt." Richard Vincent, U.S.
Army Intelligence, France, 1944

Richard Vincent lived by his stories, spinning them out as he improvised his life. There was the one about singing under the baton of
Arturo Toscanini—that fine day before World War II when Ezio Pinza,
another absentminded basso, borrowed Richard's score. There was another one about the Greenwich Village actors' pad, where James Dean
and Grace Kelly turned up for Richard's party. After that it was Albany,
that last great good place up the Hudson, drinking all night with

William Kennedy, the novelist, and Dave McKenna, the jazz pianist, roaring about art and Ireland until the clock struck three and everyone passed out. The performance was full of energy, artful, enthralling—a life crafted in place of the Great American Novel.

That life lay in fragments after World War II, the one story Richard's son never heard his father complete.

As a boy, Joshua Vincent couldn't even be sure of his father's rank during the war. Sometimes his old man said he'd been a sergeant, sometimes a colonel. Other times he just shrugged. When Richard died in his late seventies, Josh found his Army discharge papers. The form listed the Great Fabulator as a private first class. He had qualified as Expert on the M-1 rifle, the carbine, and the .30-caliber machine gun. In the box where the Army recorded PFC Vincent's military occupational specialty, a clerk had typed Entertainer.

On the few occasions when Richard did break his silence, he would say he'd landed at Normandy on D-day plus three . . . or was it D-day plus four? Dates, figures, places were vague, and they had a tendency to change. From the time Josh was a small boy, he could never be quite sure whether Richard was simply buffing up the past or trying to blow more smoke over it. One day when we were talking, Josh said, "My father was a remote figure. He really was. You couldn't get the war stuff out of him, never. Every time I tried there was this weird fog. You couldn't get hold of anything."

Alcohol threw Richard into mood swings. Nothing was more likely to bring one on than seeing his son play war. "Sometimes it was something stupid, like *Hogan's Heroes* on television. It was a travesty of life in a prison camp. He hated it and he hated seeing me laugh at Schultz and all those funny SS guys. He was right, of course." One night Richard walked into the living room and caught Josh yelling, "Go, go, go, kill the Krauts" to a good guys versus Nazis shoot-'em-up on the tube. "You don't know what you're talking about," Richard said, snapping off the TV set. Then he stormed out of the house.

I met Richard after he married my wife's twin sister in the early 1990s. He was what used to be called a man of parts—although none of them quite fit together. I liked him and spent a lot of time with him. Every night at seven o'clock he would turn on *Jeopardy,* consistently beating all the contestants to the buzzer. His mental and manual dexterity amazed me until I caught him sneaking a look at the six o'clock *Jeopardy* broadcast in a little coffee shop across town; but even when he wasn't loading the dice, he was a mad genius at the game, a one-man *World Book* of disconnected information: history and geography, science and the arts, sports, sailboats and vegetables, tuning forks, card games, or forgotten TV series like *Foreign Intrigue.*

He was eighteen years older than me and so much like my father— a fellow bohemian iconoclast with a self-deflecting sense of humor ("When my biographer arrives, just tell him . . . , um, I forget.")—that I used to practice on him. How far would he really open up? Very little. How much did he care? A lot. How much did he really hear? You couldn't ever be sure. One moment he was full of life and high spirits, then, at an instant, he was somewhere on the dark side of the moon. For all his working life after World War II—first as an opera singer, then as a writer of short stories and novels, then as a music critic, also an executive chef—he was always his own best story: a mystery, I thought in the ten years I knew him. Only after he was gone did I discover it was a war story.

The last time I had seen my own father, he was in the kitchen hitting the cooking sherry, watching Richard work behind the stove. The two old soldiers had a lot of things in common: their hard drinking, their killer instinct, their taste for deception, their fine ear for words, their infinite charm. They were both superb athletes, still edgy, unreconstructed competitors as they approached their eighties. In their time they had been world record holders in various events involving gin, scotch, and bourbon. Officially my father was dry, just not right then. Richard had also given up drinking, which meant holding himself to a glass of red or white at dinner. They were talking in low voices that night, fellow conspirators shorn of all innocence by the war, hardboiled sentimentalists of the Hemingway school who knew something that sons could never quite understand.

Like my father, Richard was distant, endlessly restless, as if his brain were tuned to a phantom radio that bombarded him with relentless bulletins. To drown them out, he was driven to odd extremes. A neighbor called him Opera Man because he was always singing. He had a deep, rich bass voice, and when he sang in the kitchen—also the bathroom, or the dining room, or out in the yard—his voice carried for miles. Sometimes he sang in Italian, sometimes in French, sometimes in the affected English of a *Voice of Firestone* radio star. "Bravo, Signor Padrone," he roared, rolling his eyes like Leporello. Then he would croon "Avant de Quitter ces Lieux" and morph into the noble Valentin undone by Mephistopheles. Shifting keys, languages, and personae, he would segue into "Myself When Young." Then, shaking the entire house, he'd blow out his pipes with a thunderous rendition of "The Lost Chord."

One day, when he was out in the garden singing to a tree, a five-year-old great niece, her huge eyes full of curiosity, tugged at his sleeve.

"Why do you do that?" she asked him

"I don't know," he said.

The feature playing at the Palace Theater was *The Longest Day*. On a summer afternoon in the middle 1960s, when Josh was six years old, Richard Vincent told him they were going to the movies. Richard was taking a break from tending bar at Mike Flanagan's Petit Paris restaurant and saloon. The Palace, on Pearl Street in downtown Albany, New York, was a dying movie theater built in 1931, a huge black cavern with three thousand seats. For the outing, father and son had the house almost to themselves. The trip puzzled Josh. His father hated Hollywood. But there was his old man, watching the screen intently as John Wayne, Henry Fonda, and Robert Mitchum stormed the Normandy beachhead and punched into the hedgerows of France. The big guns thundered, bombs and rockets shrieked down from the skies, grenades exploded, machine guns ripped into flesh and bone. Men toppled and died. In the dark, Richard leaned over and whispered to his son, "That was sort of what it was like. Not a lot—but a little bit."

A lifetime away from Omaha Beach, Josh, now on the far side of forty, remembered the moment more clearly than anything out of *Saving Private Ryan*. We were sitting in his office overlooking downtown Philadelphia, where he runs the Henry George Foundation, an international economic think tank. Josh was the same age as my daughter, so we mixed and matched generations in eccentric combinations. The first time I met Richard, we talked about opera. I asked him if he preferred Verdi to that Nazi Wagner, and he looked pained. The first time I met Josh, we talked about punk rock. Josh played bass in a group called The Lumpen Proles. He told me his first religious experience was hearing the Sex Pistols sing in Atlanta. He also said he considered Johnny Rotten his real father. I liked them both. For sheer passive aggression, only one other father and son I knew could match them: my old man and me.

"Quite frankly," Josh said half apologetically, "I'm a little obsessed with World War II." He had read all the books. His preoccupation was so intense that his girlfriend Kathy sometimes teased him about it. He was becoming so omnivorous, she once warned him, that *she* now knew all the details of the raid on Ploesti. Wasn't that maybe pushing things a bridge too far?

Josh told the story on himself with good humor. He admitted that when he was a small boy with Coke-bottle glasses, he'd numbed other kids with lines like, "Did you know that a Focke-Wulf 190 had a top speed of 245 miles an hour, but in a dive it could do . . ." He'd gotten over that. But he was still trying to understand how the war had shaped the men who fought it, how to measure the collateral damage. He said that Johnny Rotten, the Finsbury Park dead-ender, Peter Pan of yobbish boys, had taught him that everyone should be able to wake up in the morning and announce, "I'm here." "For many years of my life I couldn't honestly say, 'I'm here.' I'd have to think about it—and that I got from my dad." Later, he came to see that his father and the entire generation of soldiers who went into combat along with him did not have the luxury of answering to Johnny Rotten's roll call. The next minute—the next step under the bombs, through the mines, toward the guns—could mean you were dead. "You talk about the World War II guys," Josh said. "That was the thing that came back with them. At any moment it could be over. A lot of them thought 'Why commit to anything?' That's what I think happened. Most guys came back from the war fine. But there's a certain type of guy who didn't. That was my father."

Josh rose, pulled a folder out of a file cabinet, and brought it back to the conference table where we were sitting. Inside were his father's discharge papers. The basics were all simple and in order. PFC Vincent, Richard I., Army Serial No. 35 173 900, date of birth 21 August 1924, Concord, N.H., color eyes, blue, color hair, brown, height 5 feet 8 inches, weight 150 pounds. He had in fact gone through Normandy, and he had three battle stars (for the Rhineland, the Ardennes, and Central Europe campaigns) to prove it. But the other fragments of data were as mysterious as Richard himself. He didn't leave the United States until ten days after D-day, and he didn't arrive until three weeks after the invasion. So all that talk of D-day plus three or four was definitely Richard's new math. "My father had a very postmodern view of the truth," Josh shrugged. "Intentions were what counted. The truth was what you wished it to be."

All that Josh had been able to learn for certain was that Richard had been part of a troupe of actors and musicians in an Army road show called *My GI Back*. "One thing leads me to believe he did some kind of spook work. His Army papers all have different serial numbers. He went to five schools when most men went to two that late in the war, and he was given electronics training. But who knows?"

I handed the file back to Josh and he stowed it away. When he came back, he said he had at home a stack of letters his father had written to his mother and father on entering the Army. Reading them, Josh said, he could see the fog swirl up around his father until the draftee who had gone to war out of Westminster Choir College disappeared. "Before the war he was a straight arrow from a nation of straight arrows." Richard's father was a high school principal and coach in Akron, Ohio. His mother was the kind of proper club woman Helen Hokinson ribbed in old *New Yorker* cartoons. They wanted Richard to become the director of a choir, or, if God was good, to sing at the Metropolitan Opera House in New York. From basic training he sent them letters that were almost chatty in their innocence ("Today we learned how to take a hill"). But as he slogged through France and Belgium, he became laconic, cold. Detecting the tone, his mother wrote him a sweet V-mail letter. "I hope you find a nice girl over there," she said. "There are no nice girls," he wrote back. "I've seen so much ugliness here I don't know if I'll ever be able to look at things the same way." At the end of January 1946, when he came home to Akron, a Chesterfield dangling from his lip, his mother was horrified. "Oh, Richard," she said. "You used to be such a nice boy—what happened to you?"

When Richard died in the fall of 2001, his legacy to Josh was a bag—it weighed almost fifteen pounds—of papers: Among them were a scattering of IOUs going all the way to the 1940s, unpaid bills, threats from collection agencies. Richard hoarded dunning notes the way other men hoard bonds. He didn't pay them, but he didn't burn them, undoubtedly intending to settle up someday. Among the bills, Josh also found a number of letters from war buddies his father had touched for loans. The messages were heartbreaking. "Look, Vince, we don't care about the money. Just come and see us. Come stay with the family. See the kids. We've got a guest room. Please. Just come." Riding the Boom Years, the band of brothers wanted to help a pal who was lagging behind the squad. Richard shunned them. Eventually they gave up. After 1950 there were no more letters.

It was hot in Philadelphia. Wrapping up the day's chores for Henry George, a nineteenth-century visionary who wrote *Progress and Poverty*, Josh took a few phone calls and cleared his desk. That evening we went out to his sister Maria's apartment on the Philadelphia city line. Richard loved Maria, who called him every Sunday night. The phone in the kitchen would ring. Richard would beam and take the call out in his study. So far as I could see, he found it easier to talk to Maria than to Josh. That night she made dinner for the three of us, and over coffee we conjured up Richard on her television set. Fifteen years earlier, Pete Weinberg, Richard's oldest friend—an adman, jazz saxophone player, and paratrooper in the South Pacific—had aimed a video camera at him, trying against the odds to capture him for the ages. "I'm about to proceed into precarious ground," Weinberg announced, blowing into the mike as Maria punched play and Richard swam back to life on the screen.

"You can do it, Pete," he guffawed from beyond the grave.

Richard wasn't giving anything away to time. It was like watching a brilliant improviser vamping on Dashiell Hammett. He was wearing a dark leather flight jacket that set off the full salt-and-pepper beard. His voice was gruff, his sense of irony impregnable. His shaggy eyebrows rose dangerously whenever Weinberg started working too close to the truth.

"Why are we doing this?" Pete wondered aloud.

"Archival shots for my grandchildren," replied the Entertainer, though well into his sixties, he had none. "I have not been preserved on film as much as I'd like," he said, grinning at Pete. "The first film I made was under NBC auspices. I was seventeen years old, singing with the Westminster Choir when Toscanini recorded "Hymn to the Nations." That was my screen debut. This is my second time."

He paused, his timing perfect. Out in the living room, Josh and Maria rolled their eyes.

"Speaking to my grandchildren," Richard went on, "I just want them to know I am a great guy—and things are not always as dark as they seem."

Bravo, Riccardo, I murmured under my breath. Every time Pete tried to get him to talk about himself, he steered us toward his larger family, the Vincents of Ohio, New Hampshire, and Massachusetts, the American Revolution, the Western Reserve, the far side of the moon. There was the Vincent with much the same genes as Miles Standish, the silver-tongued Vincent who preached to the Cabots from the pulpit of the Congregational Church just off Boston Common ("A terrific act—very hard to follow"), the Vincent who was analyzed by Anna Freud and went on to establish the Chicago Psychiatric Institute ("Needs some verification," Maria said, sotto voce).

"The Vincents were essentially a loyal WASP family, very tightly knit, all good friends who remained in close touch until they all finally died. They were either teachers or they were ministers or they were farmers. There was no in-between. I don't know of anyone in our family who was in trade, which would have pleased the British aristocracy, you know, 'Not in trade, my dear chap.' "

"Wrong," Josh yelled disloyally. "There was Great Aunt Hope. She owned launderettes."

Safe on the other side of the screen, Richard went blissfully on to talk about his mother, Ruby Ingalls Vincent, who adored him as he adored her. The only time Josh ever saw him cry was on the day she died. "She was a direct descendant of Laura Ingalls Wilder, so there were lots of writers in my family. Laura Ingalls Wilder was my great-great-aunt. Maybe I'm missing one of the greats, but . . ."

Maria raised the remote, aimed it at her father, and hit PAUSE.

"I was never able to document the connection," she said. "My grandmother's name was Ruby Ingalls. Dad read somewhere that Laura Ingalls Wilder had an aunt Ruby. I remember him saying, 'How many Ruby Ingalls can there be?' There's something you need to understand about my dad. I think he got it from his father's brother. Uncle Howard thought that because his grandmother's maiden name was Bonney, we were related to Billy the Kid. Every time Uncle Howard would come home to Akron, my dad's father would say, 'What's Howard up to now? Am I going to have to lend him money?' The parallels between Uncle Howard and my father weren't lost on him for a minute."

She leaned back in her chair and punched PLAY.

Richard swam into view, unperturbed. "I got a scholarship to West-minster Choir College in Princeton, New Jersey. My father wanted me to be a singer more than anything in the world. I could have been a great baseball player—he would have been very pleased—but nothing like the way he would have felt if I'd gone and sung at the Met. He was a fine classical pianist, but opera was his bag. At his funeral they played Mozart. "Ave Verum Corpus," or something like that . . . Anyway, I was drafted out of there and I went to Fort Hayes in Columbus, Ohio. That was 1942."

Just as Richard was building up speed, Pete interrupted him.

"The war was on. You feel that? I knew my school experience was going to be brief."

"No. I was always a shallow type [delivered with a don't-believe-it tilt of the eyebrows]. I didn't think in cosmic terms. I didn't feel the breath of the draft board on my neck. It was happening all around me, but I didn't take it seriously. I never thought ahead to the next Monday."

"Yeah, yeah, yeah," Pete said, meeting the puff of irony with a friendly blast of sarcasm. "All right, then, what did *you* do in the war, Dad?"

Richard froze, then turned uneasily in his seat, looking away from the camera. When he returned to his story, his delivery was quite different. He had lost his air of easy persiflage. Suddenly his sentences became short, guarded.

"You couldn't even talk about it. I think the period was twenty years. You had to sign a thing."

Not SOP for an ordinary dogface.

"Ostensibly I was a combat engineer, and from that I was transferred to part of the OSS because it said on my Army records that I spoke French, which was barely true." Catching himself actually telling the truth, he made a quick recovery. "I had taken lots of French. Somehow, when they were looking for people to go into military intelligence—what an oxymoron—they saw that. I was supposed to be in France before D-day. I could have said 'Ouvrez la fenetre,' but I wouldn't have fooled anybody."

Where he had been surfing carelessly, staying in character with that "shallow type" he had raised as a dodge, he now became much more crafty.

"There's not much to discover. As a cover to what I was doing, I was in an Army show. I was a singer, and we traveled all over the European theater, to North Africa, Sicily, wherever. It was a legitimate show, but two of us, another guy, named Harry Morley, who had a great voice— I guess he was a first sergeant, but rank didn't have much to do with it—we were doing something else."

What, Riccardo, what? I sat forward in my chair.

"Before hostilities were over and right after, we were looking for Nazis trying to get out."

Then he started to bob and weave. "I went overseas in 1943, to England. That was in the combat engineers. Then they took me out and put me in the other, uh, deal."

Deal?

"From there I went to North Africa for a while, then to Sicily, then back to England. I went in on D-day plus three days. They sent us in as a unit. We were supposed to support the Army, but we just sat there until they were far enough in. Then we actually began to do our business. Our real business, Harry and I. The other guys had nothing to do with the OSS whatever. I was hopelessly ill equipped for this kind of stuff. It was a joke."

The second time Richard froze, it wasn't his fault. Maria had mashed STOP.

"I tried, really hard, to draw him out. It began when he started to make jokes about saving us from the Nazis. I'd ask him to talk about D-day. All he'd say was, 'It was a real mess.' Then he just went silent."

When the tape started running again, the phone rang in Pete's house and Richard was saved by the bell. Pete shut off the mike to take the call and when he got back, Richard said, "Okay, so that was the war. Next ..."

What followed was a Cubist account of Richard's life after the war. For a time, pulling down forty dollars a week from the Army to grease his way back into civilian life, he decided to not go back to choir college. Instead, he went to Oberlin for two years, then dropped out. He charmed a Connecticut deb, who married him, but they got divorced after a year and she married a rich guy, and Richard started stuffing that bag with overdue bills. For a while he moved to New York City, where he lived in a bohemian pad with the actors Jack Warden and Gene Lyons, who was going out with Grace Kelly. James Dean came around, Richard didn't think he looked queer, and he became very grumpy years later when the country started morphing its most famous rebel without a cause into a homoerotic icon.

All this time he was singing solos at St. George's Church down on Stuyvesant Square, a gig that earned him forty dollars a week, matching his earlier stipend as a Ruptured Duck. Then came Richard's big break, which he seized, and booted. He was taking voice lessons with a celebrated Fifty-seventh Street teacher, who prepped him for an audition with the Munich Opera. "I got the job," he said. "On the boat over, I met a guy who said, 'You got some time. Come on down to Rome.' So I did, and I stayed. I didn't go to Munich."

"How'd ya feel about that?" Pete asked him.

"I don't think I would have made an opera singer. You've got to treat yourself like a miler in terms of health. I've always been a great believer in self-abuse [pause for effect]. I'm speaking of drinking and smoking too much. Anyway, you've got to really believe in it, and I was boring to me."

The Freudian slip jumped off the tape. He had meant to say, it was boring to me. Could I have heard it wrong? Three replays. Nope. "I was boring to me." Richard was boring himself to death. "Anyway, it was too late," he said philosophically. His father was bitterly disappointed, but Richard moved sunnily forward, smoking, drinking, and slipping out of gear. He dubbed movies in Rome and New York, becoming swordmates with the actor who played Athos in a TV series of *The Three Musketeers*. He cruised the Via Veneto when *La Dolce Vita* wasn't even cool. When the Italian government cut its subsidies to film studios, he crashed with his Uncle Howard on the Rue Bonaparte in Paris for nearly a year. When Uncle Howard's wife urged him to move on, he returned home as a freelancer, novelizing Hollywood screenplays, writing a western called *Red* in six weeks of hyperactive creativity, scoring in the slicks with his short stories. He was successful, ready to go into the ring with Mr. Hemingway. But then writer's cramp spoiled the main event. "The Great American Novel got me," he told my sister-in-law in a moment of introspection. "I froze."

Back to the video. On the small screen, Richard told Pete that *Red* brought in three thousand dollars, enough to live on for nearly a year. After that, he sat down one day and banged out a short story about a major league umpire who makes a bad call and decides to hang up his chest pad. "I wrote it in one afternoon and they gave me eighteen hundred dollars." He'd reached the summit, conquered Everest, and then he sat down. "I never did that again."

"Nope," said Pete philosophically. "I don't sense a career path here."

Reaching for the remote, Josh stopped the tape to fill out the rest of the picture. For a while his father taught voice and creative writing at Kent State, where he fell in love with a talented student who became his second wife. In well under the conventional nine months, they had a son—Joshua. "I'm premature," Josh reported, fingering the remote. "Amazing how many of us there were in the Baby Boom—and so healthy."

In this Boomer's first memory, his father, entering a nautical period, is sitting on the patio of their house on Long Island Sound. Richard had struck up a friendship with Patrick Ellam, the famous British small-craft sailor—Ellam had crossed the Atlantic in a twelve-foot sloop—and the two of them had gone into business delivering yachts. At one point Richard managed to run a boat aground off the yacht harbor in Mamaroneck, which is where Josh's memory began. Josh was three years old and his father was sitting there with his baby sister Maria on his knee: one part Ahab, three parts captain of the *Pinafore*. From sailing with Ellam came some rollicking good times and more stories: There was the one about mastering navigation through speed-reading and making a dead reckoning landfall right on the nose in Bermuda; the other one starred Richard before the mast during a hurricane in the Gulf of Mexico. Opening the hatch, he yelled down to Ellam through the howling wind and buckets of rain, "Did someone call a cab? It's waiting."

Changing tack, he took a job as music critic at the *Albany Times Union*, where William Kennedy was financing his own lean years writing about movies. For a long time Richard prowled the Berkshires covering the great and near-great who spent pleasant summers playing at Tanglewood and other retreats away from New York and Boston. After one less-than-stellar concert, he slipped a pun about a "nocturnal omission" past his editors, and everyone in Albany except his editor had a good laugh. After seven years he quit. "It was time," he told friends. Drawing on his Italian period, he became a professional chef, working the best kitchens in Albany and teaching courses at the local university. Years later, whenever he stopped in Albany for dinner, old friends and students would come barreling out of the kitchen to embrace him. No one would let him pay.

In Josh's next memory frame, Richard is standing behind the bar at the Petit Paris in Albany a year or two later. Mike Flanagan, Richard's best friend, owned the place. It was on Madison Avenue in the Pine Hills section of town, a raffish, bohemian watering hole haunted by jazz musicians and writers. Richard is wearing a thin black tie and a white shirt. It is midday, and the serious drunks are already propping up the far end of the bar. Ignoring them for the moment, Richard carefully whips up a Shirley Temple and places it in front of his son. Then he turns around and roars, "This is my boy!" And everyone shakes hands. "I don't know what a father's supposed to do, I guess," Josh said mildly. "I can't say he wasn't around. He was around. The stock stuff— I just don't know." Whether he was acting from a split personality or simply covering all bets, Richard also had a job as sexton in the Presbyterian church on State Street. "That's a fancy word for janitor, just an image, but sexton was the word he used. He put on a good public image." Even so, he was an egalitarian, not a snob. Between shifts, Richard sometimes took Josh to Pat and Bob's, a longshoreman's bar in South Albany where he was always welcome and where he introduced his son to a life they didn't have out in suburbia. "There would be guys sitting at the bar saying shit, fuck, and goddamn, and they'd see us coming in and yell, 'Hey, shut the fuck up. Doncha see there's a kid in here?' " Man for a day, Josh wallowed in the good company.

With his fuel cells full of gin, Richard would do anything for his son. When Josh was four, he fell out of a tree, caught his leg in a crook between two branches, and wound up with a hernia that required an operation. To celebrate his recovery, Richard took him to Block Island. They drove down to New London to find that they had missed the ferry. So Richard hired a private plane and they flew across the Sound. "How he was able to charter a plane on a bartender's salary, I'll never know, but that was my old man. We did all sorts of cool, dashing things." The grandiosity sometimes backfired. When Josh was eight, Richard bought him a full-size, Willy McCovey baseball bat. McCovey was one of the tallest players in the majors and he swung a very heavy stick. Josh could hardly pick it up, let alone whip it across the plate. But it was the intention that counted. Richard bought him a glove that would have fit a giant. It engulfed Josh's hand. When the neighborhood kids came around, Richard would grab the huge basket and catch flies behind his back: Awesome, Josh, they all told him—you got one great old man.

Richard was one of the good guys, broad-minded, tolerant, though his politics could sometimes upstage his parenting. There was a white Albany and a black Albany, and the children of both met for the first time in the city's one huge middle school. When Josh was in the seventh grade, a geeky kid and an easy mark, a tougher set of black kids stopped him one day and demanded his lunch money. When he said, um, no, they knocked off his glasses, bounced him on the ground, took his change, and ran away. That night when he got home, he said to Richard, "Bunch of niggers robbed me." He'd heard the word for the first time from the white side of school, from Irish kids who told him he shouldn't let "niggers do that" to him. Richard blew up. "He turned magenta. He said, 'You never, never use that word again. Ever.' I was really impressed. I still get a little lump thinking about it. I'd never seen him really feel something, and believe me, I never used that word again." Richard had not saved Josh from the Nazis, had not risked his life fighting racism in its National Socialist form, to see his son turn into a little Ku Kluxer. But if he had given Josh a good lesson in human dignity and civil rights, it was mostly about principle and more than a little abstract. He didn't storm the principal's office or try to stop more muggings in the playground. I asked Josh whether his old man had done enough to stick up for him, to address the immediate problem: Someone had just beaten and robbed his boy. Now Josh said, "I never thought about that aspect of it." Richard, magenta, ruled.

Josh's mother Doris studied for a master's degree and got a good job with the New York State Department of Health. While Richard was bobbing from job to job, charming everyone from longshoremen in South Albany to the artists-in-residence at Yaddo, her steadiness and income kept Josh and Maria in groceries and clothes. "She was the one who made sure we were bundled up. She was always around. She provided the basics, he provided the glamour." The glamour was entrancing. In that zone, his father was world class.

To Richard, however, emotions, even the ordinary, day-to-day kind, felt roughly as comfortable as impacted wisdom teeth. This was understandable; he had constructed his defenses so fiercely that nothing, particularly emotion, could get out of his bunker. He'd forgotten the door. But that wasn't within Josh's range of insight during the years he spent debating the relative merits of Ravel and Rotten with his old man. Over and over, Richard would argue that rock wasn't even music: no intelligent structure, no complexity, nothing approaching the sublime, just three chords and a lot of brute stupidity. "He was always very technical, abstract. He tried to convey the beauty of music, but the feeling I never got from him. This was weird, because I knew his passion was real, he just couldn't convey feelings." Not about music, not about anything else. "Quite frankly, we never had a real emotional moment. He never said he was disappointed. He never said, 'Good for you.' It was like we were lodgers in the same house."

Josh geeked his way through high school, then told his father he wanted to go to the University of Puget Sound, as far from Albany as

he could get and still be within the Lower Forty-eight. Richard went magenta. Oberlin was where Vincents went, four generations of Vincents. That he had dropped out was not germane. Josh folded and headed for Ohio, but as soon as he got there, he started looking for a band. For two years he blew off the books, concentrating on the three chords his old man hated. Playing gigs from Cleveland to Lorain, he got pretty good, and then in the tradition of his father, not his grandfather or great-grandfather, he quit Oberlin and started to improvise. Flipping the bird to Richard, he went back to Albany and organized The Lumpen Proles.

The Proles had a changing cast. Josh recruited an old friend from high school and a metalhead from 288, the local punk club on Lark Street. They alternated on the band's two guitars, adding a drummer and an Italian art student percussionist, who later gave up playing conga to become a Realtor in Massachusetts. After that, he bought a bass, learned how to play it, and plugged himself into a giant amp. The competition was a New Wave band called Blotto, which had scored one hit—"I Wanna Be a Life Guard"—and a parody of a bar band called We Are the Now Tones. The first gig was at the Town Tavern on the corner of Lark and Washington. The local fanzine, *Blue Lunch*, sent a reviewer who praised Josh's cover versions of "Secret Agent Man," a Johnny Rivers hit, and "Bye Love," "a psychotic, bitter version" of the Everly Brothers' sucrose lament. Looking out over the crowd, Josh saw Richard. "I didn't expect it. I felt it was pretty cool." At the time Richard was working as a chef, but he knocked off long enough to hit the Town Tavern. He may have loathed rock, but he didn't miss Josh's opening night.

The Lumpen Proles stayed together three years. At their prime, they opened for The Bangles, who glittered more visibly on the charts. That night Josh saw The Bangles drummer carefully watching the Proles bash out their demented version of "Hazy Shade of Winter," a Simon & Garfunkel song. When he bought The Bangles' next album, there was the song again, the haze in the Lumpen Proles' arrangement.

"Direct influence," he thought. A score. Almost as good as his old man's baseball story.

The band spent its time drinking and writing songs, following its punk bliss until someone made the mistake of bringing in a keyboard player who slept with the lead guitarist's girlfriend. Not having the same financial stake as megabands, where such things were the norm, the Lumpen Proles broke up. "Chicks!" Josh groaned. He moved on to a band called E Plem Nista, Star Trek pidgin among the Yangs and Comes for We the People. (Kirk: "Don't you understand, Spock? Yangs—Yankees, Comes, Communists. This is the path our planet could have taken if they had destroyed themselves.")

The irony was that the more Josh tried to shuck off his father, the tighter he felt his old man's grip. At the same time, the weaker Richard's hand actually was, the harder he played it. After the war he had become a master of the timely default. "He didn't finish much of what he started, that's the truth," Josh told himself. The corollary was that Josh didn't finish anything either. As he advanced into his twenties, his father was closing out his fifties, and the war that had unstrung his old man was still there, warping them both, just beyond the baseline. Richard, the lame, demanded a winner. "Whatever I did was never acceptable. That's pretty standard between fathers and sons. You never measure up, I suppose. But it's hard to measure up to someone who isn't anything." If Richard had been a cop, Josh could have been a cop, or, to be ecumenical, a robber. With no steady point of reference anywhere in view, both of them lost their bearings. Richard became hypercritical, Josh went into passive resistance. He might stay up all night listening to The Clash, but the last thing he wanted was a direct confrontation with his old man.

The first real blowup came after Richard and Doris got divorced. She prospered, he wound up in a subsidized housing project called The Pasture working on the Great American Novel. Josh was pulling down $180 a week, Richard was broke. One day he turned up and asked Josh for a loan. Josh said, "You know, you still owe me from when you broke open my piggy bank when I was six years old." It wasn't actually a piggy bank. It was a Plexiglas bank that sorted coins into pennies, nickels, dimes, and quarters, with a slot for bills. Josh's grandfather had sent him five dollars, and he had pushed it through the slot a few days before Richard stuck up the bank.

"I did it for the family," he said, badly wounded.

"You didn't help the family any. It was a piggy bank, for God's sake."

"That's unfair."

Josh shut it down. He didn't want to get emotional. But he also had no intention of getting suckered into a loan. Drawing the line, he refused. His father left in a sulk. For the son, it was a more or less Pyrrhic victory. He was still living with his mother and sister, and eventually Doris suggested that he start thinking about a steadier line of work. So Josh left Albany to try his luck in New York City. Standing tall—and directly in his father's shadow—he got a job as a chef on a freighter, the SS *Andrew Jackson*, out of Fort Schuyler in the Bronx, a fine old tub that got him to Europe and back, expanding his possibilities far beyond the punk club on Lark Street. When he got off the ship, he moved permanently to Manhattan, where he thought he might still have a shot at becoming a rock star. While Josh was hustling bands and gigs, Richard reconnected. "You should go to Harvard," he said. "You should become a stockbroker." All right, Josh said. How?

"I know Jeff Bullard from First Albany Corporation. He knows all about you. Go down there, present yourself. Get a job."

"You talked to him?"

"Yes. Go down there, he'll take care of you. This is a big chance for you."

Since Josh's prospects were roughly confined to Tompkins Square Park, he got a suit and went down to Wall Street, where Richard's pal Jeff had never heard of him. This happened more than once. The next time, Richard told him Pete Weinberg would get him a job on Madison Avenue. All he had to do was show up. Pete would take care of everything. So once again Josh tried to be a suit. Pete took him to the Pen and Pencil, an ad guy's place, and bought him a huge dinner, which was welcome, because he was starving. Over coffee he said there was no job. "Here's fifty bucks," Pete said, taking out his wallet. "Thanks, but no," Josh said, and he ambled back to the East Village, telling himself that his father would never change: "If you wish it, it will be so. That's what he believes. Even though it never happens."

We now reached the final scene in Richard's Last Tape. Pete Weinberg was asking him about his divorce from Doris. True, he said. He was once again a free man. "So if anyone's out there . . ." he said, grinning seductively at the camera.

There was someone. Two years later he married my wife's sister.

Precisely at the moment Josh thought his old man was heading for the rocks, Sag Harbor offered him a snug berth. He scooted around the village in a little white Tracker with a bumper sticker that said CALL ME ISHMAEL. On Sundays he sang in the Old Whalers Church, rattling the windows from the choir loft. Pastor Chris and the church authorities invited him to deliver a guest sermon, and he said he'd do it, but they should understand that he didn't believe in God and would probably have to say so from the pulpit. The day of his performance he introduced himself as the grandson of a Congregationalist minister who had told his flock that he was going to leave the church so he could become a good Christian. The best thing about religion was the singing, and to keep the flock in Minard Lafever's Egyptian Revival landmark clear on that point, he composed a hymn for the church. A true pew pounder. He called it "For Shame Ye Joyless People."

You had to like Richard. He buckled his belt with a shark cast in bronze, a souvenir of his pirate period in the Bahamas. He'd talked to Hemingway at Bricktop's Bar in Rome, where Ava Gardner and Frank Sinatra burned out their marriage. Stored away somewhere he had a tape of the night he and Dave McKenna and Bill Kennedy all got drunk together in his living room. "I'll find it for you someday," he told me one evening. "Dave started to tell Kennedy how 'being so fucking Irish' could ruin an artist—and then he passed out."

Out in the kitchen, he could do more with a tomato than any WASP alive. Lois never had to cook dinner again. He could slice cheese thinner than Saran Wrap, feed an army on one roast chicken. He was a Red Sox fanatic, a football freak who knew all the statistics back to Red Grange, a deadly competitor. He played Hearts as if the object were to cut out yours. When he couldn't sleep, he'd get up and play through the night on the Internet, slapping Dirty Dora on hapless opponents in Bangkok or Singapore, shooting the moon. Just when you thought he was a killer to the core, he would start talking elegiacally about being a boy in Henniker, New Hampshire, where he had spent his first seventeen summers. His grandfather owned a clapboard farmhouse at the end of a dirt road on a hill where the skies were always blue. His father made the drive from Ohio in an old touring car with a trunk strapped on back. From 1924 to 1941 he spent sunny Augusts doing the chores, haying, singing, splashing in the spring-fed waters of the pond at the far end of the meadow.

While Richard was flourishing in Sag Harbor, Josh was polishing glasses behind the bar of the Irish Pub in Atlantic City. He'd moved away from New York, but this time circumstances began pushing him closer to his father. The Irish Pub was an Atlantic City landmark, though of a different order from the Whaler's Church. Cops drank there after work and so did local mobsters like Tony T, part of the old Steubenville mob—strong around West Virginia and Ohio—until Tony blew a bribe and wound up in a federal prison.

Joe DiMaggio also liked the place. When he was in Atlantic City, he'd stop by, dressed to the nines, bring in the satchel of magazines he usually carried and drop it on the bar, and shoot the breeze with Josh.

Joe D had the run of the Pub. One afternoon he walked into the kitchen to pour himself a cup of coffee and caught Josh wearing a Cleveland Indians hat.

"I thought you were a Yankees fan," he said.

"I am. It's just that my father's a big Indians fan, and I got the hat from him."

DiMaggio nodded, unimpressed, so Josh whipped out a baseball card he happened to have on him, a development, so far as I can tell, that only happens to Vincents. It was a Ken Keltner card, the Cleveland third baseman who stopped the jolting one's fifty-six-game hitting streak.

"Look at that," he said. "What do you have that for?"

Like Richard, Josh always had an ace around somewhere. So he and the great DiMaggio talked for a while, and when DiMaggio asked who was this Indians fan dad of his, Josh said his old man had once written a great sports story. *Saturday Evening Post.*

"I know that one," Joe D said. "It was about an umpire. About his eyes."

Josh, uncharacteristically, was struck dumb.

"That one was good. It read like it was real."

It didn't matter that it was the only one. Or that the story had been written before Josh was born. From out of the past, Richard had done something that mattered. You could look it up with DiMaggio.

Josh was impressed. But he didn't tell Richard what had happened.

The second break was even more amazing, as if O'Henry were working somewhere beyond the scenes to correct for Richard's Hemingway bias. The Irish Pub was a twenty-four seven saloon, and, as it happened, Josh's shift coincided with *Jeopardy*. The program was at the top of its popularity. Everyone watched it, including a squad of off-duty cops, who had noticed that Josh was even faster than his old man at the categories' Daily Doubles.

"You ought to try out for that," one of the cops told him.

"Yeah, yeah, yeah," Josh said, drawing another beer.

A few months later, a *Jeopardy* team showed up at Resorts International in Atlantic City. Merv Griffin owned both enterprises and he was holding auditions for the show.

"Hey," the cops said.

"Yeah, yeah . . ."

Josh didn't get the rest out. The cops grabbed him, stuffed him in a cab, and escorted him to the audition. Whatever Richard thought about his son, a polymath bartender looked irresistible to the Men from Merv. They signed him.

A few weeks later, up in Sag Harbor, Richard sat down in front of the small TV he kept in the kitchen. When he turned it on, there was Josh. That night and in the sessions that followed, Josh racked up $58,500 and a slot in the fall showdown of champions. This time it was Richard who got wowed. Josh rode into Sag Harbor like Destry. "We almost started to get to know each other," he says. "But I guess it got a little too much." After withholding the DiMaggio endorsement, he finally told the story to Richard, who went magenta, this time from sheer happiness. Then, Josh remembered, "I moseyed on." He also moseyed through the prize money in a year or so and wound up working as a cook on the Cross Sound Ferry.

Crossing the Sound two or three times a day, heating chili, flipping burgers, tending the deep fryer, still left time to think, and between shifts he got a part-time job doing research for an insurance company in New London. Richard had been thirty-six when Josh was born; now Josh had reached the same station with much the same hangover. "I was aping how he acted. I talked to people the way he did. I treated them the same way. I didn't have many deep or lasting relations with anyone in my life, including people I thought were friends." As this was sinking in, Doris's new husband, a successful businessman who had a lifelong interest in the economics of Henry George, called Josh and told him there was an opening with the foundation in Philadelphia. Josh caught the train south and discovered that his stepfather was no four-flusher: They were expecting him, there was a job, and he did so well in the interview, he got it. Devoting the same manic energy to *Progress and Poverty* that he had once put into the Lumpen Proles, he finally gained traction. A few years later he was promoted to director. The altitude improved his view of his father and himself. "I'd become so passive, so self-protective. I learned almost too late that you've got to stick with something. That's the way it goes. Maybe it's dull. And maybe you will get hit by a car tomorrow. But you can't assume you are going to be exterminated."

Richard reached his late seventies before his body sold him out. During the last few years of his life, even though he had a heart condition and a lot of other parts in need of repair, he was as stoical and tough as any first sergeant. After he developed cancer, I'd drive him to the vets hospital in Northport, where he'd bounce through the door for chemotherapy as if he were just getting his teeth cleaned. One evening, recovering from the chemo and just beginning to feel himself, he broke out a bottle of white wine and fixed dinner for Lois. Halfway through dinner, he said, "I don't want to alarm you, but I'm not feeling well and I think I'll just go upstairs and lie down."

He had always told her he wasn't afraid of death. It was just a matter of the screen going to black. Alarmed, she followed him up the narrow back stairs. At the top he nosed over on the bed. For a moment, he recovered enough to open his eyes. "Bye-bye," he said.

Lois called for an ambulance and then she called me. When I came running up the steps, an emergency team was pounding his chest. They worked for forty-five minutes, then strapped him to a stretcher and carried him feet first out the front door. We gave the ambulance a head start, then drove to the emergency room. The team was outside, looking glum. Inside, Lois started explaining Richard's condition to a young resident, who listened until she finished. Then he said, "I'm very sorry. But your husband died tonight."

The night Richard died, Josh was staying at the Comfort Inn in Pocomoke City, Maryland. He was on his way back from a conference in Virginia Beach. It was too late to make it all the way back to Philadelphia, so he had checked into the motel and called the number into his message machine at home. About seven o'clock, his sister Maria phoned him. I'd called several times with the bad news, and her voice was quite tense.

"Dad's sick," she said. "He's lost consciousness."

An hour and a half later, Maria called again.

"Dad's dead."

Josh hung up the phone, fighting back tears. He walked to a nearby TGI Friday's, where he had a drink and got dinner to go, then went back to his room. His sister called again, then his mother. "Obviously, you don't hate him after all," he told himself. When the calls were finished, he reached for the remote. The "Battle of the Bulge" episode from *Band of Brothers* was playing on the TV. He didn't believe in coincidences; they always seemed too damn contrived. But there it was: "I watched the whole thing. Then I turned off the TV and had a good cry."

The screen should now go to black, just as Richard wanted. But it didn't work that way. Richard's death devastated Josh. Grieving, he took several days to reach Sag Harbor. We arranged a memorial service at the Yardley funeral parlor. When I went in with Richard's blazer and glasses, the funeral director asked me for his Army discharge card. It was needed so he could get a flag and complete a few papers.

"Where am I going to find that?" I asked him.

"Don't worry," Mr. Yardley said. "It will be in his wallet. They all kept them."

He had seen it before. The yellowing card was there in the wallet along with Richard's last few bucks. At the service I read the umpire story and we played a recording of Lawrence Tibbett, Richard's favorite bass, singing "Myself When Young." Pete Weinberg was there. He got up and walked out when Mr. Yardley put on the canned recording of taps.

The following April, Josh and Maria took Richard's ashes north to New Hampshire, where the entire Vincent clan gathered for a final service. By tradition, the Vincents all had their ashes spread on the pond at the end of the meadow below Clarence Augustus Vincent's farmhouse, where Richard had spent those idyllic summers. We stood in a grove of hemlocks. On a rock, a muffled boom box played "I came like water and like wind I go." It had been raining and the pond was high. "I'm going to roll up my pants," Josh said, and he started for the depths. Doris intercepted him, gently steering him to a shallow bathed in sunlight. Josh upended a small black box, and Richard's ashes, mingled with daffodils, drifted off into the pond where he had paddled as a boy.

Henniker had always been Richard's Eden, the place from before the Fall, which was World War II. "I know there was a different guy there before the war, the real person," Josh said afterward at the reception. "My father knew it, too. He heard snatches, distant notes from the past. He knew what he had lost."

The mystery of Richard's war service seemed to have drifted away with him across the pond. But I couldn't get it out of my mind. Two years later I called Doris and asked if he'd ever said anything about the war that struck her as unusual.

"Yes," she said. He had told her something he didn't want anyone to know.

Richard had worked for an Army intelligence unit whose job was to hunt down Nazi leaders. One day he pushed through a door in a farmhouse and found himself face to face with a young German, not much more than a boy. He said the German looked exactly like him. For an instant both of them froze. Then Richard killed him. "When he told me, he wept," Doris told me. He couldn't stop. So the Entertainer shot his double and saved us from the Nazis. He paid for it with the rest of his life. The day he pulled the trigger he blew out his own center. All he had left were fragments.

Six months after the service, I talked to Josh again. "I thought we were getting to the point where my father was going to talk," he told me. "He was starting to feel the shadow. We were getting close, and I thought we still had a little time. Now . . ." The glass had run out on Richard and Josh. It was too late for them, but my father was still alive. How much time did we have left? Why was I still stalling?

Chapter 5

Frostbite

*Pvt. Arthur Nelson, back from the
dead, Long Island, 1944*

It **was** early September 1945, a season of heat and dust in the potato
fields of Long Island. Erik Nelson, a stocky boy with cornsilk blond hair
and large blue eyes, had just finished his first week in kindergarten. As
he came into his yard that day, the eyes picked up a stranger sitting on
the cellar steps. The man was holding his head in his hands.

Erik knew the man was a soldier because of the uniform. For as long
as he could remember, he had watched soldiers, thousands of them,

moving down the Jericho Turnpike in their dark green trucks, heading for Camp Upton and Camp Hero. They waved and then they disappeared—just like his father.

He could no longer remember what his father looked like, only the uniforms.

The stranger, hearing him coming, looked up.

"Come here," he said.

Erik took a step backward.

"It's me. Your dad."

Not possible. My dad is dead.

His dad had been dead since before the summer. That he knew for sure. His mother had cried when she opened the letter from the Army. She had told him and his brother and sister that their father wouldn't be coming back from the war. After that she had brought the butcher from across town to meet them. "This is going to be your new father," she had told them. Not good, Erik thought. He didn't want a new father. He didn't want his mother to be with the butcher. But there was nothing he could do. His real father was dead.

Now the stranger on the cellar stairs called to him again.

"I *said* come here . . ."

This time the voice was as sharp as a knife.

And then the memory broke off, hanging in time and space between 1945 and the next century. From across the living room in Ronkonkoma, Erik was looking at me blankly, unable to go on. He is sixty-three, and although the war now seemed as distant as the dark side of the moon, he felt its tidal pull within him the same way I do. "I don't know what happened," he said bleakly. "One day my father was dead. The next he just walked in on me."

What happened was that the War Department had made a mistake that shattered the lives of Pvt. Arthur Nelson and his sons and daughter. In the spring of 1945, Erik's father was in a hospital recovering from frostbitten feet, limping, but very much alive. He couldn't read or write, and he didn't get word home. Frostbite crippled tens of thousands of American soldiers during the winter of 1944-45. Among all

these casualties, the Army simply lost track of Private Nelson and reported him as killed in action. So his "widow" found a new husband. As
Erik Nelson was telling the story, Irene Nelson, his wife, stood behind
his chair, gently protecting his back. "I've tried to explain it to him,"
she said. "You have to understand. His mom was stuck with three small
children. She thought her husband was dead. Those were hard times.
So she remarried. Understand the times."

"My father lived to be eighty-two," Erik said suddenly, interrupting her.

Irene corrected his memory.

"Ninety-two."

"Ninety-two," he repeated, sucking in a deep breath. "And you
know what? In all those years, my dad never said he loved me."

"S'cuse me," he said, squinting back tears. And then he walked out
of the room. He had been a soldier himself, also a cop, and no one was
going to see him cry.

Irene Nelson let him go, watching sympathetically as he moved up
the hall. For forty years she has been studying the Nelsons, her husband, his father, her son. "I don't think Erik's father ever understood either," she said, speaking quietly so her voice wouldn't carry beyond the
living room. "It's hard for them to show their emotions. Erik's father
was never there for him." She paused. "Just the same way Erik was
never there for his son—until now." Then she went into the kitchen to
warm up my cup of coffee. From father to son to grandson, the damage
had spilled through three generations.

While Irene Nelson was tinkering with the coffeepot, Erik returned, his self-control in good order, and picked up the story. To understand what happened, he said, we had to go back to 1939, the year that
Adolf Hitler invaded Poland and Erik Nelson was born. His father
came from Commack, where the two cash crops were cucumbers and
spuds. It was a dirt-poor stretch of Long Island circumscribed to the

east, south, and west by endless potato fields. In the woods to the north, gray and silver foxes still roamed, along with an occasional albino deer. The village had a hotel, a garage, a baseball field bordered by Kern's Waffle Stand, and Werle's General Store, where you could buy two pounds of pork chops for thirty-nine cents. A box of black Climax shotgun shells would set you back four bits and a nickel. Five or six hundred years before the Depression, the Secatogue Indians—Pompos and Napanicks, Memsoworron and Perwineas—had given the place its name: Winnecomac—Pleasant Land. But the scattered fragments of evidence Erik had to rely on, a handful of photographs and documents, an old family story or two, suggested quite strongly that Arthur Nelson wanted only one thing from Pleasant Land—out.

There was no gene for impulsiveness in the Nelson family DNA, and it took Arthur Nelson a long time to make his break. His own father, a Swedish farmer, had come to the United States during a wave of Scandinavian immigration just before World War I. Arthur was three years old when his parents tugged him through Ellis Island. A nun gave the newcomers a rosary, which they couldn't use because they were Lutherans, and the civil authorities failed to make clear to them what they had to do to become citizens. Arthur's old man was a paternal fundamentalist: The father's first duty was to put enough fear of God into a son to keep him from hell, then enough food in him to keep him alive. Anything else was a luxury. Erik got out an old picture that shows his father standing in front of a farm wagon, muscular, stoical, tough. The look in his eyes says how many potatoes can one man pick?

So Arthur volunteered, and when he got home, Erik's mother, thanks to the War Department, was a bigamist. The problem rattled through Commack like a Long Island Rail Road milk train. "This was a small village, maybe five thousand people. Everybody knew everybody. You got in any trouble, someone would rat you out." All parties agreed that the situation demanded a quick divorce, but the plan left a crucial issue up in the air: Which husband would Dorothy Nelson keep? She had been married to the butcher for a few months; she had been

married to Arthur since 1936. Conceivably, she could have thanked the
butcher and sent him back to Fort Salonga and his shop. Instead, she decided to stick with the pork chops and leave the potatoes to Arthur.

The custody of the children was left to a family court judge. The
night before the hearing, Arthur assembled his children to discuss their
future. "My father said, 'You don't have it bad here. Gran takes care of
you. Clean clothes and everything. You want to live with your mother
or you want to live with us?' " The voice was broadcasting on the same
frequency Erik had heard out by the cellar steps. "It was like, 'You're
going to court tomorrow, kid. You better say the right words.' " The
next day the judge took the children into his chambers without their
mother or father and put the choice to them. Erik's sister Dottie, four
years old, picked her mother. Erik's older brother Ray said, "I'll live
with my father." Erik wavered, then set his compass by Ray. "I just
went along with the program. If I'd gone with my mother, my life
might have been different."

The program Arthur Nelson went on to devise for Erik yoked the
Protestant work ethic to the obedience of Army basic. Chilliness was
part of the Nelson family's Scandinavian tradition; but the war had
turned Arthur's emotions to dry ice, and with the divorce, his temperature sank to the cryogenic. When he issued his orders of the day, Erik
could follow them or be court-martialed and strapped. Love wasn't part
of the program. When he remarried after five years, he didn't tell Erik's
stepmother he loved her either.

Coldness was all. There was no furnace in Gran's farmhouse, no
lights, no toilet. Erik's grandfather upstairs was dying of cancer. "We
knew nothing about it. We always had to be quiet in the house. You
didn't say a word." Not having the price of a haircut, the way my father
had managed it, Arthur took Erik out to the garage, put a bowl over his
head, and sheared off his blond hair, leaving the boy as cleanly scaled as
any new private. "I looked like a real schmo." Then he pointed to the
goat, the turkeys, the chicken coop, and introduced him to the manual of
pails. "It was no BS. My father would tell you once. 'Okay, let's go.' He
believed in hard work, seven days a week. Work would never kill you."

Gran owned two acres, they rented another ten, and planted potatoes. Doubling up, Arthur also got a job as a carpenter. One day he came back to the farm with a war surplus jeep that he boxed in against rain and snow. He installed an Army cot in the bedroom he shared with Erik and Ray, the Nelson barracks. "Pajamas? Forget it. You had your underwear on, your T-shirt and shorts, and you ran down the steps to the kitchen where it was warm. My grandmother, old as she was, always got up and made a fire before she made breakfast." For years, Arthur skipped Christmas. Finally, one December he relented and Erik got a box of hard candy and a pair of work boots.

"Is this it?" he asked his father.

Arthur said, "You're lucky you got that."

The war's legacy to Erik was devastating in another way: The resurrection of his father cost him his mother. He saw her weekends for a while, then she moved and they lost touch. After five spartan years of bachelorhood, his father met a divorcée from New Hyde Park and asked her to marry him. He didn't, however, tell Gran; she was so strict that he didn't dare smoke in front of her, and bringing a new woman into her house, especially one with a small daughter, was almost as bad as tobacco. When she found out, she went for his throat. "You shouldn't be going out with another woman," she yelled at him. "Didn't you learn once? Don't trust women. They're all bad." Absorbing the scene, Erik found himself trapped between his grandmother and stepmother. Arthur's new wife tried hard, always keeping good clothes on the boys, dinner on the table, but even before Erik reached his teens he was miserable. "I hated her. She tried to conform me. Like with proper eating. I used to eat with my fingers—I was resentful as hell."

Gradually, as the war receded, material conditions improved around Camp Commack. Erik's stepmother sold a house she owned, bringing in some cash. Arthur had a small piece of property from before the Army. He cleared it of scrub oaks and pines and built a new house, moving his expanded family out of Gran's farm. If he was warming up, it didn't show in his color scheme: He painted the house gray. Then all around him, postwar prosperity began hitting Commack like a sonic boom. The

Long Island Expressway now stopped at Commack Road. Developers bought up the potato fields from farmers who cashed in after fighting their own losing war against the golden nematode, a particularly nasty little bug. The State of New York ran an overpass for the new Sunken Meadow Parkway perilously close to Arthur's dream house, piling a mountain of dirt in his face. He sued, collected twenty-five thousand dollars, and traded up, buying a better lot on which he built a larger house in the new ranch style. This time he painted the house red.

His moods swung wildly. One day the family was sitting around the picnic table he had set up in the yard. Erik had started smoking, always carefully beyond range of his father. That evening his stepmother picked up the whiff of tobacco on his clothes.

"You smoke?" she asked him.

Silence.

"I asked you a question. Do you smoke?"

More silence—ending in a Krakatoa explosion. "Lemme tell you something. My father comes across the table and rapped me so hard it knocked me right off the seat. I thought I got hit by Ali. You know what he said?"

I shook my head.

"He said: 'You don't like it around here, get the hell out.' "

It was 1956. Erik was seventeen years old. He went upstairs to his room and stuffed some underwear and two pairs of jeans in a small bag. He had no money. His pockets were empty when he came back down.

"See you around," he told his old man.

"You won't go far," Arthur said. "You'll be back tonight."

But Erik wasn't just going AWOL; he split for good, a getaway that was far more decisive than his father's. He hitchhiked into Manhattan. Just before the sun came up, he found himself on Washington Street, where trucks were off-loading sides of beef and crates of produce. "This guy came up to me and said, 'Hey, kid. You looking for work? I'll give you five bucks to unload my truck trailer.' " The rig was forty feet long, full of apples. Erik emptied the lot. When the job was done, he deadheaded back to Chicago with the driver. For a time he had a job painting flagpoles. He saved $250 and picked up a fake birth certificate, then he hit the road, heading west. He wound up in San Francisco, sleeping in the bus station, where an Army recruiter's office caught his eye.

Trying to sound older than he felt, he walked in the door.

"I want to join the service," he said.

"How old are you?" The recruiter looked at him skeptically. On his pipe stem legs, Erik stood over six feet tall but weighed something on the order of 140 pounds, and with his scrawny chest he didn't look like much of a warrior.

"Eighteen," he lied.

"You got a birth certificate?"

"Yeah."

The NCO looked at the paper. "How bad you wanna go in?"

"Bad."

"Where you from?"

"East Coast."

The recruiter drummed his fingers on the desk. "You gotta go back to New York to get registered. Tell you what. I'll put you on a military flight."

"I don't have any money."

"The Army will send you. You won't be in the service until you get sworn in at Whitehall Street."

"Okay," Erik said, and he signed the papers.

The recruiter returned his fake birth certificate. "You know what, kid?" he said. "A blind man could've forged it better."

Within two days of basic training, Erik was sure he had made the worst mistake of his life. He had jumped from Arthur's army into Uncle Sam's, and it took some time before he saw the significant difference between them. Erik had joined the brown shoe Army that marched between the Korean War and Vietnam, an interlude of spit and polish, not his old man's time of blood and bullets. He went to MP school, then joined the 101st Airborne, not so much because of the glory of Normandy—though his instructors had fought there—but to get ninety days knocked off his hitch. He put in his time, was honorably discharged. The whole time he didn't exchange a word with his father.

Before taking off, he had made it through his first year of high school; unlike his father, he knew how to write. He chose not to, which made his silence twice as profound. He was nineteen when he got out of the Army. A friend got him a job at Pilgrim State Hospital, a mental institution only a few miles from Commack, but he continued to observe radio silence. He liked the hospital. He had his own room, three good meals a day, a regular paycheck. Life was looking up. Then one morning, just after he'd turned twenty, he was digging into a plate of bacon and eggs in chow hall when two men walked up behind him. One of the men said: "Your name Nelson?"

"Yeah."

"FBI"

"FBI? You don't want me."

"Stand up. Turn around."

The two Feds clapped handcuffs on him and shoved him toward the door.

"You're shitting me," he said in disbelief. "I was in the service. We'll go up to my room and I'll show you my discharge papers."

"You didn't read the fine print."

"I put in two years."

"Let's go."

Erik had neglected to go to Reserve meetings. The Army had sent warnings to his last address, his father's place in Commack, but Arthur didn't forward them. A local judge told him he could go to jail for thirty years or go back in the Army. A few weeks later, he was back in uniform and in Korea. One day a friendly officer asked whether he had a high school education. Discovering that Erik had made it only just past the eighth grade, he arranged for him to get a high school graduate equivalency certificate. For two years Erik put in a couple of hours a week at the school, and when he passed the test, the officer called him to his office. "I'm very proud of you," he said. "Very, very proud."

The word must have been in Arthur's vocabulary somewhere, but he had never thought to apply it to his son. For Erik, Korea became almost snug. He was making $150 a month and he had a Korean girlfriend. "I was in love. Madly in love. Don't forget, I'm twenty-one and she's thirty, but boy could she treat you right." For the first time he wrote his father, telling him about the romance. And for the first time his father, who had by now mastered the ABCs, wrote back. The letter said: "If you ever get married to a Korean girl, don't bother to come home. I don't want to see you again."

After Korea, he ran out his second hitch at Fort Devens in Massachusetts, a base so bucolic he was able to make twenty dollars a day on the side picking apples. When the personnel officer came around to ask if he was going to re-up, Erik thought to himself, "I really don't have shit going for me except the Army. Think about it. You're getting three squares, a bed, eight hours a day, you can come and go as you please, nobody bothers you. Not a bad deal." Sensing the kill, the officer told Erik he could pick his next post. He also said there would be a five-hundred-dollar signing bonus. Erik re-upped and transferred to New York City, where he fell in love again, this time for life. And this time—fuck you, Dad—to someone who might as well have been German.

Her name was Irene Reitmann. Her father was a first-generation immigrant from Germany and she still had a million German cousins. Erik met her in a little bar on Flatbush Avenue called Moriarty's, where he sometimes drank when he was off duty. She was nineteen, with long blond hair and a ring on her finger. "Oh," he said, doing a double take. "You're engaged."

"I'm not engaged," Irene said sunnily. "*He's* engaged." Erik asked for her phone number. The next time he saw her, the ring was gone.

Just as he and Irene were getting serious, the Army sent him to a tiny village in Germany, where he guarded tunnels and acted as a courier for nuclear materials, writing Irene like a wild man. "My mailman used to get thirty letters at one clip," she laughed. "He used to say, 'What's wrong with this guy?' "

When the Army started lobbying for him to re-up again, he held back. Then someone said to him, "You got a girl back there?"

He said, "Sorta." They offered him a thirty-day pass and a free trip home if he'd reenlist.

"Sounds good," he said.

"You gonna reenlist?"

"Haven't made up my mind, but most likely I will." So he hopped a military plane and flew back to Irene. They went out a few times, and then one day he proposed.

"You know, this is bullshit," he said. "Can I marry you?"

"No," she said.

"Please?"

"Okay," Irene told him. He knew a justice of the peace. They got a blood test, a license, and then a marriage certificate in about the time it took to cross town.

"I told him, 'You're going to stay at my house tonight. Don't tell my parents—please.' "

"Am I going to sleep with you?"

"Hell no."

"Look, we're married. Put the marriage certificate under your mother and father's coffee cups. Let's go."

"No, no, no, no, no."

Irene slept in her room, he slept in the guest room. Irene finally told her father the next day while they were out for a drive. He nearly ran the car into a pole. When they got home, he took Erik into another room of the house and sat him down.

"Let me tell you something," he said, tears running down his face. "Don't ever hurt her or I'll kill you. Make her a good girl." In the Reitmann family, love ran right out to the nerve ends, not somewhere under the tundra.

When Erik got back to Germany, the reenlistment team called in the chips.

"You gonna reenlist?"

"Nope. I got married."

"Well, let me tell you something," he said, looking at the ceiling as if it might fall on him again. "You talk about every shit detail there is. They invented new ones."

It was 1964, about six months after the Gulf of Tonkin incident in Vietnam. The U.S. Army was sending advisers there, all regulars, to steer the South Vietnamese, and the American presence was poised for the massive buildup that followed a year later. Repaying Erik's re-up scam, the Army sent him on sixty days' duty to Vietnam. At first it wasn't too bad. "Once in a while you'd go out in the boonies for a night. No combat. The mortars would come in. You'd be in a foxhole and you had to stay alert. But that was it."

And then it got very bad. One afternoon he was in a chopper with a group of Marines flying back into Saigon. There was a burst of ground fire and smoke started pouring from the bird. As the chopper plunged down, Erik jumped out. "I hurt my leg something terrible. One of my ankles cracked. This wasn't bullshit like you see in the movies. Those guys were shooting real bullets. We had M-16s and M-14s, but I didn't know what to do. A couple of guys got hit. I got hit. We were supposed to save this top-security box from the chopper. This silly-ass box."

Among other secrets, the box held codes for tactical nukes.

"That was more important than your life. So there I am. I can't walk. I've lost my rifle, everything. Man, you talk about being scared. Then this guy grabbed me by my jacket and pulled me away. Except for him, I wouldn't be talking to you." A second chopper dusted him off to a hospital, where he stayed two weeks. The doctors patched up Erik's leg wound and sent him back to his outfit. When he came into the barracks, he saw that a number of grunts were missing.

"What happened to those guys?" he asked.

"Dunno," said an officer.

Punctuating the memory, Erik cleared his throat and choked off the rest. "You got killed, they just rolled up your bunk. Everything was top secret. You have no idea. I said to myself, 'I screw up one more time, they'll send me here permanently. This kid is out.'

"So I come back. I got a pregnant wife and I gotta find a J.O.B." A bank paid him $119 a week to train, but he hated "the tie BS," so he got a job roofing, then went to work for the railroad. "They called me at work one day and said, 'You gotta go home. Your wife's had a baby.' They didn't tell me what kind. I got to the hospital and called my sister and she said, 'Congratulations. Irene had a baby boy.' That ain't what I wanted. I mean, I said, 'Send this rugrat back.' I wanted a girl."

"And from then on," Irene said, "you treated John the same way your dad treated you."

"That's right," Erik replied. "I did."

So the aftershock of World War II, emanating from Arthur Nelson, coursing through Erik Nelson, now reached down to the third genera-tion of Nelson men. Looking at John Nelson, you might miss at first glance how he could have come from the same world that produced his grandfather and father. We were sitting in an apartment on the Upper West Side of Manhattan that was setting him back forty-two hundred dollars a month, one of the smaller rewards for winners in investment banking. The rent was exorbitant but also deceptive, because John was living like a soldier. No frills, no sign of any woman, just a mountain bike in the vestibule and a shelf full of books on combat.

President Bush was going on television later that night to warn the country that the balloon is going up in Iraq. "I can't believe it," John said to me. "We're going to war and I'm sitting on my ass at West End Avenue."

If ever there was a good soldier, it was John Nelson. He has been out of the Army for ten years. With a master's degree in business ad-ministration and a decade on the investment banker's fast track, he was beginning to look less like a commander than a sprinter stuffed into a banker's suit. On several fronts, he was under a new kind of assault. The dot-com boom was now a bust, and the bank where he'd made partner had just blown out all twenty-six members of his deal-or-death team. Beyond that, he had fallen into divorce hell. "They think I'm a gazillionaire banker," he says. "I told them you gotta be fucking kidding. Do I get to keep my couch?" In the hall, a stack of packing boxes rose behind his bike. The following week he was moving out. He no longer hailed taxis. "I do the subway thing," he said, managing a laugh. The wizard of the IPO had joined everyone else on the IRT.

Among the ruins, he seemed oddly cheerful, as if he had finally gotten a fix on where he'd been blindsided, armoring himself against all feelings, advancing so fast and hard he'd outrun all the maps. He traced the problem to his father and grandfather. "My grandfather was the most stubborn, opinionated sonuvabitch I've ever met in my life," he observed. "My father absolutely did not get along with him, but he became a mirror of that old bastard and made my life incredibly difficult."

His father joined the Army to get off the farm and away from his grandfather. He himself had left for exactly the same reason. Although John had gone to college before enlisting, he didn't think that made any real difference. "If I'd had to, I would have gone in as a PFC. I'm just beginning to put it together. The funny thing is that my old man mellowed out." After thirty-seven years of hostility, the son sent up a distress flare, and the father answered it. John shot me a go-figure look. "And that is the short version of the long story of how I went from thinking he was a complete prick to seeing that I was the same kind of asshole he was—and I did love him."

The longer version started to roll in John's mind when he was about three years old. For a while his father worked as a railroad cop. "The first thing I remember about him was how he had to go to work and I didn't understand where he was going or why or whether he was coming back. In my memory, I see him in uniform." Then there is a blank for four or five years, and when the lights come back on, John, home from school with his report card, is cowering in front of his father. "He wanted results and he didn't care how he got them. He didn't want to help with the homework, but if I came home with B's or C's, he'd whip my ass. One time he hit me so hard I pissed in my pants just out of sheer fright—and that pissed him off even more. Looking back, I can laugh at it, but I wasn't laughing then."

To John, his father looked mysterious, frightening. For misdemeanors, Erik applied the telephone book torture: All afternoon, to make John think about what he'd done wrong, he had to hump a stack of phone books around the living room. For more serious infractions, he had to dig huge holes out back, then fill them up, or shuttle piles of bricks in a wheelbarrow. For crimes in the first degree, John says, Erik's response was summary judgment and sudden death. "One time I gave him the finger under the kitchen table. I was so little I didn't even know what the finger meant, but he took me by the ass and threw me across the table—dishes flying everywhere—he just tossed me in the other room and pulverized me. He was a scary bastard."

The forces at work on the father were invisible to the son. Part of it wasn't hard to understand: His old man was often exhausted. Erik started civilian life paying eighty-five dollars a month for a five-room railroad flat in Ridgewood, but after John and Denise arrived, Irene started lobbying hard for more space in Ronkonkoma. For thirty-two years, Erik worked nights and overtime at the railroad; he always had a part-time day job somewhere else, leaving him no time for Little League or the needling why, why, whys of a bright young son.

"Why do I have to move the bricks, Dad?"

"Don't ask."

"It doesn't make sense, Dad."

"BECAUSE I SAID THAT'S WHERE THEY'RE GOING—THAT'S WHY."

Erik had told me earlier about the same scenes, describing them unflinchingly. Like most fathers from Adam on, he had said, "I firmly believed you were gonna do it my way. But John always questioned me. When he was seven, eight years old, I'd say, 'Start the lawnmower. Start mowing. I want straight lines. No misses.' I'd sit up on the porch, drink a six pack, watch him, make sure he did it right. Very much a discipline man. Take nothing to rap him on the ass." At that point, Irene had sighed.

"And could John ever get it right?" she asked Erik.

"No."

As Erik shrank from his father, John now did the same: If there could be no margin of error with his old man, at least there could be a margin of safety. In high school he got his own job, working after class and early weekend mornings at the local stationery store, where Mr. Strauss, the owner, liked him and treated him well. "Like a father," Erik had told me, without intending any irony. "Just like a father." He played lacrosse expertly enough to catch the eye of college coaches, then wangled an ROTC scholarship to a school in Pennsylvania. The day he graduated from Sachem High School, he came home twisting his lacrosse stick and ball in one hand and saying he was going to college.

"Where?" Erik asked him.

"Gettysburg."

"How far you think that silly-ass ball and stick's gonna get you in life? You gotta get out there and learn something."

Not a problem, John told his father. Not a problem? his father growled. Nope, John told him. He had it all worked out. He was going to be rich—that would take care of everything. "From sixteen that was his philosophy," Erik had said. "I'll be wealthy. I'll always have enough money to get things done." Then, accelerating past his father and grandfather, he did a double parlay with college and the Army. Under the terms of his scholarship, he graduated with a bachelor's degree and a commission as a second lieutenant. On graduation day, he and his father declared a moratorium on twenty-one years of hostilities. John asked his old man to pin the lieutenant bars on his uniform, and to his surprise, when Erik stepped back from completing the job, he had tears in his eyes.

Before going into the Army, John's plan was to go home for a few weeks, then move down to Baltimore, where he had a girlfriend; but in Ronkonkoma, it took only a few days for the cease-fire to break down.

John was twenty-two, Erik was forty-seven. "I don't remember what happened to start it, but he pissed me off," John said. "He was yelling at me and I told him to fuck off and walked down the stairs. And I'll never forget, he came running after me." John whirled around.

"I've had it," he said. "I'm leaving."

"You can't talk to me like that."

"Dad, I will just fucking beat the shit out of you."

John had never stood up to Erik before and it took his old man by surprise.

"I'll bust your head," he told his son.

Erik stepped forward, John pushed him back.

"I'll kick the shit out of you right now if you come at me again. I'm not going to take it."

Erik hesitated, John went upstairs. Following family tradition, he packed up his gear. Whether the first run of this psychodrama was replaying in Erik's mind, it's impossible to say, but when John came back down, their exchange did represent one small step of evolution since 1956. "I'm leaving," John snapped. Erik didn't tell his son, "You won't get far." He didn't say, "You'll be back tonight." He said, "Just say good-bye to your mother first."

When Irene Nelson got home from work, John told her, "I've just had it with this guy. Good-bye." It was their last fight. Erik could see that his son had size and reach on him. It was no longer possible to muscle him into line. If anything, John was getting even more hotheaded than he was. The memory still made John laugh. "I think my dad looked at me and realized for the first time—'Holy shit, I've created a monster.' "

Over the next three and a half years, John spent exactly two days at home. For the first part of that time, he was stationed in Germany, where his job was to lock and load a platoon of Pershing II missiles. Normally a captain commanded a nuclear missile platoon, but seeing John's promise, an alert major gave him the keys even though he was only a lieutenant. At the same time, the major said, "Little piece of advice I'll give you, Nelson. You're good, but you're not *that* good." It was a left-handed compliment, but an improvement over what he could hear above the lawn mower back home. The issue was authority; the question was how to exercise it. The major's reminder to his sharp young lieutenant was nothing more than Erik had been trying, in his way, to tell him: You still have a lot to learn.

To that point, however, John's experience had been limited to bucking his old man's orders. The Army taught him something about authority he'd never understood before. "If you think you can just yell 'Charge!' and soldiers will do it, that's bullshit. It's not in human nature. You have to build up a level of mutual respect. They won't move because you tell them to move. They'll do it because they trust you."

You didn't trust him. His own son didn't trust him.

Somewhere on the far side of my right brain, I could hear Les Ware talking to me again. My father had issued an order at the doghouse, expecting me to jump on his authority alone. If that wasn't enough for a soldier, as John was arguing, how much more so did it apply to a two-year-old boy? But there was something else: How much mutual regard can you develop when one of you is working on minnows in Mill Creek and the other is working on Germans in the Apennines? The war had provided my father with the style of command at the very moment it was depriving us of the fundamental core of authority: trust and respect.

I asked John if what he was saying about soldiers might apply within a family, between a father and a son. The contrast between the rules around Erik's house and the way John ran his missile unit was so total it made him burst into a guffaw. At first he said, "I don't know the answer," then, thinking it over, he made a connection: "The do-as-I-say mentality—that is the problem." Before I could get too heavy, he said with a shrug. "You gonna charge for this therapy?"

Whatever the Army did, it worked for John. Two or three days after talking with the major, John went out on his first exercise as unit commander. The night before the mission, stoking in the comfort food, he had picked up food poisoning. He woke up early in the morning to a cold German sky and torrents of rain. Out in the wet, eighty men were waiting for him to show his new grasp of command. "I've got an infantry squad, all my artillery guys, I've got a satcom link to National Command Headquarters in D.C., I've got three mobile nuclear missiles, and I've also got a fever, I'm puking my guts out, and it's pouring rain." As he walked from position to position, checking his defenses, he was thinking, "I've got shit running down my leg. This sucks. I can't have anyone think I'm a wimp. I'll go in the woods and clean up." At about that point, an old sergeant spotted him.

"You don't look so good," he said. "You got a fever? What the hell are you doing out here? You okay?"

"I'm fine."

When the sergeant moved on, John wobbled into the woods. "I can't control myself, I'm so sick. I remember sitting down on a log, cleaning myself up—I can still feel it. But, the Army had put something into me: I can't fail. Calling in sick isn't an option. There is no out except to be looked on as a poor leader. That's a death spiral." So he wiped his ass and kept going, and two days later he was fit and ready for the next death trip. I couldn't bring myself to ask if it had ever occurred to him that his old man and his grandfather might have been proud of him. How could you ever know?

Desert Storm swelled up just as John was finishing his tour in Germany. By November 1990 his car and personal belongings were already on a boat headed back for the United States. His unit wasn't going to war; the Army didn't need Pershing launch officers in the Gulf. "So I begged, pleaded, did everything but suck my colonel's dick, and he sent me up to the 2nd Armored Division, where they were short of officers." With another gung ho friend, he wangled a Humvee and drove three hundred miles to Gstadt, where he called his father. He told Erik he wasn't coming home and asked him to pick up his gear. "My dad said two things to me I'll never forget. One: 'Don't tell your mother.' And two: 'Just keep your head down and you'll be fine.'"

John volunteered partly because he was a professional and partly for a personal reason: He didn't want to fall short of his father and grandfather. When his mother, who was a Catholic, found out where he was, she sent him a Saint Christopher medal. "I thought for sure I had to accept death, because it was a probable likelihood it was gonna occur." He knew he would be coordinating fire from tanks, planes, and mobile field guns. Two days before crossing the line of demarcation, he went to confession, thinking before he went into battle he'd better get clean with God.

On the second night of the war, Saddam Hussein's Republican Guard came out of the wadis shooting at the 2nd Armored Division. John was so green he was standing out on the back of an armored personnel carrier as if he were still on a training mission. "What the fuck are you doing?" an astounded sergeant shouted at him, and when he clapped on his helmet, he heard the platoon leader in the lead tank yelling that he had hot spots all over their front. Enemy tanks were turning up everywhere in his thermal sights. "I'm like, 'Whoa, this is real, this is real,' and we just started shooting up tanks. The crazy part was that you had to drive past the tanks we hit, and they were still cooking off their munitions." Afterward, what he remembered most was the smell of burning metal, an acidic odor you could taste, as if you had put a copper penny on your tongue. The next time he smelled it was in downtown Manhattan after 9/11, oozing out of Ground Zero.

Up to that night, John's combat experience had been more virtual than actual: By a rough count, he had seen every war movie ever made at least fourteen times, maybe twenty-five for Audie Murphy in *To Hell and Back*. In the early hours of the war he had directed fire on an Iraqi tank and destroyed it, but the experience still felt like a training mission back in Germany. "I had this vision—I shouldn't tell this because it may be cowardly, I don't know—that I was going to be like Audie Murphy out with my bayonet, stabbing Iraqis in their trenches." Didn't happen. When his APC got stuck behind a berm and tracer bullets started scorching past him from an Iraqi position somewhere in the dark, he called for a tank, then waited until it pulled up and blistered the bad guys. "I'm like, no way I'm getting out from behind this berm until somebody takes care of that gun position. I should have got my M-16 and shot the hell out of them. It didn't even come to me to get out of my vehicle and take on their machine gun. Didn't cross my mind once." When the shooting stopped, he moved forward to a spot where he saw medics hovering over a wounded Iraqi. "This guy must have been running or something. A .50-cal went in one side of him and out the other. He was still alive, but almost cut in half. I put my flashlight on him and I'm like, 'This fucking guy's dead.' " While the medics tried to save the dying soldier, John rethought his sense of war. "I honestly thought I was going to be this Audie Murphy guy jumping from foxhole to foxhole. Now it was like, 'Fuck that.' "

John's war was over in 100 hours; his father's lasted 60 days; his grandfather's stretched out to more than 300. From grandson, to father, to grandfather, the experience of combat grew more and more intense; but to judge by the war stories they told, you might have thought it was just the other way around. Erik was always modestly matter-of-fact about the Army, treating it as a job. When he told John about the crash, it was not so much a star turn as an uncharacteristic religious experience. "He's not religious at all. Zero. But he said, being dragged across that field, 'You couldn't count how many bullets were around us,' and they didn't get killed. He's convinced it was a miracle. You ask him, he says, 'God will touch you when he wants to touch you.' " Arthur, the real combat veteran, the soldier knocked off his feet by frostbite during the Battle of the Bulge, told John only a single war story, and it was not about Sturm und Drang but German stew.

"He was talking about the Army, going through France. It was the weirdest story. He started out saying how you had to have your weapon with you at all times, and that one day he had come up on a farmhouse. The Germans had just left. There was a stew on the stove, and the Germans had left so quickly they didn't have time to poison it. He hadn't had hot food for a while, so he ate the stew. It was something that stuck in his mind, something he could talk about. I thought I was going to hear a big combat story. Instead, he had stew in some farmhouse—isn't that bizarre?" Maybe not, if the combat was five times or five hundred times worse than anything your son and grandson would ever see—and after you were carved up for all time you came home to watch your wife disappear with the butcher.

In an eerie replay of his grandfather's experience, as the War on Terror opened, John found himself watching his own wife disappear. It was late fall in Dutchess County. In the skies, squadrons of ducks were winging south above fields of skulking pheasants. One warm afternoon, after bagging a few birds at a rich man's shooting club near Millbrook, he sat in his car fighting off a deepening sense of gloom. In less than ten years, he had bootstrapped himself up from the Army to the world of the Killer Deal, but now his game plan was falling apart. At thirty-six, he could still run ten klicks in less time than it took most men to get up, shave, and flag a cab. In banking as in battle, he had not lost his command presence. But he was rapidly losing his wife. She had left a high-paying job in the private sector and was away in Afghanistan on mercy work, saving the world, feeding the poor, trafficking with mujahideen warlords even worse than the bastards he had fought in the Gulf. They both loved each other, but no matter what he said, he couldn't get her to believe that she meant more to him than the adrenaline rush of his job. He lived by a code of self-control, but now his life seemed to be careening. For an instant, feeling a kind of out-of-body amazement, he looked at the shotgun lying on the seat next to him. How easy it would be, right now, to shut the show down. And then the feeling passed. "Not the answer," he told himself. He took the shells out of the shotgun, broke it down, slipped it into its padded case, and drove home. After that, he did something that amazed him even more—he called his father.

That day in Dutchess County brought the Nelson men full circle from Arthur's day on the cellar steps. Once again a wife had gone AWOL (or free, as seen from the other side of the lines), and once again a Nelson, this time the grandson, couldn't believe what had hit him. From the Army he had aced business school, then propelled himself into the stratosphere at Bear Stearns, Solomon Smith Barney, and Bank of America. Like his grandfather and father, and at least in part because of them, he had developed a full metal jacket soul. In any war of wills—with his father, in business—he had fortified himself against all weakness. But in the war of the sexes, he was lost.

Reversing currents that had powered the Nelsons for fifty years, the crisis galvanized Erik. "All of a sudden my dad was calling me. 'How you doing? Everything okay? You need anything? Come out for dinner.'" So for the first time in years, John would go home and spend the night, and after a couple of months his feet landed on some unfamiliar but very solid ground. "It wasn't like my old man necessarily did anything specific. It was that all of a sudden, here's a guy who's trying to make sure his son's okay. That meant a lot to me. It was just that he wasn't an asshole anymore, and I had to stop being an asshole, too."

John laughed like a man who'd just received a stay of execution. "Man, you have to laugh," he said, slapping the coffee table with his hand so hard the cups rattled. "It really is funny." All of the Nelsons had guts and all of them were old-school patriots, but that wasn't the real reason all of them had enlisted in the United States Army. One after the other, in lockstep, Arthur, Erik, and John had signed up to get the hell away from their fathers, hardly noticing that they were all doing the same thing.

The pattern extended in a straight line back to World War II. Having left that cold comfort farmhouse in the potato fields, Arthur had returned from France to bend Erik severely out of shape. Instead of breaking the chain, Erik proceeded to hammer John. But when John saw his position being overrun and called his father, Erik had responded like the cavalry. "My dad was like, 'Do you want me to come into the city and stay with you?' He said, 'We could just hang out, or you could come out here and let's go fishing.' Anything. Just to make sure I was okay."

If the Nelsons could reconnect, why not me and my father? It would take something like the SETI hookup, where they link thousands of computers to radio telescopes aimed at outer space, searching for the slightest blip of extraterrestrial intelligence. Nothing in yet, but stay tuned. That was me and my father. But then again, I asked myself, wasn't it just possible that my father had been beaming signals all along, that the static was not in the transmitter but the receiver?

A few weeks later, Erik took me on a drive around the old family battle-grounds in Commack. Veterans Highway now roared across what had once been the farm of Arthur's parents. All that was left was the lane of trees that had once flanked the dirt road leading up to the farm-house. Gran's place, where Arthur had cut Erik's hair, and the gray house that had been Arthur's first success, were squeezed so tightly be-tween the Sunken Meadow Parkway and a four-lane highway that to spot them you had to risk your life slowing down among the honking ranks of homebound commuters. We made a stop at the Commack Cemetery, the immaculately green haven where Gran and Arthur's fa-ther were buried. Erik studied the headstone. "Know how much it costs to be buried here?" he said. "Sixteen grand." Forget it. He planned, when God touched him, to park his bones up in Calverton, where a vet and his wife could still get a rack from Uncle Sam. No charge.

It was raining that day, and while Erik was as hard as ever to read, the trip seemed to touch him. He looked out the window, pointing to a pond where he used to skate as a kid. Behind a fringe of cattails, you could see a small puddle, flanked on three sides by asphalt and speed-ing cars. Turning away, he said, as if from somewhere behind Saturn, "Was I a lousy father? Probably. Did I love my kids? Yes."

Then he stared out the window.

It wasn't a confession, just a statement of the facts, and it startled me. Love from a hard-ass father. Why did that have to be so hard to imagine?

When we got back to Erik's house, we went through a huge box of old photographs. He had never stuck them in an album, but for some reason he had kept them. He showed me the rosary the nun had given his grandparents at Ellis Island. When his own father was dying, he told me, he asked if he might have the beads. Sure, Arthur said. What the hell use were they to him anymore?

Among the photographs I found a tiny shot of a young soldier in an MP's uniform standing with a grounded M-14. At first I thought it was a picture of Erik. Nope, not him, he said. It was a friend from Chicago who had served with him in Germany. One day the young soldier came back from a run, checked his weapon into the armory, then went into the barracks to read a letter from his wife. After a few minutes he came out, went back to the arms locker, and signed out his M-14 again. Then he returned to the barracks, sat on his rack with the letter in his hand, and blew his brains out.

Erik stopped, as if there were no more to the story. I asked him what was in the letter.

"It was a Dear John. Shook me up. I never got over it."

A letter from the War Department to his mother. Fifteen years later, a letter from a runaway wife to a desperate young soldier. Forty-five years later, a cry for help and a rescue mission for an embattled son. Behind all of this, you could hear the rumble of World War II. But what had happened was no curse. Erik Nelson, a son, and John Nelson, a grandson, had broken the pattern. The one wasting energy on curses was me.

Chapter 6

Blue Devils

Sgt. Michael Savino, 88th
Infantry Division
Florence, Italy, 1944

Like a falcon on a crag, Teggiano perches on its mountain in southern Italy. The village overlooks the Vallo di Diano and fields once
plowed by the Romans. It is so remote that after the Germans withdrew
in 1944, no one else showed up. Then came Sgt. Michael Paul Savino.
To reach the village where his father was born, he hitched a ride, then
climbed until his knees ached. He was a stocky young soldier with

darkly alert eyes, and on the day he liberated Teggiano all by himself, he was wearing a baggy uniform at least one size too big. Old men slapped him on the back. Young women kissed him. Children swirled around him, trying to catch his eye. Someone dug out a camera, and dozens of Savinos squeezed next to their warrior cousin from America. The shutter clicked, and for the next fifty years everyone in the picture felt the same way. *"Michaele noi ha salvato,"* Sergeant Savino's cousin Giovanni would tell you. *"Si non per Michaele, tutte parla tedescho."*

So Mike Savino, a hero from Brooklyn, saved Teggiano, and to this day his relatives don't have to speak German. But the mission wore hard on him for the rest of his life. When he joined the 88th Infantry Division in 1943, he looked like an early Robert De Niro. By 1946, still in his early twenties, he had turned into a premature Paul Sorvino. More than half a century later, his son Richard followed his footsteps to Teggiano, searching for ways to understand what had happened betweeen the two of them after the war. The father was a soldier who took off his uniform and turned into a workaholic American Dreamer, remote but loving and generous behind the patriarch's glower. The son was a hyperactivist who grew up cultivating the gypsy in his soul. The booming forties and gray flannel fifties exhilarated the father, and he prospered. The weedy sixties, which did much the same for the son, set them at each other's throats. Through the worst of it, Richard couldn't bring himself to sleep overnight in his father's house.

By going to Teggiano, Richard recovered some missing fragments of Mike Savino's past. In the collective memory of the village, Sergeant Savino was still alive: young, innocently idealistic, gallant, and full of energy. Everyone remembered him. Richard was invited into a stone house where the owner had the old photograph from 1944 on a dresser. Suddenly there before him was his father, Mike the Liberator, as he looked when he was twenty years younger than Richard. It was as if the image in the frame had been developed yesterday. Other Savinos steered him to the house of the family's oldest living member, Zia Grazia. Walking through narrow streets lined with dark houses, he found her, a widow well into her nineties dressed in black. When

Mike Savino (center with baby) liberates Teggiano, 1944

Sergeant Savino had made his last visit, he carried an M-1 rifle. Richard Savino packed a Sony Super 8 Digital Camcorder. Aiming the lens at Zia Grazia, he asked if she had a message for his father. "Michael, Michael," she said, fluttering her hands. "Why did you never come back to Italy?"

The mystery was something Sergeant Savino kept to himself all his life. He never again returned to Teggiano, and he almost never talked about what he had seen or done as the U.S. Fifth Army fought its way up the boot of Italy. If you asked him if there was anything good about World War II, he would say, "The women." If you asked him about the bad things, he would shake his head and fall silent.

I met Richard after he married the daughter of a close friend of mine who died very young. Mary Quinn Savino brought him to the house, and even though he could have been my younger brother, early on I'm afraid I started grilling him in place of her father, making sure he was good enough for our daughter. On one of the early visits, searching for anything we might have in common, we started talking about our fathers and their war.

"What did he tell you?" I asked Richard.

"Not much," he said. "You didn't have conversations with my father."

"What's the first thing you remember about him?"

"Him yelling at me, smacking my head with his hand, breaking my glasses. With my father, it was always, like WHAM!"

Richard and I were sitting in my kitchen. He had come east to help his parents pack and move from the house in Lindenhurst where they had lived for forty-four years to an apartment attached to his sister's new house across town. For Mike and Mary Savino's golden wedding anniversary, the children created three photo collages of the Savino family history: the grandparents just off the boat from Italy between 1910 and 1918; the courtship of the Savinos in the 1940s; the Baby Boom children after the war, and the X-er and Next-er grandchildren who followed them. After studying the assembled photographs, Richard told me, what haunted him most was the transformation in his father's face before and after he went into uniform. "Just before the war he looks footloose, totally part of what we'd call the 'now' generation, stylish, cool suit, a smile on his face, individualistic. After the war, he tried to run his family as if he were still in the Army. Everything changed: He's stiff, severe, a conformist. The 1950s really shaped him. He felt that he had to fit in, that he couldn't be unique—I don't think he even wanted to be unique."

The words spilled out quickly, an arpeggio of memory. Richard was eating a bagel, washing it down with grapefruit juice to correct for the double-espresso he'd tossed down before breakfast as an eye-opener. He's a compact man, silvering up top at forty-six, but squirming on the chair in his blue shorts, his T-shirt drooping across his narrow chest, he has the boundless energy of a hyperactive eight-year-old. "I was a wild child, a little monster" he confessed. His grandfather had been a tyrant of the old school, and his father tried, with mixed results, to do better. Now and then he would take Richard to the office, letting his son play for hours with the Dictaphone. He took his family on vacations to the

Catskills and Montreal, Richard's first expeditions into the world beyond Long Island.

At the time, Richard admitted, the father's best efforts were mostly lost on the son. "As a kid, I could not comprehend my father's experience," he said. His father took himself and his role as head of the family very seriously. He also had to take care of his mother and, quite often, members of his wife's family. "It took a long time before I understood the full weight of my father's responsibilities." Richard started his own career in the Age of Aquarius, lifting rock and roll songs from the Byrds in a group called Arcturus (also known as Crazy Richie's Band). Now he records classical music from the sixteenth through nineteenth centuries on instruments from the period. Drumming his fingers restlessly on the kitchen table, he gave the impression of a man searching for a lost chord somewhere in the dead wood. "Looking back, I sometimes feel like a little shit who was just pissed off that he couldn't do everything he wanted to do. Other times, I think, my beef is legitimate."

In all the nonconversations Richard had with his father, World War II didn't even come up until the day Richard came home from elementary school with a Nazi book cover. He had made it out of a brown paper shopping bag. "Somewhere I saw a swastika. I didn't know what it was, but I thought it looked cool, so I copied it onto my book cover." By then nearly twenty-five years had passed since the liberation of Teggiano. The sight of the swastika on his son's schoolbook jolted Sergeant Savino out of his silence. "He freaked and tore it off, but he didn't whack me that time. He just sent me to my room. Afterward, he told me about Hitler and the Nazis, but he wouldn't talk about himself."

Richard put down his bagel and started pacing the kitchen floor, one memory prompting a torrent. The Savino house didn't have a basement when he was a boy. It was built over a crawl space that could be dug out later if you had the money and energy for the job. When he was twelve years old, spelunking the crawl space, he found an Army duffel bag. Dragging it out into the yard, he opened it. Inside he found Sergeant Savino's boots and steel helmet, a web belt and his canteen, a stubby trench knife and a longer bayonet. "He'd kept it all. The strange thing was that when he caught me playing with the box, he didn't smack me. He just said he didn't want his stuff lost. He was very uptight about me misplacing it. For some reason he wanted to preserve it." Two days earlier, Richard said, the bag was one of the things he looked for in preparing his father for the move across town. As he searched, he found a box, this one full of black-and-white snapshots. One of them showed a dozen GIs in a forest, hoisting beer bottles. At the bottom, his father had inked in A.W.O.L. Another captured Sergeant Savino clowning on top of a Sherman A-1. The caption on this one was Yank on a Tank.

Flipping through the curling photos, he found a formal portrait very much like the ones of Steven Greenberg's father and my own. In soft focus, it showed Sergeant Savino in his baggy uniform, hands folded, two campaign ribbons on his chest, an Errol Flynn silk scarf wrapped around his neck. Scrawled on the back, in fading ink, was a brief message:

Italy
Nov   1944
Your Loving Son
Love
Michael

The face under the soft cap was carefully composed, the eyes impassive, the mouth tight. From the picture, there is no way of telling what the soldier has seen. The only clue is the double use of love, as if Sergeant Savino was taking no chances on his mother's missing the message if he didn't get back.

After he returned alive, he kept in touch with a reunion group of old Blue Devils. In 1947, when one of them, John P. Delaney, published a combat history of the 88th Division, he ordered a first edition stamped with his own name. On the book's olive drab cover, a horned demon with a gladiator's sword stands with his feet planted between

Naples and Rome, the tip of his sword pointing to the Brenner Pass and the Alps, the 88th Infantry Division's last stop. Inside is a sampling of what Sergeant Savino couldn't tell Richard. In the fall of 1944 the Blue Devils provided the spearhead of the Fifth Army's offensive against the German Gothic Line in the Apennines. In rain and mud, through the cold and fog, they took Mount Battaglia and held it against seven frenzied German counterattacks, throwing rocks when the grenades ran out and the BAR gunners blistered off their last rounds. After that it was Hill 471, then Hill 435, then Mount Cerrere and Mount Grande, then Hill 581 and Mount Cuccoli.

Slogging forward, the 88th took them one by one. At Vedriano, a few weeks before Mike Savino sent the picture to his mother, the Germans received stand-and-die orders. In Delaney's combat history, the following after-action report appears:

> The stone wall came at Vedriano, where the Germans beat off every attempt to take the town. By now, all units of the 88th were in sorry shape. The constant driving, the mud and rain, heavy casualties which had cut some companies to as little as twenty men, the nervous exhaustion and low morale, all were danger signals that a crackup was coming. Commanders hated to order their weary men out—some platoon leaders risked court-martial by refusing to lead their exhausted remnants in any more assaults. Chaplains and doctors warned that any future attempts to advance would be dangerous, if not disastrous. Both the strength and will of the troops to go on were fast slipping toward complete breakdown... The 88th left its youth up there in those Apennines—left more than 6,000 dead and wounded on those bleak mountains—scrawled its mark in blood over every foot of that hellish terrain.

You didn't tell that to your mother. You didn't tell your son.

A fig tree grew outside the kitchen door of Michael and Mary Savinos' castle on Long Island. For nearly fifty years, the leafy green branches, heavy with fruit in late summer and fall, provided a flourish of Italy in a town named for its lindens. In the 1870s, German-Americans moving up and out of Brooklyn built Lindenhurst in rural Suffolk County. Along Wellwood Avenue they planted their kind of trees, perfumed in spring, skeletal all winter. After World War II the Savinos were part of an advance guard of Italians making a similar trek in upward mobility. When they arrived at 497 North Clinton Street, the first thing they did was reroot the fig tree. Just before World War I, Richard's grandmother had brought it as a cutting from Montes-caglioso, her village, in the arch of the boot. On the Lower East Side of Manhattan, she planted the cutting among the tenements of Little Italy. When she moved up to a two-bedroom house in Brooklyn, she transplanted the tree. In 1958, when Mike Savino took her daughter to the suburbs, the fig went into the ground as snugly as the new mail-boxes up and down North Clinton Street, most of them freshly painted with Italian-American names: Zito, Ferrara, DeFrisco, Rocco, Savino.

Following the best traditions of Italo-American immigrants, Mike Savino came, he saw, he conquered, working his way up from a two-bedroom house he shared with ten assorted relatives behind the old Brooklyn Navy Yard, where Richard was born. The GI Bill put Mike through night school. He earned an associate degree in accounting and got a good job as a factoring agent for Burlington Industries. Each morning he left home at 6:00 A.M., grabbed the Long Island Railroad into New York, returned at 6:00 P.M. for dinner, then worked out of his briefcase until 10:00 at night. He worked through exhaustion like a sol-dier moving forward on muddy terrain, and no one really noticed what today would be considered signals of distress: extreme rigidity, mood swings, rages.

To Sergeant Savino, an order was an order; to Mike Savino, the civilian, rules were still to be obeyed, enforced. When Richard was eight years old, he snuck his first smoke and hated it. "So one day we were walking down the street and I said, 'You know, Dad, I tried a cig-arette and it was really horrible.' And he turned around and belted me so hard in the stomach I keeled over. There I was, sitting on the sidewalk out of breath and he's looking down at me saying, 'Betcha won't smoke again.' That's what you got for being open with him."

To challenge his father on his own ground was a bad mistake. Still burned into the son's circuits is a memory of the time he decided to pipe up at a family gathering while Mike Savino was explaining the Domino Theory. Richard challenged him. On all sides uncles and aunts, cousins, and his mother closed their eyes. "Don't you sass me," his father snapped. Then WHAM, the smack in the face that broke the boy's glasses.

Did anyone ever stand in for your father—who taught you the ropes? I asked him, looking for a gentler guide.

The question made him smile. He stopped prowling. "My mom will deny this ever happened," he said. "But it's true. Most kids get sent to camp. I got shipped to the inner city for two or three weeks every summer to stay with my grandma and my Uncle Louie. I loved him. I'm like eight years old and he had a convertible, and we would cruise the streets of New York City in that beautiful car. He showed me the world. We'd drive to Idlewild Airport, it wasn't Kennedy then, and park and watch the jets land. He took me out to Flushing Meadow to watch them building the 1964 World's Fair. The whole time he'd be talking about improving the world: It was like, 'Ya know, we oughta be putting in a better transportation system connecting the subways to the express buses.' "

Uncle Louie had epilepsy, grand mal seizures that sometimes toppled him. Even so, when Richard was a small boy, Uncle Louie was able to drive a beer truck, and when the two of them weren't out in the convertible, he took his nephew with him on his rounds. "It was totally cool—eight years old and I was delivering beer." When Louie was busy, his nephew rode the elevated railways into Manhattan for a dime. "From the age of eight, I was free. It was Wild Child in the city. It was insane. My father loved Louie but had no patience with him, treated him like one of his own kids, which, given Louie's age, wasn't surprising. If I caused trouble, half the time they called me Louie by accident. It would just slip out. It was as if they couldn't tell us apart."

Where Uncle Louie was part brother, part spirit guide, an Uncle Mike on his mother's side stepped into the void. He had served in the Navy, where he'd been a boxer, and Richard Savino loved him. He had an eagle tattooed on one biceps; on the other was a heart pierced by an arrow and the word MOM. He had curly hair, a pin mustache, and a tenor voice so beautiful that he sang for the conductor Thomas Schippers and was offered an apprenticeship at the Met. When *Time* did a cover on Gian Carlo Menotti, that was Uncle Mike looking out from the newsstand as the Saint of Bleecker Street. Then his girlfriend said she'd never marry a musician. So he spent the rest of his life working as a welder. He had three of his own sons and a daughter. "He took us hiking all the time," Richard told me. "We got to be men in the woods with knives, four little boys and Uncle Mike—he'd find these tiny strips of woods, like between shopping malls, little parks with a stream and a path, and he'd make up stories, fantasies, and we'd be sitting there saying, 'Oh my God. Is this where the Indian died?' 'Yes. See this rock?' When you're eight years old, your vision doesn't go beyond the next frog you're grabbing." No one even heard the cars going by beyond the trees and stream.

After these interludes, test after test, Richard kept probing for his own father, there right in front of him but still more or less missing in action. The son's tactics were in-your-face. Nothing was sacred. He watched *The Godfather* "like thirty-five times" ("It was lore, our holy grail. Vito Corleone as King Arthur. Where was the Round Table getting all those Italians?"), then started needling his father about family values.

"Okay, Dad," Richard said. "Let's talk about the mafia."

"EVERY GROUP HAS A MAFIA!" Mike Savino roared. "They're all mafia. The Jewish mafia. The Irish mafia. It's not just Italians go wrong."

"So why is there so much heroin in Harlem, Dad? You ever hear the name Lucky Luciano?"

"You're talking garbage."

"All right, look right now at the crime bosses in America, the guys running all the big major syndicates. Why do their names all end in a vowel?"

"Why don't you just shut your mouth?"

How could he when everywhere he looked he saw another target of opportunity? "I knew who the wise guys were in our suburban neighborhood," he told me. "It was obvious. They were home all day. They had big, BIG dogs. They were big, BIG guys. Like Mr. M, six or seven houses down from us. I pick up the paper one day and find out he's part of the Bonanno/Genovese families' heroin-smuggling syndicate."

"How come Mr. M never goes to work?" Richard would ask.

"He works at night."

"How come he's up all day? Shouldn't he be sleeping? This is a guy I see a lot. I don't see anybody else's dad a lot."

"Garbage."

Then his life started imitating the movies. "One time when I was about sixteen, I was walking down an alley between a bar and the 7-Eleven and I came across this guy slumped against his car. He was covered with an inch of wet snow and I thought he was just drunk. So I'm about to pick him up and put him in his car, but his head flops back and there's all this blood on the white snow." Someone had beaten the man's face into osso buco. He was barely alive. "I call 911. I bolt. I'm a kid. I freaked. All right, a coupla weeks go by. They're looking for the 'anonymous tipster.' It's in all the newspapers and I'm getting nervous, so I call to unanonymize myself. I dial 911 and say, 'I'm the guy.' Funny thing. You dial 911 and they immediately have a tap on your phone. Ten minutes later there were all these undercover cops in my house.

"They come in, do the whole third degree. My father is standing there. This describes our relationship to a T.

"It's like, 'If he did anything wrong, take him away tonight.'

"The support—right there in my corner, Dad.

"So another week or two goes by. I had nothing to tell them. It didn't matter what I said. I mean, it wasn't like I ratted someone out. And then it turns out that someone else in our neigborhood is picked up for the murder. How was I to know? I mean the dead guy was a mile from our house. Okay, the suspect is a year or two older than me. His father and my father know each other."

"What did you tell them?" Mike asked Richard.

"You were right there, Dad. Nothing. I didn't tell them anything. First of all, the guy confessed, Dad. And even if I had said something, which I didn't, how does that change anything? Sonny murdered someone."

The confrontation is playing in my kitchen like a Broadway revival. Suddenly Richard pushes away from the table and stands up. Something is caught in his throat. For a moment his eyes mist up. "It was a very bizarre dynamic," he said, clearing the gravel out of his voice. "My father was more protective of his friend and *his* son than he was of me. In this scenario, he questioned my morals. We found out later that the guy had been hired by a local thug, a loan shark, to collect a debt. He'd just hired on as some muscle. He was supposed to go in and rough the guy up, that's all, and he went crazy. So he went to jail for a few years— he was seventeen or so—and he lucked out. A couple of years later, my dad and I were talking about law and order."

Richard started carefully, "So what do you think about the death penalty, Dad?"

"Right. I'm for it. We should kill all those murderers."

"Okay, what about that murder?"

"The boy was a good kid, Richard."

"Actually, that was true." Richard went on, "The guy was a good kid, he'd just fucked up, fucked up big-time. He and my father are still friends."

That was thirty years ago, but the pain still hurts like a rotting tooth.

Richard shook his head. "It was as if the murderer, not me, was his son."

Richard struck back, drawing on the full resources of the counter-culture for the counterattack. "I never punched him. That would have been death. He would have shot me. The sixties set up everything for me. I could just revel in them." Mike Savino liked the trumpet, so Richard told him marching bands sucked and taught himself to play an old steel-string guitar. Within two years he learned enough to form his own band and eventually to front for rock groups at the Bitter End Cafe in Greenwich Village. Reincarnated as a weed-sucking hairball, he would come home from the Bitter End to debate global issues with his father, Earth Day or Vietnam. When Mike Savino said that the Domino Theory was sound and that the Army was just trying to save good people from communism, Richard rolled his eyes at how the old man could be so naive about "geopolitical dynamics."

Not long after that, the son of one of Sergeant Savino's Army friends, a young soldier only a year or two older than Richard, came home in a body bag. "Guys just a little older than me were going, they did their duty, they got killed. And I was a longhaired rock and roll guitar player. My hair was down to my ass, and he wanted to kick that ass most of the time. I can't say I blame him." During his last year in high school, Richard registered for the draft and was assigned number 8 in the lottery. That was low enough to produce a trickle of sweat under his ponytail, even though Henry Kissinger was going to Paris to negotiate with the North Vietnamese. Taking no chances, Crazy Richie developed his own exit strategy: "I was going to Canada. That was clear to me. It wasn't exactly like escaping from East Berlin, but I had a route."

Then the Nixon administration turned the fighting over to the Army of the Republic of Vietnam, and Richard's number never came up. Instead, he devoted his undivided, if slightly out of focus, attention to expanding his consciousness with a variety of substances. His experiments baffled his father. Mike Savino drank a beer now and then, but he had diabetes, and most of the time he stayed away from wine. He didn't know what a doobie was. He thought reefer meant refrigerator car. The showdown, when it came, went like something out of *The World According to Garp.*

"It was a pretty crazy time. We were smoking grass in the high school cafeteria, out in the open. They had a smoking lounge for cigarettes. We sat in the back smoking pot, then going to class. Insane. It didn't help that one of the principals was a poet married to an abstract expressionist. I ran into him at a David Bowie concert. And then one night my father found me with a big bag of reefer. He flipped, totally freaked out. First he smacked me, then he pushed me aside and ran to the bathroom with the bag. He was holding it over the toilet, ready to flush, and all I do is think, hmm, he relates to money, corporate responsibility. So I yelled, 'DAD! That's worth fifteen thousand dollars. I'll be bankrupt.' Like I was saying a four-letter word. He handed the bag back to me."

"Get rid of it," he said.

"Not a problem."

Harvey Greenberg had addressed a similar problem by using muscle. Richard used cunning. After that night he was a lot more careful about where he hid his stash, and Mike Savino never again tried to smack him.

Richard stood up and started prowling again, as if motion were the only antidote for frustration. Looking at him, I thought, here's a grown man who owns thirty-three guitars and twelve lutes, he's recorded for Koch, Harmonia Mundi, Naxox, Stradivarius, Dorian, and Cantilena, he's a professor of music, he owns a four-bedroom house with a view of the sunset behind the Golden Gate Bridge—something must have gone right.

Eventually he reached the Stony Brook campus of the State University of New York, where he undertook his first formal instruction in music. Among a talented crowd of young teachers and performers who also taught at Juilliard and Yale, he found a surrogate father. The first time he went in to see his classical guitar teacher, the man sat him down in front of a chessboard and broke open a bottle of scotch. He said, "I want to see how your mind works." For the next three hours they played chess while the teacher studied the way his new student thought and moved. "The great thing was, you could talk to him and he would actually listen. He didn't want me to follow in the maestro mode. He gave me a ton of freedom, which was the only way I could do it." Years later, when CBS News showed Richard playing with Andrés Segovia, Mike Savino saw the story. Something within the father began to change. He counted a few blessings: His son was not a dead junkie; this hippie, miracle of miracles, had finished college, earned a doctorate; this weirdo fuckup was sitting in a master class with the great Segovia. If that old bird was yelling at Richard, what the hell: Wasn't that progress?

A father who would not let his son borrow the car until he was thirty-five—he was convinced Richard would get loopy on LSD and hallucinate right off the Sunrise Highway—finally tossed him the keys. When the son made his debut at Carnegie Hall, the father came, listened, applauded. A few years later he turned up at the Cloisters, where Richard was giving a concert of medieval and sixteenth-century French and Spanish music with the celebrated baritone Paul Hillier.

"I feel like I'm in church," Mike said.

"Uh, Dad, you are in church. This is a chapel. They reconstructed it here."

"So, do you guys do any tunes?"

Mike was thinking maybe Tony Bennett or Frank Sinatra, but for the first time Richard realized that his old man was actually trying. Not long after that, the doctors gave him Prozac. Suddenly he was a different guy. Jesus, Richard thought, they should have given him antidepressants twenty years earlier. The transformation prompted him to take a closer look at the balance sheet. His father had always provided for his family and any member of the Savino family, close or distant, who fell on hard times. Over the course of his working life, he'd accumulated significant savings, spending none of it on himself. One year when he bet on the stock market and scored big, each of his six children opened their Christmas envelopes to find a check for ten thousand dollars. When he reached his seventies, he divided his wealth equally among his three sons and three daughters, giving them part of their inheritance in advance so he could enjoy watching them spend it.

The final test came when Richard's oldest brother, well into his thirties, told his parents he was gay. One afternoon Richard came into the kitchen to find his mother fervently working over the range while his father sat at the table losing himself in the newspaper. It was one of the rare times the three of them had ever been alone together. Richard sat down to enjoy it. Then he saw that Mary Savino was upset.

"What's the matter, Mom?"

"Nothing."

She dropped a wooden spoon. "I knew she was not pissed at my father and not pissed at me. So I figured Michael had finally come out of the closet."

"Mom, you wanna talk about it?"

"Nope. Nothing to talk about."

Mike Savino disappeared behind the business pages. Finally his mother slammed down the wooden spoon and tomato sauce went flying across the room.

"I just can't stand the thought of him doing it."

"Ummm." Nothing more from Mike Savino.

Richard looked at me and grinned. "I'm like, 'Okay, well, you know, with all due respect, Mom, I really can't stand the thought of you two naked doing it, either. The thought is revolting to me.' "

With that, Mike Savino folded the paper. There had been a time when he would have flayed his son alive for making such a crack. Now he told Mary Savino, "That's the first smart thing this kid has said in twenty-five years."

The following day I was still laughing as Richard and I drove over to Lindenhurst. The fig tree was there by the side door, right where he said it would be, its green leaves shading a little sign that read MILK AND COOKIES, HUGS AND KISSES, GRANDMA AND GRANDPA. In the kitchen, Mary Savino rustled around in a cupboard and returned with an old glassine envelope. She opened it and spilled the contents onto the table: Sergeant Savino's stripes, a blue cloverleaf-shaped shoulder patch, and a Good Conduct medal still attached to its government-issue cardboard backing. I picked up the cloth stripes and ran my fingers over them.

Suddenly I felt an irrational impulse to steal them, protect them, make sure they don't get lost in the move to Babylon.

Then I heard Sergeant Savino coming up the stairs. At seventy-nine, Mike Savino is no longer the stubby little bull who climbed the mountain to Teggiano in 1944. He is wearing black orthopedic moon shoes and leaning on a cane, but he makes the ascent with an unmistakable dignity and sits down at the table. The old Blue Devil now looks about as scary as a Teletubby. His wife and son hover behind him protectively, wondering what he will say. Trying small talk, I say, "Italy must have been tough. The Germans didn't want to go home."

"They went home," he replied. "In caskets."

Richard picked up one of the old snapshots and nudged it toward his father. Sergeant Savino was the shortest guy in his outfit, five-foot-five—and that was pushing it—in his combat boots. He once told his wife that his legs were so short, it was hard to keep up with all the marching. In this picture he is standing on the side of an embankment next to a towering GI. The giant's feet are planted flatly on the road, the little guy's feet are nearly a foot up the embankment, and still he doesn't reach the brim of the giant's helmet.

"Who's that?" Richard asked him.

"Big Tiny. Friend of mine. From Brooklyn. We bumped into each other on the road that day. Just an accident."

It was all still there, the stories he never told. A lot of other things might have faded from Mike Savino's memory, but the war will be the last to go. For the next fifteen minutes he talked as if he had just come home, laughing at the Yank on a Tank picture, reminiscing about Big Tiny, explaining that he never went back to Teggiano because he knew it was the wrong place for him.

Modestly, he pointed out that he did not serve in a frontline infantry platoon. Most of the time he spent in the relative safety of a headquarters company, where his job was to keep ordnance moving to the front. The last of the snapshots showed him standing in front of a memorial of some sort with a giant wreath draped around his neck. We asked him what we were looking at.

"Dead soldiers," he said, and then he caught himself. "What's the point? Nothing you can do. Forget about it. The good things you remember, the bad things . . ."

His voice trailed off.

"What were the good things, Mike?" I asked him, setting him up for one last question.

"The women."

Mary Savino rolled her eyes, then looked at him with something like adoration.

"What were the bad things?"

"Those you don't think about."

When I got up to leave, Mrs. Savino handed me the olive drab combat history of the Blue Devils. Back in my own kitchen, I sat down and opened the book. The only time Sergeant Savino ever let down his guard, he had said that he had been shot at a few times flushing Nazis out of caves. I turned the pages looking for a fuller account. The story he wouldn't tell was there:

> The entire front was a nightmare of mud and fog. Days were
> hardly distinguishable from nights. . . . Rear-echelon units in the
> theater weeded out their able-bodied clerks and typists, gave them
> rifles and sent them up to the front. Inexperienced and untrained,
> many of these replacements were killed in their first few hours of
> action.

Sergeant Savino survived. For the rest of his life he must have wondered why. A week or two before he sent that picture to his mother, the Blue Devils had hit the stone wall of Vedriano. Another entry recorded what happened next:

> One fresh division might have been enough punch to get the
> Fifth Army through to the Po. . . . There were no fresh troops and
> the weary men who had taken the battle for more than six weeks
> had just about had enough. But the orders still came down to "get

that hill"—orders for a hill when one unit commander said he couldn't even order his men to take a house. That's where and how the drive through the Apennines was stopped.

The fresh division was parked in Camp Swift, Texas: the 10th Mountain Division. The Gothic Line had silenced Mike Savino. Now the Germans had withdrawn to the Winter Line, where they were well dug in and waiting for my father.

Sergeant Savino died six months after telling Richard and me that there was no point in brooding over dead soldiers. On the day of his funeral, they lowered the flag to half mast at the VFW hall. There was a requiem mass at Our Lady of Perpetual Help. At the end of the service, a local brass quintet formed up and blew Aaron Copland's "Fanfare for the Common Man" over his coffin. The music was commissioned in 1942, not long after the 88th Division was reactivated for the war; its premiere took place in 1943, shortly before the Blue Devils shipped out for North Africa. The fanfare is a difficult piece to perform. Resounding over Sergeant Savino that last day, it was all the more powerful for being slightly out of tune.

Chapter 7

Smoke Rings

Lt. Spann Watson, 99th Squadron,
Cap Bon, Tunisia, 1943

On a summer morning over North Africa in 1943, Lt. Spann Watson craned around in the cockpit of his P-40 Warhawk, a young man in a leather helmet and goggles, a stick in his hand, his eyes on full scan. He was flying Tail-End Charlie that day, returning from a mission with the 99th Fighter Squadron. Near Cape Bon he spotted a German Messerschmitt scorching the tail off a crippled Warhawk.

"Break right. Break right!" he yelled into his radio. "There's a plane in trouble."

"We don't know who he is," the squadron leader snapped back, refusing to alter course.

"We don't care who he is," Lieutenant Watson shouted back. "He's an American."

Breaking formation, he carved out an S-turn and flew head-on at the German. From the wings of his Warhawk, six .50-caliber machine guns raked the Messerschmitt. Trailing smoke, fragments tearing away from the nose, the pride of the Luftwaffe broke off the chase and vanished into the Mediterranean haze.

That's the way Spann handled a fight, and long after the war he expected his three sons to do the same. Even so, he was surprised the day Weyman Watson, his youngest, said he was volunteering for the military. Weyman liked jazz and crazy clothes. He spent a lot of time in Greenwich Village. He had a tendency to hang out with people who wore sunglasses indoors. Up to then, so far as Spann could see, the only thing about Weyman that stood tall was his hair. "You of all people?" the old fighter jock spluttered, his pride mixed with astonishment. "*You?*"

Capt. Weyman Watson, United States Navy Reserve, laughed as he told the story on both of them. "That was my old man. He thought I was a total hippie. He had been saying to himself, 'This is the screwup son I figured was coming sooner or later. This is the one who got away.' " We were sitting in his bachelor quarters, a large, prewar house in South Orange, New Jersey. The living room smelled pleasantly of fresh paint and varnish. When I asked him what was the first thing he could remember about his father, he said, "His skin bracer." Mennen aftershave. Forty years before Calvin Klein started getting thirty-five dollars a bottle for designer cologne, it cost a buck forty at the post exchange to buy the stinging green scent of a man. Spann Watson was born in the Deep South, but no one would ever mistake him for just another cracker colonel. Beneath the bracer, his skin was black.

To fight German master racists, he had to fight a homegrown set that did everything it could to keep him out of the sky. At the outset of World War II, the Wild Blue Yonder—in the view of the United States Army Air Corps—would always be lily-white. This did not improve Spann's mood. One time after the war, when Weyman's cousin Ronald came on a visit, he said, "Uncle Spann walks up to the picnic table and all you can see is this big black cloud." Some days he thought Uncle Spann was "the meanest, scariest man he ever knew."

The picnic table was behind the Watson house in Westbury on Long Island. When Weyman was in junior high school, he told me, the fathers of his five closest friends were all black vets who had served in World War II. On the Kelvin scale, the chill between fathers and sons ran close to absolute zero. "All my friends were going through the same thing," he remembered. "We thought all of our fathers were sore at us all of the time. Our mothers were cool, but these guys were bitter, really disappointed in us. We were never going to see eye-to-eye. They didn't approve of us. We were never going to earn their respect."

Weyman and his posse argued with their fathers all the time. "My father was a compassionate man," he said, balancing the equation. "When he was in a good mood, there was nothing like it. He'd pick you up, hug and squeeze you, laugh and joke. The only problem was, maybe 80 percent of the time, he wasn't in a good mood. He'd wake up pissed off. He'd go to work pissed off. He'd come home pissed off. And when the old man is pissed off, it just ain't a happy house. At night my brothers and sisters and I would hear the car pulling up and we'd say, 'Uh oh. Here comes Dad.' "

The black cloud mystified the sons. Weyman said he didn't understand it until he was nearly thirty.

"Why?"

"We didn't realize they were taking it on the chin every day. During the war and after the war. None of us knew."

"How could that possibly be?" I asked him.

"They didn't tell us."

The front door of Spann Watson's house in Westbury was painted Air Force blue. I had read about him in a history of the Tuskegee airmen, but nothing I had read prepared me for Spann on the wing. When I knocked, a voice from the other side called out, "Hold on. I'm coming." The door swung open, and I was looking at an older man with chestnut brown eyes and a mustache going to gray. Although he was dressed casually in soft brown slacks and a sport shirt, his command presence suggested that he could still withstand a lot more Gs than me. He appeared to be in his mid-seventies, though I learned later that he was nearly ninety. "Come on in, don't stand out there," he said, the voice a low baritone, rich with South Carolina sorghum. There was a baby grand piano in his living room, and his bookcase was full of works on the big bands.

"Ever hear of Glen Gray?" he asked me. "Casa Loma Orchestra?"

When I admitted I hadn't, he went over to a giant sound system and cranked it up.

"Smoke Rings," he said. "Listen to this."

For a few bars, a sax and a trombone, the heavy bombers of swing, laid down the bass line. Then, spiraling out of nowhere, a clarinet broke right and flew skyward in a dazzling Immelmann riff.

"My theme song."

We sat down at a green cloth-covered table in the dining room, where Spann was working on his memoirs. He started pulling out documents and old photographs. Grabbing for my reading glasses, I noticed that he wasn't scrounging for his. "Twenty-twenty vision," he said, tapping his temple. "Well, hell, almost."

He told me that when he was a child in South Carolina, once or twice a year he might hear an airplane, but he was never fast enough to actually see one until his father, Sherman Watson, transplanted him to the North. He handed me a snapshot that showed him as a kid in Lodi, New Jersey, around 1927. In his hands he was holding a model airplane.

Lodi was just one ridge away from the old airfield at Teterboro, a favorite with barnstormers and the Gates Flying Circus. On the Fourth of July in 1927, Spann and his brother Roy walked the three miles from Lodi to Teterboro, where Gates and his stunt fliers were putting on a show. In the middle of the performance, a lone monoplane suddenly appeared over the field and started circling.

The barker picked up a megaphone and said, "Fella seems to be lost. We'll send someone up to bring him down." An old Curtiss Jenny biplane took off to escort the lost flier down to the field. Spann studied the sky. A few weeks earlier, his mother had sent him to the post office to mail three dollars to some relatives in South Carolina, and the silver plane on the stamp stuck in his mind.

"That's the Spirit of St. Louis," he shouted.

"Well, get that, folks," the barker sneered. "Little colored boy here thinks that plane up there's the Spirit of St. Louis."

A huge guffaw went up from the crowd. Spann's face burned. Then the monoplane touched down at the far end of the airstrip and rolled to a stop. The window opened and a boyish face peered out.

"My gawd," the barker said. "It's Lucky Lindy."

It wasn't a circus stunt. Lindbergh had gotten himself lost. As the crowd ran deliriously toward the Spirit of St. Louis, Gates gathered all his roustabouts and the biggest men he could find, including Sherman Watson, to roll the plane into a hangar. Lindbergh escaped through the rear door, but before the getaway, Spann's father made sure that his sons touched the plane. "That was it for me," Spann said. "Lindbergh was my hero. From that day, all I wanted was to fly."

Ten years later he went to Howard University, where he enrolled in the Civilian Pilot Training Program. After completing the course, he got together twenty-four dollars and rented a Taylorcraft two-seater for three hours. Then he invited his mother, his brothers, his girlfriend, and his father to Teterboro and took everybody upstairs. His father was last in line. Sherman Watson was a farmer, blacksmith, and millwright, a good man with machines, but he'd never flown in an airplane.

"Okay, Dad," Spann said. "It's your time."

"Me?"

"Yes, you, Dad. This is for you. Let's go."

Lifting off, they crossed the Hudson for a look at Manhattan. Then Spann made a sweeping loop west back to Lodi. They flew over Garibaldi Avenue and the Millbank Bleachery, where Sherman Watson had found work. Spann said his father's genes didn't fit him for passive resistance, and he passed them on to his sons and grandsons. After a lynch mob murdered three members of the Loman family in Aiken County, South Carolina, he moved his own family to Lodi. When I asked Spann to tell me the most important thing he had learned from his father, he said, "To be a man."

"What did that mean?"

"It meant to be a straight shooter. Don't get mixed up in games, intrigues, foolishness."

After that he said he could sum up what he had learned from his father in a single word.

"Justice."

On the eve of World War II, justice for black Americans was an issue of zero visibility for the Army Air Corps. The prevailing ignorance of racism was that black men didn't have the reflexes to fly; they didn't have the intelligence to take care of machines; they didn't have the nerve for combat. So at the Army recruiting office on Whitehall Street in Manhattan, it astounded Warrant Officer Solomon when Spann started turning up once a month to volunteer. "He'd say, 'We're not accepting colored,'" Spann remembered. "Then I'd be back. 'No change.'" This went on for a year. One day Spann said, "Are there any other blacks applying?" And Warrant Officer Solomon replied, "No. You're the only one coming in here and giving us trouble."

Warrant Officer Solomon was mistaken. In the spring of 1940, the National Association for the Advancement of Colored People moved to sue the Army to break the Army Air Corps' color line. A young pilot from Howard University named Yancey Williams was the plaintiff. Spann was the backup. For five months the Army went into desperate evasive maneuvers. Then, at 5:18 one afternoon in October, one month before that fall's presidential election, a moment Spann never forgot, he heard over WOR radio in New York City that the NAACP was going to force the issue. Franklin D. Roosevelt was running for a third term and he needed black votes. The following day, the Army announced that it had decided to form a Black Eagle Squadron. In a flash, Spann was standing in front of Warrant Officer Solomon.

"We don't have any news about that yet," Solomon snapped.

"Okay," Spann said. "Would you give me an envelope and call me if you do?"

"No. We can't do that."

The Army's rearguard action kept Spann out of uniform for more than a year. When the Army Air Corps could hold out no longer, it grudgingly agreed to form a single squadron, the 99th, at a single base, Tuskegee, in Alabama. In early 1941, Spann reported for duty along with about thirty other young visionaries who had already qualified as pilots under the Civilian Pilot Training Program. Their Army physical could have been scripted by D. W. Griffith as a sequel to *Birth of a Nation*. "The doctors were all extremely interested in black men physically," Spann remembered. "One of our guys was so outstanding in his endowment we all called him 'Big Dave.' I remember the doctors gathering around him and one of them said, 'Man, you got all that for yourself?' "

When the cadets lined up for the eye test, one redneck doctor immediately started to flunk them. "He was saying, 'This guy has astigmatism. He can't pass. Here's another.' " A more levelheaded captain took a closer look. "That man's got perfect vision," he said, and he dismissed Doctor Cracker. The final interviews took place at a series of tables where officers evaluated the mental attitude and psychological fitness of the cadets. The last station was headed by a brigadier general. "We all had to go by him and his team. I was almost home free. And then this is how the general greeted me: 'What do you think of niggers marrying white women?' "

Spann held his temper. "I told myself, don't blow it. If you really tell him what you think about racist bastards like him, you won't be a cadet. Tell him something that will respect his question, not him. I didn't give a damn who a black man married. I don't think you should be white to be beautiful. In fact, I think if you put on a tan, you've got something unusual, a trophy person. The girlfriends I had could compete with any woman. What the hell, there wasn't any reason for me to go chasing white women. But marrying a white woman was a forbidden thing in those days. It could make real trouble for you. So I said, 'Well, sir, marriage is a very, very personal affair between two people. If those people think it's the thing for them and one's white and the other one's black, that's them. But for me, I would just as soon stick with my own people. I always will.' "

The general, expecting an easy kill, missed his target. Spann passed the physical, and the Army told him he would be called up later that summer. Then it double-crossed the black visionaries. Only one of the young, well-trained CPTP pilots in Spann's group was taken into the first class at Tuskegee. Most of the first junior cadets, all eager, brave, young men, had more connections within the black community than hours in the air. Pull, not experience, got them to the head of the line. This suited the Army. Lacking the flight time of the dreamers, the first recruits were more likely to wash out. Between the Army Air Corps and the string-pullers, Spann was grounded for another four months, a maneuver that put thirty or forty latecomers ahead of him in line of service. "I paid for that dearly my entire military career," he told me. Despite the lack of flying experience, seniority made the first pilots commanders, leaving more seasoned pilots to fly wing when the 99th went into combat. That was when the dark cloud began to form over Spann Watson. "I was pissed off then," he said. "I've been pissed off ever since."

The Army eventually told him to return to the Whitehall Street induction center. There, a last attempt to torpedo him failed, and he was ordered to report for duty. On Armistice Day, a month before Pearl Harbor, his mother drove him to Newark Airport, where there was an air show in honor of the holiday. The highlight was a dogfight between a sleek P-39 Airacobra and a stubby Republic P-43, predecessor of the

P-47 Thunderbolt. It was the first time Spann had heard the roar of an inline engine. Mesmerized, he watched the two fighters rip off high-speed runs. "What were you thinking?" I asked him.

"I was thinking, 'You're never gonna be poor again.' "

The Army could have trained the 99th Squadron in California or Texas. Instead it picked Alabama, where the base commander, Col. Frederick von Kimble, made sure that the barracks were segregated and that personnel did not have to wash their hands next to the black cadets. Whites had linen tablecloths in their mess hall with black waitresses to serve them. At one point, two hundred blacks had to line up for chow in a mess hall twenty feet long. Their seats were empty soft drink crates. A rope at the post theater, where Spann took his best girl, Edna Webster, to see Humphrey Bogart and Ingrid Bergman in *Casablanca*, separated the races.

The atmosphere improved modestly when a more enlightened commander took over from von Kimble. His name was Noel Parrish, and the first time Spann saw him he mistook him for a lieutenant, a slip von Kimble would have considered a court-martial affront. "I'm a pea-shelling redneck from the pea patches of Georgia," the new commander informed the stricken cadet, who said, "Yes sir." And then Parrish said, "We're here to do a job. We're gonna do it. You're gonna do it." "I said, 'Yes sir,' " Spann remembered. "I was looking all the way through his head. He had big blue eyes and I thought to myself, 'This is a man of destiny.' I didn't hate him. He was a straightforward man. He fought for you. Maybe that's why he retired with only one star. He should have had four."

At Tuskegee Army Airfield you got your wings in the chapel. After that, if you were in the 99th Squadron you went to war, while the new black 332nd moved to Selfridge Field north of Detroit for more training. If Parrish represented the best of the Army Air Corps at the time, he was as isolated as he was exceptional, and he remained behind when the squadron shipped out for North Africa.

On April 15, 1943, the 99th boarded the USS *Mariposa* in New York. The next day the *Mariposa*, a converted liner, nosed through fog into the North Atlantic. The ship was too fast to travel by convoy. For nine days it zigzagged east toward French Morocco. When Spann landed in Casablanca, he fired off a V-letter to Edna. "Was in Rick's Cafe last night." Then he boarded a freight train and rode to Oued N'Ja near Meknes and Fez, where Josephine Baker, the black torch singer and dancer, had taken refuge from the Nazis in Paris. She persuaded the mayor of Fez to throw a party, and the Tuskegee airmen quickly discovered that they were more welcome in Morocco than anywhere in Alabama.

At Oued N'Ja there was a dirt airstrip with an operational shed, a control tower, and Col. Philip Cochran, a hell-for-leather fighter pilot, dive bomber pilot, and friend of the cartoonist Milton Caniff, who used him as the model for Flip Corkin in *Terry and the Pirates*. Cochran's orders were to give the pilots of the 99th their final few hours of training before they went into combat, and he quickly sensed that something was wrong: Many of the new squadron's leaders had only 95 hours' flight time while Spann and others flying wing had as many as 240. "He called me aside," Spann remembered. "He tried to get me to pour it out. 'What's wrong here?' That's what he asked me. 'Why are you flying wing?' I didn't tell him a damn thing. I wasn't going to let a white man use me to destroy any black man who was flying in command and running the show. But he figured it out for himself pretty quickly."

Cochran took the 99th aloft and taught it everything he could in the time he had left. At that point, the 99th Squadron was flying the P-40L Warhawk. German Messerschmitts and Focke-Wulfs were one hundred miles per hour faster, but the Warhawk could turn more sharply and its six .50-caliber machine guns gave it an advantage in reach and firepower. The correct way to attack the Germans was to fly in a line abreast formation. By wheeling sharply right or left and flying straight ahead, a flight of eight Warhawks could bring to bear forty-eight guns on any bandit formation rash enough to attack it. The 99th moved to Cap Bon east of Tunis three weeks after the Germans got out of North Africa. At Fardjouna there was a dry lake bed good for Warhawks, but when Spann flew in, he saw two fields, one for whites, one for blacks. North Africa was in the hands of the Allies—and Jim Crow.

The white airfield was under the command of Col. William "Spike" Momyer, an ace with eight kills. The Army Air Corps considered this accomplishment sterling enough to offset a more embarrassing number: When Momyer first arrived with seventy-five P-40s, twenty-one had crashed on landing. The second base, about two miles off across the lake bed, was for the pilots from Tuskegee. Colonel Momyer didn't return the salutes of black pilots. Before the 99th's first combat mission, he gave Spann and the others the wrong time for the briefing. Emerging as Spann and rest of the squadron arrived, he snapped, "Y'all boys keep up," and headed for his plane. "That was it," Spann told me. "That was the way I went into combat."

The first time the Germans descended on the 99th, Spann was flying wing. "We did that famous 180 degree turn and came up line abreast." Fulfilling Cochran's fears, Spann's leader pulled too hard on the stick and spun out. Spann followed him down, but when he saw he would miss the action, he pulled on the stick and nosed up into his first dogfight. "In a minute you're sweating like a hog," he recalled. "But then you calm down. I got in some good blasts. You could see the German bullets and the shells. They were red-hot. Looked like you were flying through Roman candles. I thought, 'Damn, that little sonuvabitch could kill you,' and after that it was him or me. There wasn't time to be scared." The Germans broke off the fight, but after the 99th returned to base, Momyer reported that the unit had "panicked" and "disintegrated." The false report still burns Spann. "We didn't disintegrate at all. We were fighting until they broke away. The guy was a racist bastard."

I asked him if he'd told his sons about the way he felt. Did he tell them war stories? "No," he replied. "There were too many lousy things. As far as I was concerned, the war was over. I didn't talk about dogfights. I didn't talk about what you have to do when a lot of people get killed. There's no point in talking about that." He saw no point in talking about the eerie signature flash an airplane made when it hit the

Mediterranean. "You see it, you know one more guy is dead." He didn't talk about the night, flying above the clouds, when a wingmate's engine froze up and the pilot went down. The last Spann saw of him was a red glow up through the clouds when his plane hit a mountain. It tormented him when he returned safely after a pilot was lost. "The last time anyone saw him he was in a vicious dogfight with three or four Germans and you say to yourself, 'How the hell did he get out there all alone? Why did you let him get in that position? You should have been with him. You saw him over there, and you couldn't get to him to give him a hand and he never comes home. There's no point in talking about losing people. So many men. You come back and even five, ten years later, someone's telling you, 'Mitchell will be home. Graham will be home soon.' People do that. But you saw Mitchell hit the mountain. You saw Graham go down. They ain't coming home. You don't talk about that."

The color line in North Africa was drawn as sharply as anything in Mississippi. The day Spann broke formation to save the crippled P-40, the white pilot limped on to the white airstrip instead of landing on the 99th Squadron's runway, even though the black field was closer. He did send a message thanking whomever had chased away the German and saved his life. But the message came by phone. He wouldn't drive over to shake Spann's hand. A few months later, one of the Tuskegee airmen who had completed his combat missions was sitting in his tent waiting for transportation home. "Some guy from one of the white-area squadrons, for some reason or another, flew over our area and his drop tank hit the ground. It exploded and burned our man to death. You get all stirred up. Wing tanks don't just fall off. Did the white pilot do it on purpose? He couldn't have known the guy was going home. Nobody knew. But if he cut loose that tank, it was because there were black people below him. It did happen. You ask yourself, 'Could there be that much hate?' " The "accident" flashed through his mind one day more than fifty years later when he first heard the news about a black man being dragged to death behind a pickup truck in Texas. Shaking his head, he said, "It isn't over."

The Army Air Corps, having little interest in seeing the 99th succeed, had sharply reduced its sphere of operations and Spann had no opportunity to become an ace. After thirty missions, the Army ordered him back to Selfridge Field in Michigan and then on to Walterboro, South Carolina, to train replacement pilots. Over Christmas in 1944, he took a flat tire down to the Chevrolet garage in town, where a black worker promised to fix it right away. For the next four days Spann returned to the garage, but the tire was never ready. Finally he lost patience, cussed out the flunky, and demanded his tire. "Who are you talking to?" a short, fat white man asked him. "I was talking to him," Spann said, pointing to the mechanic. "But it could just as easily be you."

It turned out that the pudgy little guy was the mayor of Walterboro. He took a swing and hit Spann in the mouth. So Spann decked him, and when he stood up, Spann coldcocked him. At that point, everyone in the garage jumped him. He fought his way to the street, where he found three MPs, who sent for reinforcements. They were white. As a lynch mob swirled up, Spann told the MPs to be ready with their sidearms; he wasn't about to become one more black man killed in the South "while trying to escape." At that moment the deputy base commander, a fine white officer like Parrish, arrived with an escort of two dozen security troops. He ordered a special team of eight to extract Spann from the mob. The mayor's name was Sweat. When the riot was over, the Army transferred Spann, not wanting to bring any more heat to Mayor Sweat's damp white brow.

War stories, race stories, a lot of lousy things. Spann kept them to himself. He tried to be philosophical behind his dark cloud. "The war was so massive," he told me. "Probably nothing like it will ever happen again. You served. You had to live day to day at God's discretion. America was so different then. Everywhere you went someone was giving you hell on a racial basis. All that kind of crap. There's a lot of glory and flag business now. Yes, we served our country. I'm part of the Greatest Generation. We won the war. We built the A-bomb. America has bloomed into the greatest conglomeration of people in the world. And it's still a free country. But still, if we were the Greatest Generation, I'd hate like hell to see what the others were like. A lot of people who served did things that are never gonna get them into heaven."

When the war was over, Spann stayed in the Air Force. He found himself on a flight path toward the Age of Suburbia, a second American revolution that started just beyond Runway Three at Mitchel Field on Long Island. Spann knew Runway Three like groundling New Yorkers knew the Northern Parkway. Between 1945 and 1961, when the field was deactivated, he landed there more times than he could count. For the first few years, what he saw from the air was a complex of hangars, barracks, and administration buildings surrounded by potato fields; also the hospital where, later on, Weyman was born. He decided that the best place to buy a house and raise a family would be somewhere within a fifty-mile radius of the Empire State Building. Signing out a twin-engine Cessna, he started his search from Mitchel Field by overflying the New Jersey side of the Hudson River. He thought Rutherford looked promising, but no one would sell to a black man there or anywhere else along the Palisades.

One day in 1947 he saw bulldozers knocking down trees and carving streets into the fields. In the months that followed, he watched an army of carpenters, plumbers, and electricians deploy below him, escorted by an armada of cement mixers. With the same dizzy speed that had gone into covering the United States with barracks during the war, they poured foundation slabs, banged together walls, and wired all the sockets of 14,205 houses.

What he was seeing was the birth of Levittown. The development was named for a genius of prefabrication who spent the war perfecting the art of assembly line housing. The federal government subsidized Levittown. The idea was to provide reasonably priced housing for returning GIs. You could buy a starter house in Levittown for thirty-two hundred dollars. If you were white. "I went in and nobody would talk to me at all." Levitt was a Jewish immigrant, but he wouldn't sell a single house to a black family, even if the head of the family was on active service or a veteran who had fought the Germans and Japanese. He imposed the same color line on his next project in Pennsylvania. When Spann tried to buy one of the Levittown starter houses, every real estate agent he called told him to forget it. Eventually he bought a lot in nearby Westbury. Then he spent ten years between tours in Asia and around the United States trying to talk a banker into giving him a mortgage so he could build a new house. By that time he was rising past major to lieutenant colonel. He went to seventy-five bankers. All of them rejected his application. He got nowhere until the day he stumbled onto a black contractor, who referred him to a Jewish lawyer, who broke through the redlining banks and secured a mortgage. Flipping the bird to Levittown's cookie-cutter Cape style, Spann built a split-level ranch house that featured a recessed entrance and two towering white columns. Then he painted his front door that Air Force blue.

During those Boomer years, Spann's wife Edna, a devout Catholic, gave birth to two daughters and three sons. On his wall he had hung three formal portraits of his boys: Marlowe, Orrin, and Weyman on their confirmation days. As the oldest, Marlowe was first in line when Spann handed down his Four Commandments: DO WELL IN SCHOOL. DO WELL IN SPORTS. BE A YOUNG GENTLEMAN. LOOK OUT FOR YOUR BROTHERS AND SISTERS. Marlowe, easygoing, took it well. His only signal act of insubordination came after college. He had majored in pharmacy and he thought he might do well in the military. "He came to me and he said he wanted to join the damn Navy."

Spann couldn't believe it. Of all the armed forces, the United States Navy had the worst record on race. At the time, it had only three hundred black officers. What you did in the Navy if you were black was cook or serve white superiors in the officers mess. But the Navy had a good program for pharmacists, and Admiral Zumwalt, chief of naval operations, was making encouraging noises about recruiting black officers. Marlowe had taken him at his word. He applied. Then he waited.

And waited. No word arrived. While Spann laid down the law for his sons, he also stood up for them. When he found out what was going on, he fired off a heads-up to Admiral Zumwalt. "You're saying one thing, but your guys in the bureau are saying something else." In record time he got a call back from the Pentagon. "Your son will be in the Navy in the next three days." Marlowe stepped into uniform. Two decades later he was a full commander, equal in rank to his old man.

With Weyman, the youngest son, Spann's principal concern was that everyone adored him. He told Weyman he couldn't stand spoiled children, anybody else's or especially his own. He didn't want any mama's boys. So he issued Weyman his Baby Brother Commandments: BE A STRONG LITTLE MAN. STAND ON YOUR OWN TWO FEET. WHATEVER YOU DO, DON'T ACT LIKE A SPOILED BRAT IN FRONT OF SOMEBODY OUTSIDE THE FAMILY. If Weyman didn't polish his shoes, if he wasn't polite, if, worst of all, he fell and cried, Spann was all over him. Basic training lasted until Weyman was around eight years old, a robust little kid who could land on his tail, dust himself off, and get back into the game.

During the 1950s and early 1960s, the happenstance of being sons in a black military family sharpened the perils of getting along with Spann. The household was tense because Spann himself was always under an Air Force microscope. Wherever he was stationed, there were seldom any more than two or three other black officers. Spann pressed his family to make a better impression than anyone else. For Weyman and his brothers, it was like being preacher's kids. Their father wouldn't let them wear jeans or dungarees because he associated them with manual labor. When he'd been a small boy in the South, the uniform for black people was a set of overalls that he didn't want to see on his sons. When they went to picnics, they couldn't roughhouse because they'd be gigged if they got their pants dirty. If they went to the base officers club, they had to speak only when spoken to. When Weyman was nine, Spann took them to see the Mets play at Shea Stadium. For the game, they had to wear white shirts and dress shoes. Weyman thought it felt like going to church.

After Spann retired from the Air Force in late 1964, he finished his house in Westbury and started looking for a job in New York City. One day he stopped in an office on Sixth Avenue to sound out the personnel department for an executive job. He presented his credentials and asked if he might explore job possibilities with the company. The interview ran on for about fifteen minutes, and then the man across the desk said, "You've done a lot of things and you have a lot of good experience, but we don't hire any colored people for stuff like that." He at least was candid and reasonably polite. As Spann made the rounds, others said to him, "Look around. You see any colored people here? You might as well leave right now. We're not gonna hire you."

That was precisely at the same time the 1964 Civil Rights Act and the 1965 Voting Rights Act were supposed to put an end to discrimination. The reality was that at forty-nine, with more than two decades of service to his country, Spann couldn't get a good job in Manhattan. So he planted his family in Westbury because the schools were good and went to work for the Federal Aviation Administration in Washington, D.C. For the next twenty-seven years he commuted: five days and four nights in D.C., weekends at home. Over those years he integrated the skies of commercial aviation in the United States, placing dozens of black pilots, including several women, up in the cockpit along with four hundred young black women in flight attendant positions that had always been restricted to whites. And after he retired, the National Aeronautical Association made him an Elder Statesman of Aviation, the first black American to receive an honor that placed him side by side with Admiral Byrd and Gen. Jimmy Doolittle.

During much of that time, Weyman was cultivating a towering Afro that put him closer to the side of Shaft and Huey Newton than Booker T. Washington or Martin Luther King. Around Westbury, white and black kids who had played Little League side by side divided the school cafeteria into opposing war zones. You had to choose. To stay in the middle was to get your ass kicked by both sides. And as the sixties bled into the early seventies, arguments over the nature of black power opened a deep gulf between Weyman's generation and Spann's.

Spann and the other fathers who were vets couldn't tell whether their sons were just crapping out or whether they really wanted to burn down the house: They lacked focus; they had lost their commitment to improving life for the race. They were putting up Black Panther posters, pimping in black leather jackets as if they'd forgotten how to walk straight. They were calling anybody old enough not to buy their rap Uncle Toms, lackeys, house niggers. For half a century, Spann and the others of the generation of Dr. King and Roy Wilkins of the National Association for the Advancement of Colored People had been opposing racism with dignity and courage. Now these teenagers were telling them the solution was simply to "Do your thing."

So fathers and sons squared off. The sons didn't think they had to prove anything to anybody, particularly to white people. What they felt was an urgency to be black, to be who they were, to do what they wanted, which quite often meant simply having a good time like anyone else. The irony was that over the years since the war, the fathers had succeeded all too well. Bewildered and angry, they believed their sons were letting down the race. The sons counterattacked: They were only seizing the opportunities their fathers had created. Now and then Weyman would say to his mother: "We're just doing all the stuff they used to do. If it was them in our shoes now, they'd be doing the same thing we're doing."

He was sure he was right—but he never said it to Spann's face.

Of Spann's three sons, Orrin in the middle was the most precocious. As early as four years old, he started exhibiting sharp curiosity and mechanical gifts. Most little boys will pull toys apart, but not many can reassemble them so they still work. Orrin's brothers called him Butchie, and when Butchie put something back together, no parts were left over; everything hummed. At Westbury High, Butchie won prizes for his science projects. When he was fourteen, he talked the Civil Air Patrol into letting him apply for a flight training scholarship. Up to then, you had to be sixteen before the CAP would even look at you. Spann blew up when the CAP sent Butchie on a cross-country test flight that took him from Long Island, down the Jersey shore, and across Delaware Bay to Maryland and back. "Thirty miles of open water. It was wintertime. Dangerous. I didn't want to snatch the boy out of class, but I was damned if I wanted to see them drown my son. So first I got him a Mae West and then I briefed him: 'Don't get so far out over the water you can't see land. Tune your radio to McGuire Air Force Base and never go east of McGuire.' He got home that night at about nine o'clock. His first night flight. I was mad, and his two instructors were sitting there looking at me frightened to death." Butchie had stopped in Atlantic City because he was running low on fuel. He landed safely, and the two instructors made it home that night alive.

In 1967 a local congressman promised Spann that he would appoint the talented young flier to the Air Force Academy; but then a constituent with more influence got to him, and the congressman welshed. Spann went into action as if he were taking off from Cap Bon. He secured the help of a congresswoman from California who appealed to the Pentagon, and Butchie was given the appointment of a young man who had died. He wanted to be a fighter jock like his father. During the Vietnam War, when he was still a cadet, he flew combat missions incountry; but on graduation, the Air Force seized on his scientific abilities, made him an expert on nukes, and put him into a B-52. He put in eight years of active duty, then flew for American Airlines. But singleseaters were still his dream. So Spann wangled him a slot with the District of Columbia Air National Guard, and he took a six-month leave of absence to retrain on F-4 Phantoms. One night when he was well on the way to shooting past Spann in his Air Force career, he and two friends decided to go into town. A drunk driver, white, plowed into their car, killing Butchie and one of the other passengers and crippling the third for life.

The drunk walked away from the wreck.

"No-fault law," Spann said. "We couldn't do a damn thing."

"That must have broken your heart," I said.

"It does."

Butchie was killed in 1981. The tense his father used was the present.

On a warm April morning in the spring of 2003, Spann and Weyman went for a walk in the pines outside Johnston, South Carolina. Spann was eighty-seven years old, Weyman, forty-seven. The sun filtering down through the pines fell across Spann's stocky shoulders. He wore green pants, a light flannel shirt, and sneakers. He had a baseball cap pulled down over his eyes. The cap was black. Embroidered on the crown was a fighter and the logo of the Tuskegee airmen. For the expedition, the son carried a camcorder ready to roll. Spann carried a shotgun ready for anything. Before they set off, he borrowed the gun and a pocketful of shells from a cousin. Crossing the line of departure into the loblollies, he turned to Weyman and said, "You never walk around the woods in the South without a gun—can't be sure who you might meet."

Rednecks, moonshiners, Grand Dragons—the thought added a whiff of excitement to what would otherwise have been a sweaty hump through the woods. Weyman had to suppress a smile. Padding among the pines, his father looked as exuberant as a small boy hunting birds and rabbits. Every now and then, for the pure joy of it, he would raise the shotgun and blast a branch or shoot at the sky. "Dad, you keep shooting that way, somebody might think we're shooting at them," Weyman called out, but his father just laughed. "Don't worry about it, boy," he called over his shoulder. And firing for maximum effect, he sent another tree burst booming through the pines.

Weyman wore rimless glasses. His head was shaved in the style of Michael Jordan and his mustache was trimmed to the lines of Malcolm X. At 180 pounds, loping along in jeans and a T-shirt, he was spotting his father no points. Even so, Spann was moving so rapidly through the trees that it was hard to keep up with him. "Where you going, dragging me through these woods?" Weyman called after him. "We're getting lost." Up ahead, his father kept pushing forward, swift, as if he were pacing off boundary lines only he could see. "Just a little bit farther, just a little bit farther, just a little bit farther," he kept saying, the repetitions driving home the urgency of the trip. As Spann turned at the next bend, Weyman suddenly thought to himself, "We're heading for ground zero." The matrix of his father's mystery and strength.

Early that morning they had piled into a rental car, Weyman at the wheel, Spann riding shotgun, and set off to untangle the family roots. As the crow flies, they were about twenty-five miles to the northwest of Aiken, but they had driven and walked the better part of a century back in time. They'd found Spann's oldest living relative, Gertie Lee Dean, who was ninety-six and living alone in a small house at the end of a dirt road. Spann had pulled out a notebook full of names and they worked through the Watson family tree. Weyman watched his father and thought, "He's making sure everything is put into place so it's not lost, totally forgotten, gone with the wind." Spann was born in 1916, halfway through Woodrow Wilson's war to end all wars. His birthplace was a post house, or cabin, built by slaves about the time James Monroe took office. The first thing Spann could remember was a visit that his grandmother, Amelia Campbell, who had been a slave, had paid to his family. "Grandma Amelia was telling us stories about activities during the slave years—of outfoxing the master. She had a couple of young women with her, and they were splitting their sides laughing. Yes, that's it. That was my first memory. I never forget."

The days of bondage were an enormous leap from the Days Inn where Spann and Weyman had started the morning. Their first objective was that old cabin, and they searched for an hour, but the red earth of the Deep South had swallowed it: no walls, no root cellar, nothing left but the memory. They pushed on, looking for a larger five-room bungalow that Spann's father, Sherman Watson, had built to replace the cabin. Spann's woods sense and navigation impressed Weyman. The old fields were now overgrown with pines, oaks, and gums, but Spann's inner compass simply ignored all the trees. "This was the tobacco field," his father said, pointing through the shadows. "This was the cotton field. This is where Pop grew sugarcane." He seemed intent on touching every corner of the old place. Finally he stopped, took his bearings, and said, "This is where our land ended, and this is where Uncle Mingo's farm started. You used to be able to see his house from here." To mark the discovery, he fired a 20-gauge salute to Uncle Mingo.

Spann's grandfather, on his mother's side, was light and fair and could have passed for white, but he chose not to. His name was David Holt, and he had prospered in the years leading up to World War I. In an area called Fruit Hill, he owned a plantation of four hundred acres and an antebellum mansion, a white house on a hill with green shutters and columns in front and two magnolia trees out back. He also owned a cotton gin, a sawmill, and a general store. In the horse-and-buggy days, when Spann went up to Granddaddy Dave's house, it was so big he made echoes in the hall. His grandfather had a carriage and riding horses, and on Friday night he brought in fiddlers to play for the kids and the hired hands. But during the depression that followed the armistice, Grandpa Dave lost everything. He wrote Henry Ford in Detroit asking for a job and went up north, but Ford had nothing for him. He died of a stroke. Spann hoped to find his grandfather's house, but it was gone. All that was left was the barn. Of the whole Fruit Hill empire, the only item to survive was a foot-pedal Singer sewing machine that Spann had stored in his basement back in Westbury.

Even though Sherman Watson came from rough stock, Grandpa Dave liked him; he raised no objections when Sherman came courting his daughter. Sherman owned his own farm, forty acres that produced eight bales of cotton in good years, five or six in bad. He used to tell his sons, "I'm poor, but I'm stout." He cut railroad ties for ten cents each, and he could cut eleven in a day. Across from the farmhouse was a blacksmith's shop where Spann pumped the bellows to fan a soft-coal furnace while his father shoed the neighbors' mules for free. During World War I Sherman went to Fort Jackson sixty miles away to report for duty, but the Army deferred him, so he returned to the farm and after a few years built his bungalow, the newest and best house anywhere near Johnston: a country T-house with a living room, a poor man's parlor called "the visiting room," two bedrooms, and a large kitchen out back. The iron stove burned wood kindled with back issues of the

Atlanta Constitution. "You gotta learn to read," Sherman Watson told his sons. "You gotta learn to count, and you gotta know what's goin' on. I pay a dollar and sixty cents a year for that paper, and I want you to know what's in it."

Backtracking through time and the trees, Spann and Weyman found the bungalow. The place was abandoned. Opening the door, they stepped into Spann's childhood. The place hadn't changed since the 1920s. Reminiscing, Spann wandered from room to room. "This is where we slept. This was my parents' room. This is where we got a whupping for tracking mud in the hallway and putting our shoes on the couch. This is where they brought the little neighbor girl who was sick, so we put her in this room, and she stayed for a while, and then they took her home and she died."

Coming out of the house, they stopped for a while on the porch. This was the place to be when Spann was a child. On the evening of October 9, 1926, he was sitting on that porch when he heard his father say, "There's someone coming through the woods."

A black man on a horse came out of the woodlot, rode past the barn, and jumped out of the saddle. He led the horse up to the porch.

"Mr. Sherman Watson?" he said.

"Yes."

"I just came to notify you that they lynched the Lomans last night."

The Lomans, two brothers and a sister, lived in Ridge Springs a few miles beyond the Watson farm. Earlier in the year, Henry H. Howard, the local sheriff, had accused them of running a still. Sheriff Howard went to the Loman farm and kicked in a door where Miss Loman was taking a bath. Someone shot the sheriff. The Lomans were black, and therefore guilty, according to the mores of Saluda County. But a lawyer from the National Association for the Advancement of Colored People defended them, and in court, it turned out that the deputy shot the sheriff. The bullet that killed him matched bullets from the deputy's gun. The state supreme court ordered a new trial. The Ku Klux Klan ordered a Roman holiday. The day before the horseman emerged from the woods, white Klansmen all over South Carolina started taking the license plates off their cars. "I wondered what those crackers were do-ing," Sherman Watson told the outrider, who was warning black farm-ers to keep their heads down. "I heard cars hitting the wooden bridge over the brook. Flivvers. Ford flivvers."

The Lomans were being held in jail at Aiken. The mob used a ram-rod to knock down the jailhouse door. A cop tossed over the keys to the cells. Someone took a shotgun and blasted one of the brothers under the chin. Someone else took a .38 and shot the other brother in the chest. The sister was killed by a round fired point-blank into her ear. The out-rider reported the news and climbed back on his horse. Sherman Wat-son watched him ride off. Then he turned to his sons and said, "We're getting out of this place."

Now Spann and Weyman were standing on the same porch. The night of the Loman lynching, Spann was nine years old. Although the murders happened thirty-one years before Weyman was born, Spann didn't tell him the story until Weyman was forty-four, three years be-fore their walk in the woods.

As they pushed on, Spann came to a halt on a stretch of ground that looked more or less ordinary to Weyman.

"Pop gave each of us a walnut tree," he said. "One for each of his three sons. So we planted them one, two, three, right here."

The ground was empty. Spann had outlived the walnuts.

The depression that wiped out Granddaddy Dave and the lynching that murdered the Lomans drove Sherman Watson north to find better schools and a better life for his sons. Each fall after his crops were in, he went to New Jersey to earn money for Christmas. On returning from these trips, he taught Spann and his brothers their first lessons in geog-raphy: You rode the Southern Railway to Washington, D.C., changed to the Pennsylvania Railroad at Union Station, then it was Baltimore and Chesapeake Bay, Wilmington and Delaware Bay, and on through Philadelphia and Trenton to Newark. He had a job at United Piece and Diework, a rambly factory nearly a mile long, in Lodi, New Jersey. He worked from late October until Christmas Eve. Then Mrs. Watson would start humming "Santa's coming," and he'd come up the front walk with a wallet full of cash and an armload of toys.

About a year after the Loman catastrophe, he started looking for permanent work in Lodi. Everyone turned him down. Finally he reached the Millbank Bleachery, a huge laundry on a rail spur from Hackensack. The foreman said, "We don't hire colored." "That's because you haven't given anybody a chance," Sherman replied. On the spur was a coal car. Someone said to the foreman, "Give the guy a chance." Reluctantly, the boss handed him a shovel and said, "Let's see what you can do." Sherman shoveled coal for a year before anyone discovered he could fix any broken machine. The boss started taking him along when he bought new equipment. Sherman stayed for more than thirty years, eventually becoming the first black man in New Jersey to earn an engineer's license for heavy power machines.

Having established a foothold, he rented half of a small house on Garibaldi Street across from the bleachery and sent for his family. The Watsons were the first and only black family in Lodi. Sherman gave Spann two weeks to get his feet on the ground, then he asked a local cop for directions to the colored school. "We don't have anything like a colored school," the cop told him. "Take your son to the school nearest your house." The next day Mrs. Watson put him and Roy in their Sunday best and went unannounced to Lincoln School, where she caught Mrs. Miller, the principal, by surprise. They were greeted royally. Mrs. Miller talked to them for two or three hours, then took them to every class and laid down the law: no discrimination—from teachers, custodians, students, anybody—and in the weeks that followed she enforced it so firmly that no one crossed her line. Chief Witty, head of the Lodi Police Department, lived in their neighborhood. He made a point of stopping Spann and his brother after school to ask how they were making out, whether there were any problems. When they were walking home, Mrs. Witty would come out on the porch and wave to them and call out, "Hello, boys. How you doing?" South Carolina fell behind them, though it remained deeply planted in Spann's mind.

Now he took Weyman to the Penn Creek Baptist Church, where they found Granddaddy Dave, his sons, his daughters, and all their children lying side by side in the graveyard. The church was a small wooden building in the shotgun style. Someone had put aluminum siding on it to protect it from the sun. Spann walked among the graves talking about people who had died needlessly from mystery diseases that would never kill them today, a stab of death that was only appendicitis. "For black folks it was just so easy to die," Spann said. "Nobody thought anything of it. You'd get sick for two or three days. Maybe the country doctor would get there to see you, maybe he'd get there in time, maybe he wouldn't. And the next thing you know, they're gone."

The ornateness of the Holt family tombstones surprised Weyman. Even the Holts who had died as infants had markers. And then it struck him that even though Fruit Hill had vanished like Tara, unlike Tara it had been real. Spann was touching the earth, regaining contact with the lost world of his father and grandfather. It was as if he were trying to regain his own paradise lost, no matter how bad conditions might have been beyond the fields of Fruit Hill. The mood was elegiac. Watching the father, the son suddenly found himself sharing an old man's sense of loss. "His family had everything. They had the world by the balls and they let it slip away. If only they could have kept everything going. If only the depression hadn't come. If only the family had stuck together, it wouldn't just be down to one eighty-seven-year-old man. We had it. We lost it. We didn't have to lose it. But now it's gone." Spann's parents and brothers were dead, so were his aunts and uncles, and all but his cousin Gertie Lee. Of all that tremendous family, Spann was the last one left. "And nobody else in our generation knows anything about it," Weyman reflected. "Nobody other than me, now."

Spann never indulged himself in pan-African chic. He didn't talk about griots. But wasn't that why he had wanted Weyman to go on the trip with him? Wasn't Spann the Silent, Spann the man under Cousin Ronald's black cloud, entrusting the Watson family history to his youngest son? Weyman thought, "No question about it. I get the message."

From Penn Creek they drove to Mine Creek Baptist Church, where

Sherman Watson's side of the family was buried. The second cemetery wasn't as fancy as the first; some of the markers were worn away, others had fallen down. But the Watsons all lay under impeccably marked graves. Spann had seen to that. It wasn't that he was a deeply religious man. When Weyman was small, he thought his father was just too lazy to go to church on Sunday. Not until he grew up did he see that Spann had stopped going because he'd become disillusioned with Southern Baptist fundamentalism. His father's mother was so devout, she didn't believe in the space program—the Mercury and Apollo rockets were shooting up too close to heaven.

Edna Watson had given Spann a rosary, and he took it with him when he went with his family to church on Christmas and Easter, and for first communions and confirmations. Beyond that, he was content to let Edna deliver the spankings and make sure his sons took confession and got to Mass. But whenever Weyman stayed with his father, at home or out in a hotel, the older man would kneel down by his bed at night, in front of anyone who happened to be around, and say his prayers. His favorite passage from the Bible came from Isaiah. "I heard the voice of the Lord saying, 'Whom shall I send and who shall go for us?' Then I said, 'Here I am. Send me.' "

Spann had taken Isaiah as his text when he composed a prayer for the Tuskegee airmen to use at their reunions:

> Send me, oh Lord, send me . . . Send not my youthful sons to fight and die for causes and reasons not yet understood. Send not my youthful sons who are seeing the world unfold and never had the chance to enjoy the blessings of God's Good Earth. Send me. I know the task before us, for I have seen the world as it is. Send me. Send me.

If Spann had trailed a black cloud, if any father-son conversation with him tended to be one-way, here was what he'd been feeling. His silence had been part of an armor plating as rugged as anything on a Warhawk. It had shielded the son even as it protected the father.

Hadn't my father done the same for me? The possibility was unsettling. Any son who heard that prayer and went on nursing a grudge against his old man could only be soul-dead.

After Sherman Watson left South Carolina, he held on to the family farm, not selling the property until the 1950s. Over the years, the brook Spann had forded to get to school dried up and there was asphalt on the main roads, but the wife of the man who had bought the place was still living with her son and grandson in another house on the property. The grandson appeared to be about sixteen, an athletic kid who looked rugged and smart. He said he made money raising and selling coon dogs. As Spann and Weyman were talking to him, his father came out. For a moment three generations stood in front of the house shooting the breeze.

The father noticed Spann's hat and asked him about it.

"Yeah, well, I'm a Tuskegee airman, a Tuskegee airman from Johnston, South Carolina. The one and only."

The new owner of the Watson family farm knew all about Spann's old outfit. He turned to his son.

"This is a Tuskegee airman," he said. "You ought to shake his hand."

The boy stuck out his paw and Spann took it and they stood there talking for a while. Then, as Spann was getting back into the car, he stopped for a moment.

"I don't know what you want to do, son," he said, pointing back to the woods through which he'd come. "But all you gotta remember is this: If I can do it from over there, from that old broken-down farm back in the woods, then you ought to be able to do it from here."

After that, Spann nodded to his own son and they went home.

A few months after the trip, I drove over to New Jersey to ask Weyman what he had discovered alongside his father. He had just returned home from a post-9/11 Reserve call-up. The eight-month mission was to keep ships, planes, satellites, and "some other stuff I can't tell you about" on the tail of al-Qaeda. He is a tall, lean man in a T-shirt, black shorts, and running shoes: At forty-seven he drives race cars to fend off boredom. No one would call him a sentimentalist, but when he told the story about his old man and the boy who raised coon dogs, his voice grew hoarse. "It really got to me," he said. "As you can see."

We talked for a while about the war. I asked him if he thought the shock of combat had been compounded by racism. He said the answer was yes, but not in any simple sense. "The majority of black political leaders in the 1950s and 1960s had experience in World War II or Korea or both," he said. "I've always wondered if the war wasn't an incubator, a force that propelled them farther than they might normally have gone. Up to then, the only white-collar jobs for black people went to dentists, doctors, and insurance guys who were selling to a captive audience. Or the guy who owned the funeral parlor. In the 1950s you suddenly see black guys getting to be professors, lawyers, black guys going into private industry, government, the civil service, black guys doing well in the military. That came later. My old man always said the Tuskegee airmen showed the way by going into combat."

From an altitude of fifteen thousand feet and a distance of sixty years, Spann had cast a long shadow over the second half of the twentieth centry. Hoping Weyman wouldn't detect my ulterior motive, I asked whether he had found it hard to get out of his father's shadow. God knows it was a problem for me. I had competed with my father, almost as if I wanted to eliminate him as a force in my life. "It never really bothered me to be in his shadow," Weyman told me. "I can't speak for my brothers, but I think they felt the same way. I don't know if I could outdo him if I was dead set on it. Maybe. But I never felt any compulsion to do that. If I didn't respect him, if I couldn't look up to him, I suppose I would have felt the need to eclipse him, but to this day I don't." This was something I had never been able to say.

It didn't hurt that as time passed, Spann mellowed. Butchie's death made him rethink everything. "It was the one piss-off he couldn't do anything about," Weyman said. "But he didn't let it stop him. He wasn't going to let it get him down." A few years later, Weyman's cousin

Ronald stopped by to see Spann. After the visit, he called to give Weyman a report. He said, "I look at Uncle Spann now and I just can't believe it's the same person." The dark cloud was gone. Weyman's father had become warm, almost jovial. He could really light up a room.

Just before Christmas, Spann and Edna Watson celebrated their sixtieth wedding anniversary. When I thought about it, it suddenly struck me that they had lived out the kind of marriage I had always expected from my father and mother. And then I began wondering how much I had needed, or even worse, demanded, that kind of happy ending from my old man. Could that be why I'd gone postal when he'd gone south on my mother? Whose life was it anyway?

I had to drive in to New York the week of Spann's anniversary, so I stopped and knocked at the blue door to give him a present. I had found a man in St. Louis who called himself Big Band Bill. He had an enormous collection of recordings by Glen Gray and the Casa Loma Orchestra. I'd asked him to burn all of them onto a set of compact disks. He sent ten CDs with everything from "Casa Loma Stomp" to "Smoke Rings" to "Under a Blanket of Blue."

Spann came out and stood on his front walk. An arctic cold front had swept in from Canada. The old flier looked up at the cobalt between the clouds.

"Sky's coming back," he said. "I thought they'd ruined it. Depression. Dust bowl. Then all the pollution. But now it's back. Good thing to remember."

I handed him the package. "Well, look at that," he said, jamming his hand into his pocket. "How much do I owe you?"

Not a thing colonel. It was exactly the other way around.

Chapter 8

Nucci's Diner

*Cpl. Frank Martinelli, infantry-
man, "Somewhere, some unit,"
1944*

On the far side of the crossing over Great Egg Harbor and the In-
tracoastal Waterway, Ocean City had vanished in the fog. Visibility
along State Road 52 was rapidly approaching zero: You had to take it on
faith. When The Crossing Motel loomed up through the mist, I lost
mine and pulled in for the night. A snug, safe landing. From the park-

ing lot, fog drifted through the open lobby door, beading the glass and cash register. The fog of peace—a million miles from Vietnam.

I had come down to the Jersey Shore looking for Sgt. Ron Martinelli of the 4th Battalion, 39th Infantry Regiment. Long before the Pentagon came up with its fantasy commercials about an Army of One, Martinelli was the real thing, a legend among grunts of the 439 Hardcore Battalion. More than thirty years had passed since a rocket-propelled grenade blew him out of his foxhole in the Mekong Delta. On that particular day, his men had watched gloomily as the chopper dropped in to dust him off from his last firefight. In less than a year he had won the Silver Star, six Bronze Stars, and now his third Purple Heart.

One of the things that impressed the grunts was that Martinelli hadn't gone to Vietnam because soldiering was his idea of a great job. He was no Army lifer. What he really wanted to be was a fireman. When the exploding RPG riddled his legs, hips, tail, and chest, collapsing one of his lungs, it occurred to him that passing the physical for the fire department back in Vineland was no longer a sure thing. Before the lights went out, a medic, misreading the look in his eyes, said, "Don't worry, Sarge. You're pretty messed up, but I'm gonna shoot you so full of morphine, you'll fly out of here all on your own."

Colonel Hackworth was Martinelli's commander in the Hardcore Battalion. When Hack found out that I was sorting through the manual of arms for fathers and sons, he called one afternoon and said in his cut-the-crap way, "Find Martinelli. True stud. Draftee. Didn't want to be in Vietnam, but his old man served in World War II, so ... you figure it out."

The next morning the fog rolling over Ocean City was still so murky that it was almost impossible to read house numbers from the car. Along Asbury Avenue, fine new beach houses, two stories with faux-Victorian turrets and dormers, porches and trim, were squeezing out the last funky bungalows of an earlier, more innocent era at the Jersey Shore. I started looking for 3610. From the corner, the numbers appeared to run 3606, 3608, 3612. Where the coordinates were supposed to fix Martinelli's place, there was a blank. Was this sergeant a ghost? I got out of the car to take a closer look. Next to the second house from the corner, a motor pool of six bicycles hid a modest side staircase, and next to the stairs an even more modest sign read 3610. At the top of the stairs, parked next to the door, was a huge pair of moccasins, big enough to shoe even the shyest yeti.

I knocked and the door swung open. There was no mistaking the man. Framed in the doorway, Martinelli gave the impression of a guy who had given up very little to the corrosion of time. He was solidly built, a six-footer in gray denim shorts. He wore a dark blue T-shirt with the logo of the Vineland Fire Department and a message on the sleeve that said, REMEMBER OUR BROTHERS 9/11. His hair and mustache were black with just the first hint of salt. His brown eyes peered over the top of a set of steel-rimmed cheaters. In one fist he held a sheaf of official-looking papers, in the other a bright yellow Nextel handset that kept him the push of a button away from the Cumberland County 911 Center. "You made it," he said, the voice even, a midrange baritone that gave nothing away. "Come on in. I was just sitting on the computer—homeland defense." I had to stifle an impulse to say "Yes sir." For command presence, Martinelli, even in shorts and bare feet, blew away any corporate suit.

The night before, he said, he and his wife, oblivious to the fog, had driven to Ocean City with some friends. At the Acme Supermarket, just beyond The Crossing Motel, they had stopped for groceries. The news that day had been full of reports about the Pentagon's logistical breakdowns in Iraq, shortages of water, young soldiers collapsing with heatstroke. As Martinelli went into the store, he saw, stacked against one wall, towering cases of bottled water, a portable reservoir of soft drinks, oceans of Snapple. "Hey, what's wrong with this picture?" he thought out loud, looking at me. "I don't know," I said, groping for the dunce cap. "Maybe it's because we've got a commander in chief, a vice president, and an undersecretary of defense who never went anywhere near Vietnam. . . ."

Sergeant Martinelli cut me off.

"Hey, that's right. Where *were* you guys?"

For an instant I felt a smug tickle of pleasure, and then the ricochet from this, my best shot, hit me squarely between the horns.

Where were *you?*

It wasn't just George, Dick, and Paul. Where were you, Tom? To be strictly accurate, the year Sergeant Martinelli was blown up for the third time, I was in Hong Kong on a graduate school fellowship, practicing my Chinese on bar girls, covering the waterfront in Wanchai. The closest I got to Vietnam was the world of Suzie Wong.

If the truth was written in lipstick across my forehead, Martinelli didn't see it, or if he saw it, he chose to give me a break.

"Where *were* you guys," he repeated. "Shame." But then, as if embarrassed at allowing himself that single word of rebuke, he shrugged and pushed back his steel glasses.

"It's always the same," he said. "It never changes."

Behind Martinelli's broad shoulders, the top-floor condo, painted in light beach colors, was immaculately neat, cheerful despite the fog at the windows. Renee Martinelli, Ron's wife, a warm, attractive woman, came out to see what he was up to. After thirty years of marriage, knowing her soldier inside out, she had to be the only person in the world who could issue him an ultimatum like the one that kept his moccasins out on the landing. ("They're always full of sand. I don't allow them in here.") Not wanting to spoil her morning with a public belly flop into the past, Martinelli suggested we go up the street for a cup of coffee. He grabbed the Nextel and we hit the sidewalk roughly at the speed of a hook and ladder responding to a four-alarm call. If he wanted to get it all over with ten minutes of polite java jive, I wouldn't have blamed him; so it surprised me when he agreed to my counterproposal that we set up camp in The Crossing Motel's complimentary breakfast and conference room. It turned out that in the years before the condo on Asbury Avenue, he and Renee had spent many weekends at The Crossing. It was neutral ground, safe—the last late risers crumpling their Styrofoam cups and heading for the parking lot, the Little League World Series playing on the wall TV. Martinelli drew the dregs from the coffeepot and we sat down at a small table. "All right," he said. "We can talk."

I asked what his father had told him about World War II.

"Not much."

"How much?"

"Just one story, really."

I leaned forward, expecting, I suppose, a conflagration.

This was an error.

"We had some snow when I was a kid, and my father said he was going to take me out and teach me how to ski."

"Ski?" I said, totally blindsided. You had to look awfully hard to find an Alp in southern New Jersey.

"That's what *I* said. 'Ski? Pop, where did *you* learn to ski?' " All he said was, 'The Army, let's go.' " That was it. I'd really have to push to come up with any other story.

What? No guns, no glory—no duty, honor, and the Great Whamdoodle?

None of that.

"But didn't he lean hard on you to go to Vietnam?"

Error number two.

"Not really," Martinelli said, studying his cup. "It wasn't that simple."

Frank Martinelli, Ron's father, was a compact man, comfortable in his own skin, easygoing until someone lit his fuse. But he was so tight-lipped about the war that you could print the record he conveyed to his son on one terse business card: He was a corporal (somewhere). He was in the Army (some unit). He learned to ski. Nothing more. Ron's mother has a photograph that shows him looking into the camera from under an old-fashioned saucer hat, probably sometime after basic training. "He wasn't highly decorated—just a regular grunt," Ron said. "He was a good physical guy—a tough guy with a broken nose. He looked like a prizefighter." For a long time Ron thought his father might have been in the Signal Corps, but then one day, on closer inspection, he saw that Corporal Martinelli's insignia bore the crossed rifles of the infantry.

Around Vineland, everyone called Frank "Nucci." The nickname rhymed with cookie and might have been the source of a few jokes, except that it could be dangerous to rib Nucci too hard. His broken beak came from football. In the era of leather helmets, thin pads, and no face masks, Vineland High School took no prisoners. Nucci was a running back and punter. He made all-state twice. When he took the field at Gattone Stadium, built by Franklin Roosevelt's WPA to fend off the Depression, fans in the fine new concrete bleachers cheered. His grandson Richard, Ron's son, has an old scrapbook full of Nucci's clippings. A cartoon from the sports pages shows a lost pilot looking down at a pigskin flying just under his wing. The caption says, "We must be over Gattone Stadium. That looks like one of Frank Martinelli's punts." Scouts from the Philadelphia Eagles and the Cleveland Browns came to size him up. But he was in love with Josephine DiFranco, who didn't love the idea of road trips, broken bones, and a house reeking of wintergreen balm. "You go professional," she told Nucci, "we're not getting married." So he hung up the cleats. Ron still calls his mother—fondly—the Little General.

Frank Martinelli had enough relatives to field his own football team, at least eleven by Ron's count, so many uncles it was easy to lose track of them all. Some were farmers who worked the fields around Vineland, others were blue-collar working guys, like the Martinelli who was a welder and the Martinelli who drove a truck. Scattered among the city Martinellis were a beer and soda bottling company, a gas station, a used car lot, two restaurants, and a hotel. After Pearl Harbor the Martinellis contributed a one-family division to remind Adolf Hitler and Emperor Hirohito what Italian-Americans were made of. "My father served, Uncle Johnnie served, Uncle Del served. My Uncle Larry was a master sergeant in the National Guard for years. On my mother's side, her brother, my Uncle Frank, was in the Navy on a destroyer. Uncle Rollie was a pilot. He got killed." The honor roll shook me. When I asked Ron who else in the family was on it, he said, "Basically, everybody."

Frank Martinelli married Josephine DiFranco in 1946, when he was nineteen. Ron was born in 1947, two years after Corporal Martinelli came home to Vineland, and for a while, when he was little, he shared in the Great American Boy's postwar obsession with soldiers. Vineland, set between the pine barrens of New Jersey and the farmlands that stretched southeast and southwest until they ran into the marsh country of Delaware Bay and Cape May, was an urban anomaly, a mill town. Its redbrick and wood frame factories—DiRossi & Brothers Clothing, Tursini, Jordan Clothes, Chinnici Brothers, Model Coat— were fitted out with fire sprinklers and Defense Department contracts. By the millions, these factories supplied the War Department, later the Department of Defense, with the most basic item of a GI's identity— his uniform.

Ron's Uncle Frank and his Aunt Creda had jobs in the mills. His mother worked for Tursini and Model Coat, where discarded seconds wound up in the yard out back on a fascinating pile of junk. "As kids we used to collect the buttons. Every once in a while you'd see the little buttons from the dress uniforms—the ones with the eagles on them. They'd be smashed. Lying in the yard, they weren't in the best shape, but we'd grab them. You'd hear one kid shouting, 'I got a big one.' And another kid saying, 'I got a silver one.' And over there someone yelling 'I got a gold.' "

Knowing from the Army that all that glitters is probably brass, Ron's father never encouraged playing soldier. He got his first glimpse of a tank the day his Uncle Larry took him down to the Vineland Armory to show him around. Uncle Larry was a mechanic, a genius with any kind of tool. "He had the Midas touch. He could do anything. Not a college guy. He'd say, 'Tell me how that tape recorder works. Oh, yeah, I could fix that. No problem.' You need him to wire your house, he could do that." When Ron thinks back, the uniforms, hats, and soldier's talk he remembers all trace to Uncle Larry and his warrant officer, Orlo Cox. "They talked Army all the time." His father maintained radio silence.

If Nucci was tough, he wasn't a hard-ass. Most of the time he was working too hard to waste his energy on small talk. He saved his money, never flaunted it. Through the entire era of swept-back tailfins and Turbo Drive, he never bought a new car. He always bought used. "He was happy. He had a nice, successful business. He could dress sharp when he wanted to, but most of the time he was very casual, always in work clothes. He was never ashamed about work. He would work, come home, then work some more. When he slept, he conked out." The one thing he never did was complain. He had a lot of sayings. The one his son remembers best is this: "I've got enough money in my pocket for a cup of coffee today. We'll worry about tomorrow when we get there." He saved enough to buy a restaurant that became a popular fixture in Vineland. The place was named Nucci's Diner.

Ron stirred his coffee and thought a while. A vagrant memory of his father watching the *Late Show* made him smile. "He loved King Kong movies." Cheap horror flicks, the cheaper the better. Some nights he'd go out and buy cookies, then set Ron and his brother down in front of the television for something like *The Dragonfly that Took over Cleveland*. All the classics. "He'd sit in his chair and we'd stay up until one or two in the morning and watch those stupid things, and he'd laugh like a crazy man. My brother and I loved it. Mom thought he was nuts." If he had a dark side, it appeared only now and then on the ball field. After the war he played third base for three local teams: the Vineland Eagles, a semipro club; Melini's Goodyear, another hardball team; and the Landis Country Club, a softball outfit. "He played with tremendous intensity—headfirst slides, diving for ground balls, knocking the catcher over at the plate, arguing with the umpire at the drop of a hat." Eventually he scrapped his way into the South Jersey Baseball Hall of Fame. "Dr. Jekyll and Mr. Hyde," Ron said, a smile crinkling the eyes behind his steel rims. "On the field it was 'Let's go' at all costs. Off the field it was 'Let's go have a beer. Relax.' That type of guy." Ron, cast in the same alloy, looked about as soft as carborundum. But you couldn't help noticing that his voice got just a decibel hoarse when he remembered Nucci at the plate.

Nucci's Diner was open twenty-four hours a day, every day of the year except Christmas. Families came for Sunday dinners. Drunks loved the place because the lights were still on and the grill smoking at 2:00 A.M. when the bars closed. Sometimes they bent Nucci out of shape. "Numerous times I watched him stretch out a guy. Somebody would walk in, make a crack at one of the waitresses or my mom—she worked the late shift—and *bam!* If you lit his fuse, it was about *that* long." He held up a thumb and forefinger and tightened them like a micrometer. "He never laid a hand on me, but I saw him lay a hand on plenty of guys in the diner who came in and didn't know when to shut up." So if Nucci took care of business, he also took care of people close to him. One day, leafing through back issues of the *Vineland Daily Journal*, I found the obituaries of a waitress and dishwasher who listed their job at Nucci's Diner as one of the good things they wanted re-membered after they were gone. The Vineland police respected the owner as someone who never cried wolf after hours. If they got a call to the diner, they hustled, because if Nucci couldn't handle whatever was going on, they knew he needed them. He returned the respect and the backup. State troopers ate free in his place. Vineland cops got all of their coffee, doughnuts, and snacks on the cuff, and he cut them a 50 percent discount on anything else they ate from the menu. They didn't have walkie-talkies on their hips in those days. At night they would park their patrol cars behind the diner, jacking up the radio so they could hear it through the kitchen, where they knew Nucci would always be ready to make sandwiches for them and shoot the breeze.

He also joined the volunteer fire department. "He wasn't a good member, just a member," Ron said objectively. If the police came first in Nucci's mind, very early on, fires, fire trucks, and firemen began to outshine soldiers and cops in the eyes of his son. Ron started to hang out at the firehouse, where older firemen like John Schenck introduced him to a world of hoses and nozzles, axes and pikes, the world of American

LaFrance, pumpers and hook and ladders, fire engines polished to such a brilliant burnish you could comb your hair in the reflection. They taught him how to ventilate a burning building and when to get the hell out. He finished high school and enrolled in community college, intent on moving up from volunteer fireman to full-time pro. Then he came home one day to find a letter from General Herhsey of the United States Selective Service ordering him to report for an entirely different line of duty. The year was 1967 when the draft started rustling once again through Vineland. He was nineteen years old, the same age his father had been in 1944. "My mom was very upset. I think she would have driven me to Canada. But Pop said no go."

Nucci was no barn-burning superpatriot. "He was just a genuine guy," Ron said, stirring the last of the coffee, which had gone cold. "He was never a flag-waver. He was just a card-carrying member of the VFW and Foreign Legion. He'd say, 'Yeah, I'll go down and have a beer with the guys.' But he didn't wear the hat with the insignia and he didn't march in parades." When Ron's induction notice came, Nucci didn't say anything at first. "He kind of thought it through. Then he said to me, 'It's the right thing to do. I know it's rough. I don't want to see you go. But I think you need to do this, Ron.'

"I went."

His story shook me. Ron Martinelli had answered the call at the time I was calling, "Absent." What was I going to make of that? This late in the game, for a middle-aged guy to wallow in guilt seemed cheap, as easy in its way as ducking the draft forty years ago. The one thing worse than copping out is to say feeling bad later makes up for it. It doesn't. So let's call my absence a fact, not a guilt trip. But then, why, echoing through the prefrontal cortex, did I keep hearing Martinelli's question?

Where were *you guys?*

Whatever else Vietnam meant to Ron Martinelli, he came out of the mangle with his sense of irony intact. "It was one of the few lotteries I won." When he reached Fort Leonard Wood for basic training, one of the first things he saw was a base fire truck. Hey, he thought to himself. He'd say to the Army, "Put me in the firehouse." They gave him a battery of tests and told him he was born to be an MP. "Not a bad deal," he thought. "I'll accept that," almost as if it were up to him. He did basic training in a group of 250 young men, but when the cycle was complete, only eleven, including Ron, got the infantry. So like Nucci he pinned on the crossed rifles and pushed on to Fort Polk, where there was still a coal stove in the wood-frame barracks. "Holy mackerel. What is this?" he asked himself. His old man would have recognized the setup. Ron had moved back to the future with Willy and Joe, Bill Mauldin's immortal cartoon dogfaces.

He soldiered on through advanced infantry training, where the Army, observing his assets and nerve, picked him for its Noncommissioned Officers School at Fort Benning. Having chalk-talked him through the basics of leadership and tactics, the Army posted him back to Fort Polk, where he trained a cycle of grunts bound for Vietnam. After that, it was his turn for the trip. When he arrived in the summer of 1968, MACV, the U.S. Military Assistance Command, Vietnam, was still mopping up after the Tet Offensive. He was a draftee, not a lifer, a citizen soldier like his father, and what he saw at first of the Vietnamese he was risking his life to help didn't impress him. For a while he was stationed at an oil redistribution depot, where huge tankers off-loaded petroleum that was funneled into fifty-five-gallon barrels and trucked into the badlands. One night the Viet Cong pegged a lucky round into a barge that burst into flames. When the Vietnamese wheeled up with a fire truck, the spectacle staggered Sergeant Martinelli. "I was just a young pup, but these guys couldn't get the truck to pump water. They didn't know how to make foam. It took them forever to get their act together. They didn't have a clue." By then the barge was just one more well-lit trophy for the Viet Cong.

Shaken, he moved on to street-fighting, where the spirit was more gung ho and the lighting out of *Apocalypse Now.* On one sweep through Cholon he came under sniper fire, and a wild man with a shaved head

and earring, swinging a cutlass, rode to his rescue. This officer was leading a band of grunts whose blue shoulder patch featured two swords
crossed over a skull. The grunts said their boss admired Taras Bulba, the
blood-soaked seventeenth-century Cossack. Nikolay Gogol wrote a famous story about this role model. It begins with Taras Bulba kicking
the hell out of his son, then kissing him for putting up a good fight. The
unit's APCs had six 106mm recoilless rifles welded to their sides. "Let's
go," yelled Captain Bulba, and as he flourished his cutlass, the APCs
leveled everything in sight. "I was like, 'What is *this*?'" Martinelli said.
"They were like, 'We don't care. Blow the block apart.'" For a while,
like Custer, he allowed himself to believe that the Army might actually
have the Indians on the run. "I know it sounds sadistic. People might
say, 'Hey, you might have hurt some innocent people.' Well, you know
what? War *is* hell." So nobody was innocent anymore. Was that the lesson Nucci thought Ron needed to learn? Perhaps that was all there was
to it, but I didn't think so. Nucci and Ron ran deeper than that. There
had to be more.

The Army then sent Martinelli to join the 439, a sad-sack outfit in
the Mekong Delta. The unit was run by a tall, thin colonel who scored
closer to Mr. Rogers than Taras Bulba on the testosterone meter. "He
was a decent guy, he thought about his men, worried about them a lot,
but he didn't seem to have any let's-go-get-'em, know what I mean?"
Viet Cong mines and booby traps were decimating the 439. Morale was
in the latrine. Weed, hash, opium, heroin were cheap and no farther
away than the next *ville*. With a soft whistle, Martinelli said, "Some of
those kids—whew—you didn't know where they were coming from. It
was very easy for them to say, 'Hey, you know what? Not today, Sarge.
Let's fake it.'" Sergeant Martinelli told shitbirds that he didn't care if
they got drunk as long as they slept it off and could head out the next
day. If they got stoned and stayed stoned, he smoked their ass so their
dope wouldn't kill his flankers. His approach was far more ethical than
most things out in Indian Country. Piss on me, piss on my people, I'm
gonna stretch you out—more or less the same Rules of the House back
at Nucci's Diner.

Despite his best efforts, the Viet Cong regularly beat up his side. During one break in the fighting, he and his men were holed up at a small artillery base north of Dong Tam, where the ground, at least, was firm enough to support the big guns and they could get hot food. "We had a lot of guys with ripped uniforms, pants especially, and I remember looking up and seeing this stack of boxes that said Replacement Uniforms made in Vineland, N.J." Courtesy of Mom, Aunt Creda, Uncle Frank, and everyone back home, where the war was popular. "People would say, 'It's keeping everybody employed.' Yeah, but look at what else it was doing. You began to wonder if the whole rationale behind the thing was to keep people in jobs." The boxes haunted him. "Eerie," he said. "Pretty eerie."

Martinelli didn't see himself as a war hawk. "Whether you believed in what we were doing or not, you were trying to get these kids back in one piece." The prospects improved when a new commander took over the 439. His name was Hackworth, his rank was colonel, and his approach stunned the grunts. The day he arrived he stripped them of all toys and comforts: everything from transistor radios to cots. In the first twelve hours he made them dig new positions, twice. Sweating in the heat, they cursed him all day; then that night they watched as a Viet Cong rocket barrage wiped out the positions Colonel Hackworth had abandoned. For a change, under the new guy, the VC missed. Even so, a few grunts still saw him as one more crazed Army lifer out to get them killed. They took up a collection to reward anyone who would frag the motherfucker.

Martinelli quelled the mutiny. "We were a broken-down outfit, but whether we wanted to wear Bermuda shorts or Madras pants, Hackworth made it clear that we were there to kick rear ends. It gave you a lot of confidence in him. He had a sense of purpose. We were going to be a good outfit. They were going to tighten up. And we were going to get everybody home alive." Within less than six months, the limp dicks of the 439 dropped their cocks, pulled up their socks, and turned themselves into the famous Hardcore Battalion, scourge of the Delta. Whatever secret Hackworth understood, it worked on young soldiers.

Martinelli was barely drinking age when he encountered Hackworth in Vietnam. I was nearly fifty when I first ran into him. Some people thought his mystique flowed from an astounding reservoir of physical courage. I once asked him about it. Hack's balls were the size of those old leather Spaldings that made basketball the game it was before rubber and the slam dunk. He told me that while guts were critical, they couldn't be the deciding factor, because the true nature of combat was terror and no one could escape it. But he did have a secret. He told green commanders that they should always carry a cigar into battle. When the mortar rounds started thumping in and bullets began to buzz past their ears, the thing to do was sit down on a rock or log, take out the cigar, bite the end off, and light it. That way men would think you were one hell of a stud, they might even do what you told them to do, and they'd never know that the whole time you were pissing in your pants.

So guts in isolation might give you Taras Bulba, but it didn't give you the extra dimension that Martinelli saw in Hackworth. What counted was the way courage, under the most extreme conditions, offset fatalism, resignation, a form of paralysis. This was almost inevitable in Vietnam. But a soldier who gave in to his sense of fatality could very quickly become one. The principle didn't apply just to firefights. Two days earlier, before I started looking for Martinelli, I had gone to see Hack in the hospital, where he was engaged in a fall offensive against cancer. The doctors were putting his odds at 50/50. He said he liked them. "Try rushing a machine gun sometime. Give Martinelli my best." Then he looked up from the bed and asked if everything was all right with me. Was he just biting off the end of the cigar? No way to be sure, but the effect had lost nothing since Vietnam.

On another occasion, I'd asked Hack if he saw a common denominator between the Good Commander and the Good Father that explained the Good Soldier. "In some ways the experience is like family," he'd told me. "But it's even more intense. There's a romantic side to war—the young stud who's seen the elephant and stood his ground. It's all about the company of men. You could call it a brotherhood forged from danger. It goes deeper than any other family thing." Whatever it was, I would never know. But Nucci knew it, and this was what he wanted his son to know. When I delivered Hack's respects, Martinelli nodded and said, "A true soldier, isn't he?" He asked if Hack had ever considered teaching, at West Point perhaps, or somewhere else. I told him Vietnam had burned out Hack so badly that he'd spent the 1970s and much of the 1980s in Australia struggling against the temptation to veg out.

Martinelli said, "I can understand that."

His education began the day his radio operator stepped on a trip wire, detonating a booby trap that hit him in the head and arm.

BOOM, BOOM, BOOM.

The explosions ringing in his ears, he patted himself down, looking for wounds, talking to himself: *"I'm okay. Concussion. I'm all right. I'm bleeding. I've got pain."*

"We've got to get you out of here," the medic said. "This is something the Doc can't fix in the field."

So they dusted him off and a week later he was back. "They stitched me up, got all the metal out." No problem.

The next time it was a mortar round splashing down while he was crossing a river. This time the shrapnel sliced into his arm, the back of his neck, and his back. "Same thing. Four of us got whacked. Okay, the Doc says. Can't get that metal out." Once again the dustoff birds carried him away. Once again he came back.

"The third time was the big one. Their guys were across the water in good strength and we were getting beat up pretty bad. We called for artillery support and couldn't get it. They sent us four-point-two mortars. The ammunition was from the Korean War. We watched the shells bounce off the ground. I was in a foxhole. An RPG came in and knocked me out of it. I got it in the legs and the back and the hips, the rear end. A piece went through one lung."

At the field hospital, through the morphine, he looked up and saw a major who had been sent to check on the wounded. "That's three strikes for me," Sergeant Martinelli told the major. " 'I'm not going back.' Just before they started working on me, he looked me dead in the eye, and I said, 'That's it. I've had it.' "

He was so badly wounded that the issue was largely moot. A C-141 med-evacuation plane flew him back to Washington, D.C., and Walter Reed Hospital, where he did some rest and rehab and got his discharge papers. At that point, Nucci parked his used car outside Walter Reed and went into the hospital to gather up his son. During the ride back to Vineland they didn't talk much.

They didn't have to. Sergeant Martinelli now knew all that Corporal Martinelli knew. If anything, he had outdone his old man. In his nerve and in his silence, Ron seemed more like the fathers than the sons I had been talking to. In Vineland, half the Martinellis in New Jersey were waiting for the two of them at the house of Ron's grandmother; but on the way, Nucci made a detour to the firehouse. "The guys had chipped in for a big banner, professionally made. It said WELCOME HOME RONNIE, and I'm looking and thinking 'I'm not even a member.' Just a kid who hung out around the fire station." This wasn't an easy club to join. At the time, the fire service in Vineland had no vacancies, but Schenck had written Ron in Vietnam and told him not to worry: "The minute you get home from the service, I will retire with the codicil that you get the slot. Everybody agreed." At the firehouse, Schenck stepped from the crowd.

"Meeting night's next Thursday," he said. "You better be there."

Thursday changed his life. Lightly drumming the table between us with his fingers, Martinelli said, "I thanked Johnny up and down until the day he was buried."

The pay was Vineland's gratitude, not a check. Nucci wanted Ron to join him in the restaurant business; he offered to send his son back to school. For both of them, it was a defining moment. "Just out of the clear blue sky, I went and had a talk with him in his office. It was about eleven o'clock at night. I said, 'Look, Pop, this ain't for me. You could turn this restaurant over to me, but if the place is packed and the fire engine rides by, I'm like . . . I got to go to the fire." The son thought his independence day would destroy his father, but Nucci understood. Ron had taken his advice and gone to Vietnam, and it had cost him. All dues were paid in full. The kid had become his own man.

If the rite of passage was crucial, it still didn't pay for the groceries. Ron found a day job clerking, stocking, shelving, and manning the cash register at an Acme Supermarket. Nights he played drums, brushing the skins for a band good enough to have a piano player who'd worked for Louis Prima. He said to Renee, "Look, I got a shot at making a lot of money, but it's gonna be working at the Acme during the day and playing the drums at night and the rest of the time at the fire station. So let's work like crazy, and the minute they confirm me as a paid fireman is the minute I'm gonna ask you to marry me." It wasn't exactly a moonstruck, down-on-the-knee proposal, but it won Renee. She was working in a law office. Doubling up, she started to work nights in real estate. By the time the Vineland Fire Department came through two years later, the couple had enough money to buy the small, three-bedroom ranch house where they still live. On their wedding day they rode past the firehouse, where the gleaming trucks were lined up in a guard of honor, and at the reception Ron took the mike and said, "This dance is for the fire department," and everyone cheered.

The Little League game on the wall TV was a mismatch won by a bunch of kids who looked like they could have held their own with the Boston Red Sox. I stood up and turned off the set. When I got back to the table, I asked Martinelli about his 9/11 REMEMBER OUR BROTHERS T-shirt.

"I'll never forget," he said. "I was chief then. We were downstairs. One of my buddies was mopping the meeting room and kitchen and he hit the page button and said: 'All personnel come to the second floor.' "

Martinelli and his men ran upstairs where the fireman was standing in front of the TV. Transfixed.

"You all right, Paulie?" Martinelli asked him.

"Yeah, I'm fine."

"What's the deal?"

The fireman just pointed to the screen. A huge cloud of black smoke was curling up from the World Trade Center's south tower.

"So how would you fight this one, Chief?"

"Holy mackerel," Martinelli blurted out. "What happened?"

"A plane hit it."

Looking more closely, Martinelli remembered the B-25 that had smacked into the Empire State Building during the war. That skyscraper had survived. Now he started to dope out the World Trade Center's prognosis.

"Well, Paulie," he said, "if the sprinkler system's holding out and the standpipe system is holding, they got a shot. If not, they are in deep doo-doo."

At that moment the second plane tore into the north tower. Martinelli and the other firemen crowded around the set at first thought they were seeing a replay. Then someone shouted, "Wait a minute, that's another plane."

The phone started ringing off the wall. At the other end of the line, the mayor sounded like a man who had just seen Pearl Harbor.

"Get up here."

Martinelli got in his car and drove to city hall, calculating the possibilities almost as if he were back in Vietnam. The mayor was padding around his office, nerves sparking like ass-backward jumper cables.

"We gotta get together," he said.

"No nonsense we gotta get together," Martinelli told him. "We are at war here."

If Vietnam had seemed remote to a good many people in Vineland, 9/11 was just up the road: In the space of a single morning, al-Qaeda had wiped out the comfortable buffer between American civilians and combatants. There had always been something slightly smarmy to the expression "home front," a phrase that rang of the ad agency, not of any real trenches. But now all distinction was gone: The home front *was* the front. "I need a plan of action," the mayor told the fire chief. "No holds barred. Get whatever you need. Don't worry about finances." So Martinelli and the fire department went on overtime, stockpiling for the defense. "It kind of went back to a military operation. Same thing. Vineland is a pretty good sized town. But you say to yourself, 'They're not going to hit us here. Most likely we're going to be asked to help. We had to come up with two plans: one to take care of our own town and make sure it was secure, the other to send guys to Ground Zero." He brought in all his district chiefs and said, "Look, pick me out five or six guys and some of our better equipment." From the list he assembled a little task force for deployment if needed. There was an unmistakable difference between this call to action and the day Martinelli had received his induction notice for Vietnam. "I had mothers calling me directly on the chief's line," he told me. The mothers weren't attacking him. They were saying, "Why didn't you pick my son to go?"

Everyone wanted to help, fending off the sense of vulnerability that threatened to magnify al-Qaeda's success. "I don't know if they were scared, whether they were shocked, but they wanted to do something." At the hardware stores, rental agencies, and supply houses, it was, "Take the stuff. Don't worry about it. I'll write down you got twenty saw blades. Don't worry about paying. And we have more." Martinelli called a friend who worked at the town's big Progresso soup factory. He said, "Johnny, can you get us some canned goods in case we need to bunk guys in the firehouse for a coupla days?" Within an hour a tractor-trailer loaded with soup, spaghetti sauce, and just about everything else in the Progresso larder pulled up to the fire hall. The driver got out and said, "Tell us where you need the stuff." No charge. Individual Vinelanders brought so much bottled water, so many rolls of toilet paper, so many boxes of Tastykakes to the firehouses that the firemen had to tell them, "Thank you. Please keep it. We're full up."

The City of Vineland sent EMS units to New York. "We had two guys from town up there in the first forty-eight hours working the pile. One of those guys still has problems." The pile had become a human compactor, indiscriminately crushing hundreds of police and firemen with thousands of office workers. The body count was twelve times higher than American casualties in Gulf War I, ten times higher than those killed during the first nine months in Iraq. The Vineland fireman, a young captain, and all the others among the rescue team at Ground Zero absorbed what the sanitized news accounts, photographs, and patriotic speeches left out, as they always do: the body parts, the rats, the smell.

If you wanted to be fancy, you could call what happened post-traumatic stress syndrome, but in the essentials, it sounded a lot like the combat fatigue that mystified doctors used to call "soldier's heart." "It beat him up really bad," Martinelli said. "He just wasn't himself. He came into my office and I sat him down and said, 'Look, you all right?' I could tell he wasn't. He didn't want to open up." Something like the way Nucci had been about his war. Martinelli had seen it in Vietnam. "Do what you gotta do," he told the young captain. "If you need anything give us a buzz. I don't want to pry. I don't want to come over to your house all the time. You know where we are. I know you want some space.' A couple of fellows who had come up through the ranks with him and were close to him personally stayed close, kept me informed, and the city was very good. The mayor and business administrator gave him as much sick time as he needed. They didn't harass him, jeopardize his promotion. They stood by him and he seems to be getting a lot better now."

When Chief Martinelli retired, he took with him two pictures that he said he cherishes. The first one, taken just before he stepped down, caught him in his helmet—the one with the large gold shield—and the vest with INCIDENT COMMANDER written on his broad back. "That's a pretty good one. I got the glasses down and you can tell I was deep in thought. Like things weren't going too good and I was trying to figure out how to straighten out that mess." A shooter from the Atlantic City press caught him that way, and they put the picture on the front page. The other image shows him in shorts and a T-shirt with the fire department crest. It's Community Day in Vineland. Next to him stands a young boy, entranced because the fire chief has let him work the fire hose. "He was fascinated by the water coming out of the nozzle," Martinelli said to me. "You can tell in his eyes." That was how Nucci's son started out and how Richard's father meant to complete his tour.

In much the same way that Nucci had seen Ron as his heir at the diner, Ron always assumed his own son Richard would be a fireman. It didn't work out that way. When Richard was young, it soon became clear that he had Uncle Larry's genes. He didn't play with toy trucks. He preferred screwdrivers and pliers.

"What do you want for Christmas, Richard?" his father would ask him.

"Get me a set of Craftsman rachets, Dad."

He volunteered for the fire department not so much to quell flames but to go into the rescue zone, where the machinery was more elaborate and interesting. It wasn't the thrill of sliding down the pole or careering across town in a wailing fire engine or watching the flames go out and the black smoke turning to gray toward the end of a job done well. It was more, "How do you cut that poor guy out of the car with this hydraulic tool?" One morning, Chief Martinelli had an eight-thousand-dollar cutter that wasn't working right. He asked his son to have a look at it, and Richard took it to the shop where he worked. "The union would have screamed that I wasn't sending it to a certified factory, but I kind of took a shot."

"No problem, Dad," his son told him. "Hydraulics are hydraulics."

When Richard got home that night, he was fully pumped.

"How did we make out," Ron asked him.

During the lunch hour, everyone at Richard's shop had gathered around the cranky cutter. They field stripped it, took everything out, put in new seals, replaced the O-rings, changed the fluids, miked the cutters, then lasered the whole works to perfection.

"Try it," Richard said.

Martinelli grinned. "He fixed that thing like it was brand-new. That's his deal." And in much the same way that Nucci had stood down when Ron didn't want to take over at the diner, Ron encouraged his own son to follow his bliss, even if it wasn't a fire engine.

"How much did you tell your son about Vietnam?" I asked him.

"Not much. Not much at all."

To be strictly accurate, almost nothing. When Sergeant Martinelli got home, he stowed away his medals. He told no more war stories than Nucci. "I tried to keep it close. The guys in the firehouse tried to pry it out of me. When I retired, the local newspaper dug out that I had the Silver Star and three Purple Hearts. I didn't want that." Friends showed him the paper and called him a hero. "Yeah," he said skeptically. "Well, it still costs me seventy-five cents for a cup of coffee." Despite his honors and his wounds, he always felt he hadn't done enough. Every now and then, when he tuned in the History Channel to revisit Vietnam, the feeling returned. "Man, we had a cakewalk compared to what they had in the jungle," he'd tell himself. In the Delta you were always wet, your feet were always rotten, you had to sleep in the mud. You had to eat in the mud. Sure, he reminded himself. But he'd had it easy in the 9th Division. (Multiple wounds, that collapsed lung, and the three Purple Hearts.) "Nope," he'd say. "The First Cav, the 101st Airborne, and the 173rd of the 4th Division, they all had it harder."

He told his son no more than Nucci had told him.

"I guess if someone asked Richard, 'How many medals does your father have?' he would probably say, 'Oh, he's got a bunch of fire department plaques hanging in the office. I think he was in the Army. He was in Vietnam.' That would be it."

About the time of Gulf War I, an old buddy who was active in the Vineland Marine Corps League asked Martinelli to deliver an address during Memorial Day. The thought scared him more than the Viet Cong. "There's gotta be somebody better than me," he said, backing away. Later, the friend called and said his daughter was doing a project on Vietnam and asked Martinelli to talk to her senior high school class. More than twenty years had passed since he'd left Walter Reed Hospital. "I didn't want to go, but he kept breaking my chops, so I finally went. I took a Purple Heart with me. The kids had never seen one. I was amazed. The day I was supposed to speak, I was all thumbs, cold, sweaty, but I went and I talked freer than I thought I would. But I had to do it in a humorous fashion, like, 'Oh, I met a girl and fell in love with her, and then I went overseas and then we shot a water buffalo thinking it was an ambush.' With the kids, I didn't want to get into the blood and guts."

Another twelve years passed before the next break in his long silence. Then his old platoon leader, Carl Hedleston, a lieutenant, wrote to tell him that ten men from his unit were planning a reunion. Martinelli didn't want to go. "They had kind of put me on a pedestal and I didn't really like that. That was number one. Number two was, 'Maybe we need to let it go, really not go back there.' " But Hedleston kept calling on the phone ("Come on, you gotta come. We're going to Atlantic City."), and eventually he pushed aside three decades and got in his car. "To be honest with you, driving down there I was sweating." He looked at me, then looked down at his knees. "I was dressed like this. I decided I was not gonna get all primped up. I just wore a nice pair of shorts and a T-shirt and walked into the place and it didn't take me but ten seconds to change my whole perspective. BOOM. BOOM. BOOM." He clicked his fingers. "I recognized a couple of guys right away, then some others I'd had problems relating to, but they surely knew me. And they were a great bunch of fellas."

He could now see what war had done to the Martinellis, father and son. Nucci died early, at sixty-two, of emphysema. He was a heavy smoker, Luckies, three packs a day. ("Lucky Strike Green has gone to war," sang the ads.) Not long before he died he was still lighting up defiantly, his son uneasily watching the oxygen tank by his side. Then, the mayor led a campaign to refurbish Gattone Stadium, brand-new walls, restrooms that worked, bleachers that didn't cripple you by the first quarter, an irrigation system for the field, lights for night football.

When Richard Martinelli trotted out on the field for his first junior varsity game, his father felt like Vince Lombardi. Richard was no Nucci. His real sport was track, where he was a good pole vaulter.

("What the heck is that, jump up in the air fifteen feet, fall down and get hurt, but that was his thing.") Every time he plunged into the line, he got clocked. Every time he came back for more. His spirit, if not his yardage, reminded Ron of Nucci. "I remember looking across the field and saying, 'Jeez, if Pop was here, it would make it so nice just for him to see Richard out there.' But it didn't happen."

I thought, for just a nanosecond that Martinelli was going to lose it, but then the NexTel beeped officially, almost as if he had put in a fix for it to interrupt him if he got too far out on dangerous ground. Grabbing the yellow hand mike, he stood up and paced the room until he found a good signal. When he came back to the table, he was beaming. "Great news," he said. Five men from the fire academy had just passed the state test to join the fire service. On retiring, Martinelli had taken over the academy for little more than gas and sandwich money, and now his fresh recruits, who had flunked their test the first time around, were straightened out and good to go.

Where were *you guys?*

This was a hook I couldn't wiggle off. What was it that Hack had said long before I started looking for Martinelli?

You ought to cut your old man a little slack.

Wasn't that the least I could do? Like, maybe, the very least?

Chapter 9

Oracle

Sgt. Louis Simpson, warrior, poet,
after V.E. Day, 1945

A **poetry** reading? Are you nuts?"

Even over the telephone I could hear John Nelson's disbelief meter cranking into the red zone. John read military history, books on strategy, tactics—the prose of muzzle velocity and valor. He probably hadn't heard a poem since "The Midnight Ride of Paul Revere." I held the phone at arm's distance, listening to him fire for effect:

"I don't do poetry readings."

"Not once? Never?"

"Never. And with you? Forget it. They'll think we're gay."

"Only an hour, John. Who's going to know?"

"All right, all right," he said. "Should I wear a tight dress?"

At the bookstore that day, I had picked up an anthology called *Poets of World War II*, a new book published by the Library of America. The only poem I knew from World War II was "The Death of the Ball Turret Gunner" by Randall Jarrell. It was only five lines long, which didn't take away too much time for a boy who was going to hell and back with Audie Murphy. All my life I had believed that the poem's last line—"When I died, they washed me out of the turret with a hose."— had the tone of World War II pitch perfect. No off-we-go-into-the-wild-blue-yonder stuff, just the way it was. I put it right up there with "Live fast, die young, and leave a good-looking corpse." So it surprised me to discover that Jarrell had spent his war with the Second Air Force in Tucson, Arizona. The poem was fabricated from the safer reaches of imagination, not the flak-filled skies over Europe. Jarrell had never shot in anger, never been shot at. He taught celestial navigation to men like Murray Greenberg.

This small eye-opener came from Harvey Shapiro, editor of the book, who knew the full story. Shapiro, also a fine poet, survived thirty-five combat missions over Europe, which gave him more than enough equity, I thought, to let some air out of Jarrell's tires. Facing the contents page, the publishers had printed a photograph of the editor as a young tail gunner with the Fifteenth Air Force in Italy. In the picture, Shapiro stands with his arm draped over the twin barrels of a .50-caliber machine gun jutting out of the real turret of a real B-17. I had assumed that Shapiro and all the other great poets of World War II were dead. As it turned out, not only were he and some of the best still alive, to get the book up and away, they were doing a reading the following week at a local library in the Hamptons.

Every war story, to point out the obvious, is told in words, and these men were the wizards of words. I wanted to hear them. But to correct for poetic license—I had taken that ball turret gunner straight for too many years—I needed an expert witness. So I had called John Nelson.

The next Saturday, when John and I walked into the Morris Meeting Room downstairs at the library, we found ourselves looking at two hundred empty chairs. A stricken look crossed John's face—no place to run, no place to hide. We were early. But George Bush had just sent the Army, Air Force, Navy, and Marines after Saddam Hussein, and, war no longer being an abstraction, people were ready to listen to Harvey Shapiro and his squad of war poets. They wound up with a full house. The woman who had organized the reading was wearing a micro miniskirt. Down at the VFW, her legs could have put an entire platoon into the emergency room. Fiddling with the microphone, she announced that we had gathered together on the day that Franklin D. Roosevelt died.

John frowned. He must have been the only man in the audience younger than sixty. "Yeah, yeah," he said, scanning the room. "Look at them. So they've all come to hear these old World War II vets because it's April 12. They'll listen to a few poems and remember their friends. For the reality check, they should go home and turn on the TV." What he himself remembered from a TV broadcast a few days earlier was the sight of a wounded grunt outside Baghdad shooting from a stretcher to cover the men carrying him out of the line of fire. The grunt later died, he told me.

"Score one for Paul Wolfowitz and the Pentagon," I said. While we were waiting, someone, idiotically, had put a Billie Holiday torch song on the sound system for background music.

"You know what? That grunt never heard of Paul Wolfowitz. You think he knows who the assistant secretary of defense is? He was doing it for the men next to him."

Scowling, he opened the copy of the anthology I had given him on the way over and started thumbing through the pages. He stopped at an entry entitled "Carentan O Carentan."

"I know the battle," he said, his interest pricked. "Never heard of the poem." He knew about Carentan because the battle figured in the history of the 101st Airborne at Normandy, his father's outfit, men with paratrooper wings, the same that had been pounded into his own chest after jump school. Quickly scanning down the page, he said, "Look at that" as he put his finger on four stanzas that had caught his eye.

> There is a whistling in the leaves
> And it is not the wind,
> The twigs are falling from the knives
> That cut men to the ground.
>
> Tell me, Master-Sergeant,
> The way to turn and shoot.
> But the Sergeant's silent
> That taught me how to do it.
>
> O Captain, show us quickly
> Our place upon the map.
> But the Captain's sickly
> And taking a long nap.
>
> Lieutenant, what's my duty,
> My place in the platoon?
> He too's a sleeping beauty,
> Charmed by that strange tune.

"The grunt's scared shitless, and he's looking to the men who trained him, and they're sleeping. Huh. Sleeping. Think about it. That's one long, long nap. I wonder what this Simpson is like."

We had to wait an hour for Simpson to read; he was the day's star, and the organizer put him next to last on the schedule. From a seat in the middle of the audience, he stood and walked to the microphone. He was wearing a blue sweater, a red shirt, and plain trousers. In height he was closer to five feet than six, a man of Audie Murphy's build, compact but confident, a man of considerable presence even though you could see only his head and narrow shoulders bobbing above the crowd. "I have too much to say," he told the room. "So I'll just read three poems." As he started into "Carentan," I looked over at John, who was looking down at the floor, studying his shoes. As Simpson reached the whistling in the leaves that cut men to the ground, John's eyes lifted and lazed the podium. Simpson's voice was soft as he caressed the last lines.

> *Carentan O Carentan*
> *Before we met with you*
> *We never yet had lost a man*
> *Or known what death could do.*

John was tapping his finger against his right knee, mesmerized. "Jesus," he said. "The guy knows what he's talking about." Outside in the parking lot, he said, "You ought to put some poems in that book of yours. I'll pick 'em." That Simpson was a stud.

To find Louis Simpson's house you have to wind among the back roads of Stony Brook, working your way through the woods until you reach a sign that reads DEAD END. At that point it is important to not lose your nerve. "Don't stop," Simpson said over the phone, offering precise directions in something close to free verse. "People get confused. They make a mistake. You'll be on course when you reach Dead End." First house on the right. A burning bush—an azalea in full flame—marked the path to the door. On the other side a dog growled, but when the door opened it was only Lottie, a brown and black guard beagle, sizing me up from between the legs of her master. Lottie was graying at the muzzle, Simpson at the temples. "Come in, come in," he said mildly, pointing the way down the hall to a cavernous room full of books. He wore pale brown pants and an indescribable sport shirt. At first glance he looked more like the dormouse than George Patton. Patton favored spurs. Simpson was wearing carpet slippers.

Camouflage. The impression couldn't have been more misleading. Simpson was a poet warrior, the elements so mixed in him that you couldn't separate his guts from his pentameters. He wrote about combat in words any dogface could understand, even a few good officers like John Nelson. Simpson's infantrymen were as real, as down and dirty, as the mud that sucked at their boots.

> *They halted and they dug. They sank like moles*
> *Into the clammy earth between the trees.*
> *And soon the sentries, standing in their holes,*
> *Felt the first snow. Their feet began to freeze.*
>
> *At first dawn the first shell landed with a crack.*
> *Then shells and bullets swept the icy woods.*
> *This lasted many days. The snow was black.*
> *The corpses stiffened in their scarlet hoods.*
>
> *Most clearly of that battle I remember*
> *The tiredness in eyes, how hands looked thin*
> *Around a cigarette, and the bright ember*
> *Would pulse with all the life there was within.*

I had looked into the warrior and the poet before driving over to Stony Brook. Simpson had been awarded two Bronze Stars and Purple Hearts for his wounds and, nineteen years later, the Pulitzer Prize for his words. As an additional test, I tried his poem out on Hack. "Real fucking thing," he said. "The way it is." After fighting across France, Belgium, Holland, and into Germany, Simpson came home with what the medics were beginning to call combat fatigue. The diagnosis was a euphemism, as if getting tired was a nicer way to describe what really happened. When he walked to work he silently checked cross streets for ambushes; when he saw a field, he wondered how he would get across it. He heard voices. He was hallucinating. He'd look down at the floor of his room and see dead bodies, arms and knees jutting toward him. He offered a cigarette to the dead German officer who dropped in some nights to sit on a chair and talk. Eventually Simpson's relatives had him committed to Kings Park Hospital on Long Island. At the asylum, he had shock therapy and came out "cured," but for the next thirty years he dreamed every other night of firefights and death. A new wife woke him after their wedding night, badly frightened. In his sleep he was imitating the sound of incoming rounds, tossing the shrieks like a ventriloquist, making them advance closer and closer toward their bed. He married three times. At eighty, once again a bachelor, he was keeping house with Lottie.

In a novel, Simpson once created a soldier who sits in a foxhole after battle telling himself, "It will be a wise father after this war who knows his own child." Delphic, for a dogface. Who was Simpson really talking about? Did he have a son? In his *Selected Works,* I found the following brief entry: "I married and had a son, but the marriage lasted only a short time." A single sentence. Ransacking the rest of his books, I could find only two other short references to this son. Then, in the dedication to the book that won Simpson the Pulitzer Prize—*At the End of the Open Road*—I found his name. Who was he? What had happened between this wise father and his phantom son?

Simpson showed me into his writing room, where Lottie curled up at my feet, keeping an eye on me.

"Do you use green tea?"

The phrase and the accent were in some sharpened key I didn't recognize at first, an inch off center and with a faint lilt. Scottish? No. It was Caribbean. Simpson was born in Jamaica in 1923. Although he had moved to the United States in 1940—he went into the Army two years later at nineteen—he still had a faint trace of high Kingston in his voice. The voice was, at that moment, very soft.

"Lots," I said,

"Then you can have quarts, gallons."

While he went off to the kitchen to put on the kettle, I rustled in my little black bag and pulled out a package in a brown paper bag. Over the phone, when I had asked if there was anything I could bring, he had said, "Nothing. No. Maybe a barrel of scotch. No. Nothing." On the way over, I had stopped at the liquor store and bought a bottle of Single Barrel, a single malt scotch. Poets make me nervous. In this case it was not a matter of flashing eyes and flowing hair. Most of Simpson's was gone, and his dark eyes were impassive, calm. For some reason they gave the impression that he knew in advance why I had come. When he came back with the green tea, I handed him the brown whiskey, an offering to the oracle.

"A bribe."

"Ah," he said, examining the label.

"Closest I could get to a barrel."

"No need, but quite nice," he said. "Let's talk. Were you in Vietnam?"

His voice was soft, but the question was to the point, and it ran me through. I had never seen combat; there was no way we could talk on level ground. Lamely, I explained how a surprise pregnancy and marriage in 1964 and a child in January 1965, just at the beginning of the American buildup in Vietnam, had dropped my classification in the draft. My number had never come up, and I hadn't volunteered. "Lucky." He said the word mildly: no compliment, just a fact of life, my own, spared from what his eyes had seen.

I told him that my father had been a soldier, and he nodded, and then I told him the story about the day my old man came home from the war, the doghouse, the outstretched arms, the word "jump," the soldier scowling at his cowering son, wheeling, and disappearing.

"You mean, he left? What a terrible thing."

The voice was sympathetic—for the soldier or the son, you couldn't quite tell. "Coming back, the first time he sees you, to say that, oh Lord." I stumbled, hurrying to explain that I knew now that I had misunderstood the moment. Mercifully, he broke into my ramble. "I think you understood the moment, but it was a very sad thing for him to say, sad for him, sad to do it. To do it to himself. There must have been some grief afterward."

Grief? The possibility had never occurred to me. From my own angle of vision, fixed at the doghouse in the mind of a two-year-old boy, fixed so powerfully that everything still looked the same today, grief was never in the equation. I mean, this father was a soldier, he had three guns in his duffel, he'd killed bad guys, he wasn't crying the day he fired the word coward at me. A bit uncannily, as these thoughts were jostling silently in my head, Simpson intercepted them, began to answer them. "For such a thing to become a tremendous block, unmovable from what you're telling me, it's so strange." He stopped, considered the scene. "Usually, just in the daily rubbing of elbows, you'd get over it. It's remarkable that it should still be standing there, that you couldn't change it." He looked at me curiously.

A bit defensively, I said I thought I wasn't alone. I told him about the day Steven Greenberg and I had put the photographs of lieutenants Mathews and Greenberg side by side and seen the same man. "Soldiers like them didn't talk," I said. "They had a code." And then I blurted out, "I suppose I was hoping to get from you what I couldn't pull from my own father . . . there were sticking points . . . I was hoping . . ." Quite gently, Simpson signaled me to stop. If I had flunked the Vietnam question, the damage wasn't fatal. "We can talk," he said. "Let's talk about what you call the sticking points."

From my black bag, I pulled out my copy of his *Selected Prose* and started flipping through the dog-eared pages until I found the passage that had put me on the road to Stony Brook: "I will speak only with reluctance. I will resist any expression that is not the truth. And rather than say what is not true, I will be silent." Was his silence the same as my father's, the same as Ed Persan's, Spann Watson's, and all the others?

"You talk about a Code," he said. "The Code is you don't brag. If anybody brags, believe you me, he's not going to be a soldier for very long. In fact, I never met a soldier in my life—a combat soldier—who boasted about what he had done. I never heard a man do that. Because he knew that what he had done had been done because of the guy next to him, or that the guy on the other side had done more. You were never to show that you had done this or that. It was an indecent thing if you went home and talked about your Army experience." He paused and thought for a moment, as if he had been transported through time to a

scene he had put in his novel, the elements of a division poised to return home ("A liberty ship was tied to one of the piers. Platoon by platoon, carrying their duffel bags over their shoulders, a line of men went
up the gangplank. Then it was our turn. We hefted our bags and moved
off.") Returning abruptly to the present, he repeated the first article of
the Code: no phony talk. "It was an indecent thing to do. A real guy
wouldn't do that."

Ed Persan must have felt much the same way; why else would he
have been so hard on the VFW? "Let's look at it," Simpson went on,
picking up the same thread. "I'm assuming the men we're talking
about have been in a serious part of the war, not headquarters. They've
seen action." I nodded—some on the ground, some in the air, but always in action. Simpson looked down at Lottie, then back at me. "One
of the things that happens, especially in the infantry, the first time you
come up against it, action itself, you don't know—you may be dead in
five seconds from now—it's terrifying." As he spoke, he slipped into the
present tense. His high forehead furrowed, as if those five seconds were
all he had. And the war came flooding into the room.

"Your first impulse—the impulse of an animal to avoid danger, to
run back into the forest, I suppose, or a human being confronted with
something really dangerous—is to get out of it." He hammered the last
four words like a blacksmith banging on iron. "But you're a soldier, and
it's not just that you're a soldier, you're with other men. You simply can-
not give way to fear." He looked at me oddly, as if to make sure I was
following him. "I'm putting this all in spelled-out sentences," he said.
"But this is something that happens at once. Instantaneously. You shut
down a part of you. The part of you that gives way, that avoids danger
and runs with the other wolves back into the forest. You shut down. You
become a different kind of person. You can do all sorts of things in that
condition. You can run, you can shoot. You become a man who has
stopped being afraid."

"Then, you have a time when it stops, and you get down into a foxhole or some safe place, and you relax a bit—and it comes again."

As terror reappeared, his voice rose and fell with his words. It was as if I were no longer in front of him. He was talking aloud to himself and to the soldier he had been at Carentan. "The next morning, the next night, two nights from now, two days from now, it comes at you again, and what you went through last time doesn't count a bit. Terror doesn't say, 'Oh, well, you've done this. You can go through it again and not be afraid.' NO. Every time it is death facing you, wounds—suppose I go blind, suppose . . ." He drew up short in front of the big one: Suppose they blow my balls off? His voice sharpened. "Now what are you gonna do when you go home? You gonna talk about it? You're not gonna talk about it because . . ."

He didn't finish the thought. Instead, he told a story, imploring me first to understand that he was not boasting. "I was wounded at Carentan. A machine gun had my place. A machine gunner was shooting right over me. About three inches. The man next to me was dying. I'll never forget that. He was calling on his mother in Italian: *'Mama, mama, mama mia'*." Whispering the words now, there in France; then, as if someone had slapped him, jolting himself back into the room. "I don't know why this should be, but wounded men, men who are dying, call on their mothers." He laughed, veering away from sentimentality. "It's true."

"Fortunately," he went on, "those machine gunners, those Germans, were taken out. I didn't have to stand up. But on another day, I did have to stand up. I was a runner. That meant I carried messages or did whatever was needed at the moment. A mortar was out of ammo. We were under severe fire by the Germans. Full fire. The first sergeant called me over and said, 'Take these shells to the mortar.' I made that trip I forget how many times. And every time I made it, machine gunners were trying to kill me. And I had no fear. I had no fear at all. I was running. I was doing something. I was showing that I had courage. I couldn't have put it in sentences like this then, but that was what was in my body and in my heart. I gave the mortar shells to the guys in the foxhole. I went back for another load. I came again. Bullets were whistling all around me. Shells. I wasn't afraid. It was like a great release. I was proving something to myself . . ."

His voice fell to a whisper.

"Yeah, but . . ."

For a moment he stopped, and then, once again, from the past tense he shot into the present. "A few days later I'm in a hole being shelled, and JESUS, I can't stand it. It's too much." His voice rose to a shout— "HOW COME WHAT I DID YESTERDAY DOESN'T COUNT? I'M OFF THE HOOK. I'VE DONE IT"—then sank. "You're not off the hook. Two weeks from now, when you're going through this again, you're going to shut down inside of you. You don't feel happy. You don't think you've proven anything. You're going to think, 'JESUS CHRIST, ARE THEY GOING TO EXPECT ME TO DO THIS ALL THE TIME? I swear, I'VE DONE IT.' "

"You've never done it.

"The American Army made a big mistake in that war. They thought they had enough men. But in the winter of 1944, they found out that they were wrong. They were really running short in the infantry. You don't get better at it, you know. This is a thing some people don't understand. You don't get better at being a soldier the more you're exposed. You don't get better the longer you go into foxholes. You get worn out. And my God, they wore you out. In the American Army, unlike the British, which was more experienced and drew its troops back from the line for rest periods, you went on and on and on. You went on until you were absolutely exhausted and you couldn't take it anymore. You become like a worn-out part. That's a fact. Soldiers have so many days in them of first-rate energy, first-rate thinking, and then the parts start to go."

Simpson had volunteered for the Army. In January 1943 he went to a tank regiment in Texas, where he learned how to hump shells and operate a radio. Observing his high candlepower, the Army then picked him for the Army Specialized Training Program and sent him to the University of Louisiana. The idea was to turn him into an engineer. He was part of the same ASTP that had netted Richard Vincent. A poet and a choir singer. But in the fall of 1944, with bodies piling up and not enough replacements for the front in Europe, the Army emptied its classrooms and handed the extra-bright boys the same rifle as everyone else. When I told Simpson about Richard, he laughed. "They couldn't afford to have all those mathematicians and physicists and artists and musicians. The Army needed the guys in the cartoon—Willy and Joe. Riflemen. The guys who fought in North Africa, Sicily, Italy. God what an awful slogging mess that was."

Like Ed Persan, Simpson crossed a field that he would never be able to leave, not when he got home, not after the rest of the century had expired. Simpson's field was in Holland, and the memory, in shards, stayed in his brain like needles of shrapnel. "In that field, German infantry and American paratroopers—they must have been paratroopers, I keep thinking . . . yes, they were paratroopers—had shot each other at very close range. And that field was covered with dead bodies. I had to walk over men with their faces shot half off lying on top of other men with their entrails on the ground. I had to step over them every night for at least two weeks." The stiff legs and arms of the rotting corpses stuck in the air, beckoning to him. In the moonlight, the putrefying faces gleamed.

"Now what am I going to do—talk about that?"

The rhetorical question hangs in the air, answers itself.

"You can spend the rest of your life thinking about it. Why is it so important to my life, that particular place? A field. I didn't tell anybody. I can talk to you about it. I told a few people. I've written a little paragraph about it now and then. But . . ."

The thought trailed off and Simpson fell silent. He had seen more combat than most men because he was not killed, and because he was never badly enough wounded to be taken off the line for good. His feet froze and he was hurt badly enough to be evacuated to a hospital for a few weeks. Then they patched him up and sent him back to the front. This is the way it was for every combat infantryman. You advanced. You advanced until the enemy shot off one of your essential moving parts and you could advance no longer. You advanced until you were killed. Those were the rules, pal. You advanced until the war was over or you were dead.

You didn't get off the hook.

"You're not gonna talk about it because of something else—thinking that if you'd really done your job, you'd be dead. You start to wonder, 'Am I exaggerating? Was it that bad? Was it that dangerous?'"

"Maybe I'm a coward."

His words stun me. A doghouse flashback intersects Simpson's soliloquy. ("Mama, what is a coward?")

"You have to fight this idea that you didn't do enough: 'I didn't get killed. The guys who are real guys are dead. The guys who really faced danger are dead. If I had been braver, I wouldn't be here. I must have been a coward.' "

Simpson returned to the worst days of Bastogne. "Thinking about men who probably died could make me weep. Any mention of somebody doing something—it doesn't have to be something terrible—the idea of a man doing something wonderful makes you want to cry. You don't get to know the guys in other companies too well, but I was a runner and I saw this one young man, a BAR man who used his BAR to great effect one day. He won the Silver Star for bravery. I would have loved to have had that Silver Star. I got the Bronze Star twice, but it wasn't the Silver Star, and when I think of what he did and what other men like him did, I could cry. What they did was so wonderful."

When the war was over, a few of Simpson's fellow dogfaces wrote him from time to time. He answered the first letters, then stopped, disconnected, tried to turn off the images flickering in his brain. "You shut down the part of you that remembers too well how it feels to huddle in a hole and be shelled. You are going to forget that. You are going to make yourself forget that. Make yourself forget."

His voice drops to a whisper so low it is hard to hear him, but that is beyond the point, as he is clearly whispering aloud what has been silently scourging his mind since 1945.

"Sure, make yourself forget that. You're going to make yourself forget the accepting of others, of loving other people. You're going to shut down a lot of things. You were afraid, so you shut it down. You became a brave man, others would say. You shut it down. The whole machine—you shut it down. And you don't talk about what you did, because it will bring everything back. If you did talk, God knows what thoughts, what memories, you'd release. God knows what demons."

Demons, night sweats, artillery rounds creeping toward the bed. "You never know when you'll want to check out," my father had told me. A Fitzgerald riff, a Hemingway gesture—I'd always pegged it that way—but these demons were no fiction. The Beretta in the nightstand had been there all along against the moment they overran his position.

In *The Soldier's Tale*, the best book on war stories, Samuel Hynes, a Marine pilot in the Pacific during World War II and then in Korea, observed that "most war memoirs come late in life, that memory dawdles and delays." Except for the small paragraph or two Simpson mentioned, he didn't really get the demons down in prose until 1998, when he made a run against them in the *Hudson Review*. He called his attempt at exorcisim *Soldier's Heart*. The expression goes back to the Civil War and military doctors' groping to diagnose an illness whose wounds were internal, invisible. After World War I, they called it "shell shock"; after World War II, "combat fatigue"; then "post-traumatic stress disorder" after Vietnam. "Soldier's heart," Simpson wrote, "strikes me as the best, for it describes an illness that involved my heart as much as my head. My heart would beat faster, I would tremble and sweat and, on occasion, pass out."

Sitting in his room of books, he seemed invulnerable to me, but the impression, once again, was misleading. He was discharged from the Army in 1945. After the war, he returned to Columbia University. He read like a man possessed. He wrote poems and essays and a wild short story set in a beauty salon that *Esquire* bought and published. A banging typewriter replaced his rifle. He didn't eat, he didn't sleep. The demons surrounded him, and he went down. "I was physically and mentally a violent man. So one day I broke down. I went violent. I tackled a policeman." Or something like that. The memory is still blurred in his mind. "I got the shit beat out of me by the police and then I got put in the hospital—where did that come from?"

In the hospital they put him on a table, attached electrodes, and pulled the switch, driving his body into convulsions. In retrospect he thinks shock therapy helped him, though there was collateral damage. "I was cured, theoretically, but I couldn't remember anything that happened between my going into the hospital and my coming out." Over the next few years his memory came back by fits and starts, but only in bits and pieces. "Carentan O Carentan," World War II's answer to "Kubla Khan"—a shot in the guts of romanticism—arrived as a dream in Paris one night more than three years after his discharge.

The next morning Simpson got up and realized that the night vision was a memory, not a dream. He wrote the poem in one sitting. To remember was his objective, to regain his voice. Many years later, in an essay called "Dogface Poetics," he wrote, "To a footsoldier, war is almost entirely physical. That is why some men, when they think about war, fall silent. Language seems to falsify physical life and betray those who have experienced it absolutely—the dead." He had found himself on dangerous ground, a man of voices trapped between words and silence, "close-mouthed, almost sullen." He wrote, "I wished to show the war exactly, as though I were painting a landscape or a face. I wanted people to find in my poems the truth of what it had been like to be an American infantry soldier. Now I see that I was writing a memorial of those years for the men I had known—who were silent."

The afternoon sun had left the windows of Simpson's room of books. Lottie had fallen asleep. Could it be possible, I asked of the oracle, that every father who has seen combat comes home a mystery to his son? Whether we call the syndrome soldier's heart, shell shock, combat fatigue, or post-traumatic stress disorder, are we making a fundamental mistake? Do we recognize only the most spectacular cases? Do we miss everyone else?

The answer came instantly.

"Yes."

Simpson looked out the window, then at me. "The war I'm describing, the frontline war, makes you a very angry man," he said. "You've been trained to be angry. You've been trained to kill. It is a terrible thing to see death all around you, and you're involved in making death.

You have to untrain yourself. You see men who live to be ninety and don't give any visible signs. They seem wonderfully adjusted.

"Adjusted?" He murmured the word again, turning it around in the air, reexamining it as if it were a rare plant or stone. "There had to be an *adjustment*," he thought out loud. "You can't see action and get away with it without paying some price. I'll make a big statement here. People are all very different from one another, that's true. But my bet would be that anyone who's seen real combat would have for the rest of his life something going on inside him. Some wound. Some secret."

The secret.

I listened, transfixed. "What is it?" I asked him, sounding like a small boy. What did the soldier in his novel mean when he said, "We are the sons of a gun and a hole in the ground"? What did he mean when he predicted that after the war, only a wise man would know his own child? He looked at me carefully, as if to weigh me alongside the secret.

"I meant there was going to be a big difference between those who had been in the war and those who had not—between the fathers and the sons."

There were only two of us in the room as he began to lift the blackout curtain.

"Yeah, there would be a difference. How can you understand this child?" An edge in the question. "You've been in the war. This child knows nothing about war. This child thinks it's a fun thing. This child thinks it's just a big game. This child has to learn my hard experience, what I know." The voice grew harder. "But this child doesn't want to learn what I know. This child doesn't want to know. This child doesn't want to know the enormous secret I have inside me."

Eerie now, his mind visible, out in the ether somewhere between us, as the soldier in him talked out loud to the poet, repeating the phrases, varying them slightly, as if he were composing a song, something slightly cracked out of Bertolt Brecht.

"I have a great secret, but I can't tell people about it."

"Because if I tell people about it, I'm going to have a nervous collapse."

"So I shut down."

"I have this big secret."

"How can I tell him about it?"

"He's a little kid. He doesn't know anything."

"He runs away from me."

The cadences are hypnotizing. Suddenly there are three of us in the room. The voice is no longer his alone. It is my father's. He holds out his arms. I run away.

"I spent the best part of my life learning not to run away. He thinks it's nothing. Nothing. You can live without that, he thinks. And a whole generation is not going to know what I did. A whole generation is not going to know. Not going to give a damn. The bastards. You little bastards."

I don't think that, I tell myself. Who is he talking about now? It dawns on me. His son. There are now four of us in the room, two fathers, two sons.

"A man goes out there."

"He stays there."

"He doesn't kick."

"But my son doesn't know."

"He doesn't care."

"He's ignorant."

"He doesn't know what it's like."

"He'll never know."

"I'm not going to tell him."

"Why should I release my treasure?"

"My secret. My treasure."

The voice is low, furious. My heart begins to pound, my hands are sweating.

"Why should I let him have it?"

"This is my secret. My treasure. That nobody has but us."

"Wives don't know."

"He doesn't know."

"I'm not going to tell him. I'm not going to tell any of them."

"Why should I let them have that precious thing?"

"That only God knows about. And since there is no God—or maybe—God, I don't know."

"This is a treasure I have. This terrible thing I went through."

"I'm not going to share it. I'm not going to share it with anybody."

"This big treasure."

"Valuable. Incredibly valuable."

"That field in Holland."

"The dead bodies I had to walk around."

"Nobody knows but me."

"NOBODY IN THE WORLD KNOWS THAT FIELD."

"What a treasure I have. I'm not going to tell."

With that shout, Simpson broke himself out of his trance. The medium collapsed, vanished from the room. Simpson was staring at me. He said, "That's pretty close, isn't it?"

Simpson's son was born six years after the war. The marriage didn't last, and the son grew up with his mother. In a memoir called *The King, My Father's Wreck*, Simpson took note of these events in something less than a single paragraph: "According to the terms of the divorce, my very young son, could visit on weekends. We would go to Central Park and the Zoo or the Museum of Natural History, perhaps a movie. I played with him, made dinner, and put him to bed. Then I worked at my writing." When I asked him what year his son arrived, he was at first a little vague about the date, though it came back to him later. He loved the boy, he dedicated books to him; but one thing baffled him: His son, to his way of thinking, was an absolute pacifist.

They had recently argued over the American invasion of Iraq. As Simpson remembered the fight, the lines of battle were drawn up this way:

"Should we just let Saddam Hussein murder and torture people?"

"No. We should stop him."

"How do you stop him without using a gun?"

"Give the United Nations more time."

"You are not making sense."

Simpson gritted his teeth. "He, of course, thinks I'm not making sense. So you're restraining all this anger at your son. I am. I don't want to be angry at him. He is a wonderful boy. He's a good man. He's a perfect father. He's good with his kids. I was never that good with my kids, I know that. But, tell me, my son, how do you deal with somebody who's a murderer? How do you deal with Hitler? You tell him nice things? YOU HAVE TO KILL THE SONUVABITCH."

The chasm between the warrior poet and the pacifist son opened the day Simpson came home and said he was leaving. "He wasn't more than three years old, maybe a little younger. That really made a big hole in me. I saw a lot of him, but I gave him a wound, a real wound. He can't take it." In the sixties, when his son reached Yale, Simpson said, he enlisted with protesters who threw stones at the Administration Building. Later he fell in love with a "very, very good woman," a biologist, and regained traction. Then he astounded Simpson by quitting a good job in California when his wife got a job in Boston. "In my generation, you didn't give up your job for a woman going across the country," he said a bit grumpily. "But my son did. He loves her and he moved east." To Simpson's double amazement, his son then decided to get a doctorate in literature. Books eventually drew them closer, but when his son started to have second thoughts about his dissertation subject, Simpson regressed. "You remember in the opening scene of *The Godfather* when the guy who's a singer goes in and says to Don Corleone, 'I need this job, I'm perfect for it. He won't let me have it, this guy in Hollywood. Godfather, I don't know what to do.' And the Godfather goes, 'You can be a man, that's what. Don't cry about it. You can be a man.' That scene remains in my mind because that's how I felt about my son."

That day, when the son took his troubles to the father, the son looking tired, the father trying not to look pissed off, what went through Simpson's mind was this: "You're gonna be a writer? Writers have to take chances. That's what you have to do in this world. Be in it." The father said nothing out loud. He didn't want to hurt his son, or make things worse. But the soldier's ethos was at work. Private Simpson's voice was shouting, "YOU'VE GOT TO TAKE A CHANCE. I TOOK A CHANCE."

The exasperation is expressed as an irony, not a condemnation. Simpson didn't kill Nazis to turn into a Hun. But the gap remains. "My son is a nice guy. But as far as I am concerned, he doesn't know the secret I know."

Lottie shook herself awake and Simpson looked at her fondly. "Ay yai," he said with a Jamaican-Jerusalem sigh. "The world is a complicated place, isn't it? It could almost make you believe in God."

When I got home, I called Simpson's son and tried to invite myself to his home. He said he'd have to think about it. After a week had passed, I called again.

"I've thought about it," he said. "I just don't think it would be a good idea."

Chapter 10

Where Have You Gone, Audie Murphy?

PFC Hollis "Red" Ditterline,
Baker Company, 15th Infantry
Regiment, France, 1945

The Garand M-1 was an air-cooled, gas-operated, clip-fed, semi-automatic rifle. For fights at around two hundred yards, you set the sights at battle zero and pulled the trigger. If the job got more up close and personal, you fixed a bayonet under the barrel and lunged. Gen. George S. Patton Jr. called the M-1 "the greatest battle implement ever devised." All the United States Army had to do was attach it to enough riflemen like PFC Hollace Edwin Ditterline.

The Army considered him Serial Number 2690999833. His friends called him Red. In 1945, when he came limping home from Europe, he had won the Combat Infantryman Badge, a Purple Heart, the Bronze Star, and the French Croix de Guerre with Palm. Even so, it took the Army clerk who filled out Red Ditterline's separation papers only thirty-six words' worth of typewriter ribbon to sum up his war: "Military occupation: Rifleman. Loaded, aimed and fired rifle at enemy personnel and enemy targets. Assisted in capturing and holding enemy positions and changing positions as situation demanded. Thoroughly familiar with weapons and hand to hand fighting." That was it. Gen. Dwight D. Eisenhower's *Crusade in Europe* on the head of a pin.

After the war, Dennis Ditterline, Red's older son, tried to extract a few more details.

The result: "Not a peep."

For Dennis and Bob Ditterline, his younger brother, being Red's son offered certain advantages around Griffith, Indiana. Ditterline would do anything for a friend, and his drinking buddies felt the same way about him. He stood just under six feet tall, all muscle, with blue eyes, a ruddy complexion, and the carrot top that gave him his nickname. Because Red drank with the local barber, his sons got their crew cuts free. Because Red drank with the owner of the Ben Franklin Store, they could play with all the toys down at the five-and-dime. Because Red drank with the guy who owned the bowling alley, they never had to pay for a lane. Actually, Red drank with everybody. Dennis and Bob knew they had the run of Griffith because their father drank with the police chief. Everyone loved Red.

No one but Dennis and Bob and their sisters Sandy and Dianna knew what happened when Red came home nights from the tavern. His wife Myrtle slept in a separate bed. In the middle of the night, the sons would hear their father yelling at invisible enemies. "You're not gonna fucking do that to me," he would shout. Then he bashed the wall with his feet and fists. The next morning they would watch him hobble off to work, his toes broken, his knuckles covered with scabs.

When Red drank, his moods swung out of control. On a tear, he would beat his sons until their backs were striped with welts and blood. Dennis hated him. Over and over he asked his mother, "Why don't he just die, Mom? Why don't he just go away? Why did he have to come back and make all this mess? Why didn't he get killed in the war?"

The reason he survived was a secret he kept from his sons for many years. Red might have been killed the first time he saw combat. Slashing out of Riedwihr Woods in the Colmar Pocket, he had taken part in the single most famous firefight of the war. On a freezing January afternoon in 1945, a baby-faced lieutenant from Texas stood in the flames of a burning American tank destroyer and fought off six German tanks and 250 advancing infantrymen. By virtue of his courage in battle that day, Audie Murphy won the Congressional Medal of Honor—and saved Red Ditterline's life.

The story obsessed me. Audie Murphy was buried in Arlington National Cemetery, the infantryman's garden of stone. The favorite stopping place for Arlington pilgrims was John F. Kennedy's eternal flame. The second most popular stop was the grave of Audie Murphy. Red Ditterline was buried near Hebron, Indiana. Only his sons and family paid attention to his last resting place. Whatever the connection was between the war's most venerated hero and this all-but-unknown soldier, it had everything to do with the conundrum that had always separated me and my father: Who had the whip hand—and who had the balls?

By accident, the first collision between me and my old man took place just after *Life* magazine put Audie Murphy on the cover. Murphy's cherubic face was all over Salt Lake City and everywhere else in the country. Bathed in the megawatts of Henry Luce, he was a young, all-American Achilles, triumphant, home safe, to all surface appearances unscarred by the war. The cover was a superb work of portraiture; it was also a masterpiece of uplift. Audie Murphy was real. He was a genuine hero. By virtue of the exaggerating lens of the popular media, he was rapidly becoming a demigod. Later on, starring in the movie Universal-International made from his autobiography, and undoubtedly the best thing in it, he crossed over from reality to Valhalla.

If you were a son of the Greatest Generation, you might hesitate over whom you wanted to play at Cowboys and Indians: Roy Rogers, the Lone Ranger, Hopalong Cassidy, the Cisco Kid—there was a lot to work out. But when the fantasy was soldiers, you knew the instant you grabbed your BB gun there was only one way to go—to hell and back with Audie Murphy. What Sergeant York did for the Great War, Audie Murphy did for our fathers' war. In action, his virtues—innocence, steadiness, selflessness, guts—were as indestructible as his body. And in the flesh, he contributed something even more important to a boy's sense of manly possibilities. At five-foot-six and 120 pounds, not only was he like you. Shit, man, you told yourself—he *was* you.

Audie Murphy came from Texas. I came from Utah. When I was eight years old that seemed to be the main difference between us. I first read about him in one of the Landmark Books, a series Random House published for boys. I owned a plastic bazooka that shot armor-piercing Ping-Pong balls. Great for blasting the bumpers of a Chevrolet Suburban Carryall. Later, when *To Hell and Back* came out as a movie, I saw it six times. Studying his moves, I came out of the Marin Theater imagining myself atop the tank destroyer, looking for a fight.

This case of mistaken identity was way over the top, but back then, for reasons of my own, I gloried in it. So far as I could see, the opposing poles of manliness were Audie Murphy on top of the burning tank destroyer and Tommy Two cowering on the doghouse. It wasn't Audie Murphy's fault that he had one foot in Alsace-Lorraine and the other on Hollywood and Vine. It wasn't even true that I couldn't tell the difference between a man and a movie star. I just didn't want to. What was the point of winning the war if it meant the collapse of fantasy in our time?

The result, of course, was my own kind of battle fatigue. Having never seen into the head of a real soldier, I didn't have the first clue about courage: what we take it to be, what we need it to be, what we insist that it be, and what, despite all our needs and illusions, it really is.

What the hell, maybe Audie and Red could get me squared away. When I fired up the computer and Googled Audie Murphy, I discovered that his oldest son, Terry M. Murphy, had set up a foundation to keep the best of his father's spirit alive. To find the real Audie Murphy, all I had to do was punch in audiemurphy.com. And when I clicked the mouse, there was the real Red Ditterline.

Navigating through the newsletters of the Audie Murphy Research Foundation (AMRF), I discovered an old news clipping. In 1951, the year of *The Red Badge of Courage,* a Murphy star turn directed by John Huston, Audie Murphy had made a stop near Griffith. The *Gary Tribune* reported that he had spent several minutes shooting the breeze with "a veteran who was identified today only as Ditterline." Forty-six years later, Larryann Willis, a lawyer and rancher from California who was the foundation's executive director, had tracked down this veteran and talked to him. Next to her interview was a photograph of Red Ditterline in uniform, clean-cut, square-jawed, beagle-eared, and smiling. His precisely knotted tie was ready for the closest inspection, and his eyes beamed out a challenge: Go ahead—you figure me out.

Red had grown up near a village called Grantsboro, where the gas station, grocery, and post office were all in one building: Fifteen seconds and you were out of town. He dropped out of school after the sixth grade and had to make his own way through the Depression. At foundries in Kankakee, Illinois, and later in Griffith, he had been a squeeze molder, turning out footrests for barber chairs. At just about any barbershop in the Midwest, when you looked down and saw your feet resting on the logo of the Emil Paider Company, cast in iron, you were looking at Red's work. When the war came he thought about joining the Navy, where he'd heard you could earn good money as a molder. But the Army drafted him, trained him as a dogface, stuffed him onto the *Queen Elizabeth,* and shipped him to the 3rd Infantry Division.

On January 25, 1945, according to the interview, he jumped from the back of a truck and hit the frozen ground of the Colmar Pocket. His orders were to join Baker Company of the 15th Infantry Regiment. A sergeant pointed out his new company commander, a runt lieutenant who looked to be about seventeen. Jesus, the squirt had freckles. Red was twenty-seven. His first thought was, "Who is this little kid and why the hell is he giving me orders?"

Lieutenant Murphy had recently taken command of B Company. On paper, its combat strength was supposed to be 235 men. On the ground, it had opened the siege of the Colmar Pocket with ninety men and six officers. By the time Ditterline arrived from a replacement depot ten miles behind the front, Murphy was the only officer left and the enlisted men were down to thirty-two. He told Ditterline to move forward and take over a foxhole abandoned by the Germans in the Riedwihr Woods. Shouldering his rifle and gear, Red moved along a path through the trees. He passed the swollen body of a dead German. Although he was seven years older than Murphy, he had never faced combat or seen a shot-up corpse. He spent an icy night thinking about it, so scared he threw up. Wondering what it would feel like to be dead, he shook in the foxhole until dawn.

I clicked back to the AMRF's report for the spring of 1998, where I'd seen Murphy's own account of what happened next. It went like this:

> The snow was knee deep and we were miserable and cold. I had my men mark time and keep moving to keep their feet from freezing while we awaited ammunition and orders to attack. Neither arrived. At 10 A.M. the Krauts attacked. Six tanks moved toward us from the direction of Holtzwihr. They were supported by about 250 infantrymen. I knew that we couldn't hold our position against that opposition because casualties were high and our two tank destroyers had been knocked out. So I ordered my men to go back 500 to 600 yards to take cover and prepare to make a stand. I was scared. I didn't think there was a chance of getting out of there alive, but for some reason I didn't give a damn.
>
> One of our tank destroyers was not far from me. It was burning and there was a danger that the gasoline and ammunition

would explode any minute. But the Germans were getting so close there was only one thing to do to give my men time to get set. I climbed onto the tank turret. I pushed aside the bodies of a lieutenant and his gunner who had been killed when the tank was hit, and began firing the machine gun. I was pretty well hidden by the turret. The flames made it hot, but that felt good after being cold for so long. I had a good supply of ammunition and kept firing. I was too busy to worry . . . By that time the artillery was going good. Most of the German infantrymen had been killed or wounded, and the tanks began falling back. I had been on the tank turret for an hour, and my ammunition was gone. So I dropped over the side and sat down on the snow. I was puzzled: How come I'm not dead?

Dug in with the other enlisted men, Red Ditterline saw it all, and he was asking himself the same thing about Murphy: "He was wounded and on that TD," Red told the Audie Murphy Research Foundation. "He could have missed doing that. He would have got killed himself to protect us. Five or six tanks and a couple of companies of Germans is hard for one man to bat up against. I'd have got off and run, if it had been me."

I reran the movie, set the screenplay against the reality.

"I was scared."

Audie Murphy, scared? Where was that on the screen?

"I didn't think there was a chance of getting out of there alive."

Neither did Red.

Maniacally, I hauled down the *Oxford English Dictionary*'s giant Volume C. First I looked up courage: "that quality of mind which shows itself in facing danger without fear or shrinking."

"*I was scared.*"

Then I checked out coward: "one who displays ignoble fear or want of courage in the face of danger."

"*I was scared.*"

What was this? Either Audie Murphy was yellow or the accepted definition was full of shit. You didn't have to be a genius to cipher it out. Shit it was. Without fear there could be no courage.

On this point, the *OED*'s article on the word coward was more instructive. It offered a reference to an obsolete word from Old French referring to an animal's tail as you saw it between its legs or from the rear when it took flight.

So the question had nothing to do with fearlessness. The issue was, when your balls quite sensibly wanted to shrink up into your armpits, would you or wouldn't you hold your ground? If fearlessness wasn't the point, what were we talking about? Audie Murphy's own answer was this: "There are a lot of things that can make a man brave. Wanting to go back to Texas, lack of sleep, anger, disgust, discomfort and hate— those things won me my medals, and they've won many other medals for many other guys."

And after that, he said, "I won't be sent into combat again unless I request it. And I won't. I'm not a fighting man. From here on, I want to like everybody."

Introducing the account, Terry Murphy had written a short note on what his father had just said.

"I was pinned by the last sentence: It was so hopeful and so plaintive. It was so innocent. I know what he had gone through, and I know what he would yet go through, so that last sentence pins me every time. That last sentence kills me."

Terry Murphy was born in 1952, about a year after *The Red Badge of Courage* meeting between Audie and Red. In that long 1997 interview with the Audie Murphy Research Foundation, Red said that he and his old commander had talked for roughly half an hour that day. Murphy told Red he had visited a busted-up officer in an Army hospital. Red had found him after one of their battles. He had lost his helmet and his guns. "He was all nerves and had about lost his mind," Red remembered. "We brought him back with us and Murph sent him to the hospital . . . but I don't think he was doing too good. He had posttraumatic stress disorder."

Post-traumatic stress disorder? That wasn't a phrase I was expecting out of Red. It didn't enter the vocabulary of doctors and psychiatrists until Vietnam. Where had he gotten it from? What he said next also startled me. "Years later I heard that Murph had PTSD, too. I think every one of us who was in that company had it." Not something they put in the movie. I called the *Gary Tribune* looking for any other trace of Ditterline, but I drew a zero, so I started working my way through the suburbs, barraging local newspapers and libraries with e-mails. Finally a state library sent me a message. They had a report on someone named Hollace Ditterline and it was only three years old. I sent for it, but when the envelope arrived, I saw I was too late: What I was looking at was an obituary.

Even so, the obit was fascinating. It turned out that the Army didn't send Red his Bronze Star until fifty years after he had won it. No matter how much he had felt like running while Audie Murphy was shooting Germans on his behalf, he had held his ground, pushed on, and completed his own experiments in heroism. There had to be more. The obit mentioned two sons as survivors. I burned up 411, looking for all Ditterlines within a hundred miles of Gary, leaving messages on every answering machine that bleeped. A week passed. Then one day I came home and a red light was flashing on my own machine. When I punched the button, a man's voice, identifying himself as Robert Ditterline, said, "I think I can help you with Hollace Ditterline." He left an area code and number near Hebron, Indiana. The line was busy the first time I called. The second time someone picked up the phone.

"Are you the guy who knew Hollace Ditterline?" I asked, ready for another strikeout."

"I'm his son."

Under a pale robin's egg blue sky, Indiana Route 8 cut its way through fields of corn and soybeans toward the small town of Hebron. To get to Bob Ditterline's place, you took your bearings from a huge silo, turned right on West 250, and stopped at a modern, ranch-style house set like a gift box on a lot cleared from rich farmland. Out back, the new mown hay was waiting for the baler. Bob was standing in the driveway. He was solidly built, over six feet tall, with a bull neck and broad shoulders that gave the impression of a linebacker pondering whether to sit tight or rush the passer. Not a man to cross. He was wearing a flannel shirt, blue and white plaid, open at the neck, jeans, and running shoes. His hair was blond, his eyes were blue, and he had the grip of a railroad switch-man. "So you found us," he said in a gruff but friendly baritone. "Dennis is on the way."

Red Ditterline was buried in a cemetery about half an hour to the west. The plan was for the three of us to go to his grave and pay our respects. Along the way we could talk. A few minutes later a car turned into the drive and Dennis stepped out. He was shorter, more compact than his brother, nine years older, and he wore glasses. Beyond that, the Ditterline brothers were a matched team: same wavy blond hair, silvering at the sideburns, the eyes sharing an intensity that unsettled me. These weren't spill-your-guts New Men. I wasn't sure what would happen. "Sorry I'm late," Dennis said. "Let's go."

Dennis took the wheel and Bob piled into the backseat, and we eased on down Route 8 at a middle-aged pace that seemed unusual, because everything else about Dennis was so sharp and quick. On the seat next to him was a small cardboard box. He pointed to it. "I kept everything Dad brought home from the war in there. I'm one of those kind of people who does that. I don't know what they call me. Sick?"

"Hermit," Bob called from the backseat. Pack rat.

"You can look through it," Dennis told me. "No family secrets in there."

"You sure?" Bob said, ribbing his big brother.

"Yeah."

Holding the wheel with one hand, Dennis opened the box with the other and started pulling out items. The first to appear was a Purple Heart, then a Bronze Star. After that, he handed the box to me and concentrated on the road. Rummaging carefully, I found a Combat Infantryman Badge, a Croix de Guerre, shoulder patches for the 3rd

Infantry Division, and a set of campaign ribbons with two battle stars. There was a folded uniform hat, the kind GIs called a cunt cap, and a small shriveled ball I couldn't identify.

"That's Dad's orange," Dennis said, peering over my shoulder. "He actually brought that back from Germany. Still has the seeds in it. That and all the medals—it's about all I have left of him."

I was expecting bitterness, but Dennis's voice was fond, almost tender. Wherever we were going, it wasn't on my map.

Dennis thought and spoke in short bursts. "I have his hat. I have his tie. I have his complete uniform. My boss owns a lumberyard. I'm going to trade for some lumber to make a case for my dad's uniform. Then I'm gonna have it professionally cleaned. Put it in the case. Put all the ribbons on it where they belong. Dad wanted my son to have it. I have to fulfill my dad's wishes. No choice. I'd like to keep it for myself, but you give your word, you know. A man's only as good as his word. I didn't have anything to give Bob's son, so I gave him Dad's flag from the funeral, so he could have a piece of his grandfather."

"He treasures it," Bob said from somewhere behind us.

"Does he?" Dennis asked his brother. "He got a case for it?"

"Yes."

Putting back the orange, I found a small notebook that private Ditterline had kept during his last few weeks in training. At the end of the notebook he had scribbled a few names: Zeller, Roche, Grifton, Elfin, Grelneck, Hangeman, men he wanted to remember. After that he wrote a list of gear: 1 web belt, 1 wool nightcap, 1 fatigue cap, 1 blouse, 1 overcoat, 3 pairs cotton shorts, 3 wool drawers, 1 pair OD gloves, 4 hankies, 1 field jacket, 1 pair of leggings, 2 neckties, 1 raincoat, 2 OD shirts, 2 pairs of shoes, 1 pair light socks, 1 pair wool socks, 1 fatigue coat, 2 cotton socks. He'd stuffed the works in his duffel bag, then shipped for France.

I asked Dennis if he'd seen the interview his father had given the Audie Murphy Research Foundation, and he said yes, the experience had brightened up Red's last years. "The war bothered Dad a lot," he told me, easing up on the accelerator. "I'm a psychology nut—oh, God,

I read all the books. PTSD is a terrible thing to have. And I'm sure that anyone who's been in combat has it. Whether they'll admit it or not, whether they recognize it or not, they have it." In the 1990s, Dennis started nudging his father toward an outpatient clinic that treated vets. "I said, 'Damn, Dad. They got psychologists down there. They got psychiatrists down there. They got people down there who can help you with your problem that *you* won't admit you have.' "

"How did your old man take it?" I asked, guessing the answer.

"He said, 'I don't want to talk about it.' That's all they ever say. They never want to talk about it."

It wasn't until Red was nearly seventy that he took his son's advice. Dennis started driving his father to the clinic, where Red recognized the company. "Dad would always say, 'Look at that guy over there. I bet he was shot up pretty good.' I couldn't tell. I thought they were just old farts. But Dad could see it. He said you could recognize it miles away. Like it was tattooed on a man's head."

Red started talking to a therapist he called Dr. K, who probed his psyche, looking for hidden shrapnel. After a long stretch of treatment, he gradually began talking to Dennis and Bob about the war. When he opened up, one of the things he told Dennis was how he felt the night before he went into combat for the first time. "It was a pretty good guarded secret. He talked about being afraid in the foxhole. They dug in. He knew his buddy was a little ways away. But they were alone. He knew that at any second his life could end and he was so scared to death that he wet himself, threw up, and just sat there all night shivering." The following morning, B Company, moving across a field, came under German machine gun fire. Red's best friend, a BAR man like Ed Persan, wounded the German gunner, then blew his head off. After that the Germans counterattacked, and they would undoubtedly have returned the favor if Audie Murphy hadn't stepped up onto the tank destroyer.

In the space of less than twenty-four hours, Red had seen his first corpse, thrown up, pissed in his pants, watched a man's head bounce across a field, then faced over two hundred Germans, more than enough to annihilate him. Was it any wonder he didn't want to talk about it? Having wet his pants, he then saw Audie Murphy's heroism, not knowing that Murphy was scared, too, until rage and adrenaline kicked in. A fresh meat replacement watching a seasoned combat warrior is only human if he feels a burst of shame along with his admiration. He gets over it if he lives through a few firefights. Is he going to talk about it when his son says, "What did you do in the war, Dad?" I don't think so. But in saving Private Ditterline, Audie Murphy pushed Red up a notch in wisdom: There is nothing about terror that disqualifies you as a soldier so long as you keep your finger on the trigger and keep shooting.

The next lesson was more complex. Away from the battlefield, a man may talk a big game about his killer instincts. But when the shooting starts, only a psychopath is totally fearless; only a nut actually enjoys it. Red got his initiation a few days later. "Dad was going through a town and they were fighting house to house, one in front of another, ducking forward, around corners. To make a long story short, Dad went around this corner and smacked right into a German. The German took the brunt of it and fell down. And Dad shot him. He made it sound really mundane; 'He fell, and I shot him.' " That's all? Dennis persisted. "I took my weapon. I aimed it at him. I fired my weapon. And his head flew that far off the ground and his brains came out." Having won the fight, Red got sick and spilled his guts over the dead man's brains.

"Straight ahead?" Dennis called back to Bob, who was doing the navigating. Bob studied the road.

"Straight."

I remembered the lines carved into the Memorial Amphitheater at Arlington National Cemetery, not much farther than a grenade's throw from Audie Murphy's grave.

Dulce et decorum est pro patria mori.

It is sweet and glorious to die for one's country.

No self-respecting dogface would ever write a line like that, in Latin or any other language. General Patton was less sentimental, more accurate about the issue. In stoking up the Third Army a week before D-day, what Old Blood and Guts told all those riflemen like Red was,

"No bastard ever won a war by dying for his country. You win it by making the other poor bastard die for his country."

It was more or less in that spirit that Red won the Bronze Star. Dennis couldn't remember all the details, but the whole story was there in the annals of the Audie Murphy Research Foundation. Lieutenant Murphy promoted Red to a bazooka team. Red, Louis DiGiuseppe, Maurice Minton, and a tanker sergeant who had lost his mount set off to block a road while the rest of B Company attacked a German barracks. "I wish he'd have said to me, 'Go fly a kite,' " Red thought. "But he didn't and I would have done anything for him."

The ground next to the road was frozen and shells were bursting everywhere, but before long, Red was guarding twenty-one German prisoners. Suddenly three infantrymen in winter camouflage came down the road. "They were wearing snow suits and so were we," Red remembered. "I don't know if God talks to people, but I think he told me to tell Minton, 'Don't trust 'em.'

"Minton said, 'Oh, Murph's sending us three guys to help out.' And I kept telling him, 'I don't believe it.'

"With all the shelling going on, there was a lot of noise, and Minton hollered to those three, 'Are you Americans?'

"We couldn't hear their answer and they probably couldn't hear Minton. They walked right up to Minton and were about three feet away when we realized they were Germans and they realized we were Americans."

Two of the Germans swung up their burp guns, cutting down Minton and the tanker sergeant point-blank.

"I knew the minute they hit Minton that he was dead. When a guy's killed, he'll fall a certain way that is not natural. He'll fall with his arm crooked underneath him. And that's what Minton done . . . DiGiuseppe hollered over, 'Are you guys all right? Are you all right?' I hollered back, 'Oh, yeah.' We had burp guns shooting at us. We ARE NOT all right!" Minton was dead and the tanker sergeant had seven holes in his chest. Terror and rage cooked Red's circuits. He raised his

M-1 and exploded, killing the two Germans with the burp guns and wounding the third.

"I'd have finished him off too except my gun was empty."

Another moment not for Sharing Hour. Red didn't talk about it until Dr. K had gentled him into confronting it. From then on, a hot stream of fury ran just below the surface in his mind. Anything could set it off. Dennis said, "Dad told me he killed them two out of anger. Not being scared. He said, 'I wanted to hurt 'em, to kill 'em. And I did.' "

It wasn't quite that simple, Dennis went on. "See, you can justify something like that in your mind: He was gonna kill me, I killed him first. You can rationalize. You can say, 'I'm alive. That's good.' Then Dad flips the coin and he feels bad because his friends got killed. Two men died and he lived. Why didn't he die, too? In your mind it's like you're going around in a big circle. After you catch your tail, you wonder what you're doing with it. Turn it loose, you gotta catch it over again. In the next couple of seconds, you're right back there in the war."

So Red pushed on, a GI Everyman following the path of a Rifleman's Progress. In the weeks that followed, he told the Audie Murphy Research Foundation, he was wounded for the first time, a nick in the shoulder. He didn't put in for the Purple Heart because the dogfaces had a superstition: If you took a Purple Heart for a scratch, the next one would be "REAL bad." As it was, his life couldn't have been much worse. He survived the day a mad colonel ordered B Company over a treeless hill and the German gunners zeroed in on them and blew away sixteen men. Red had a spoon in his pocket. The spoon blocked a needle of shrapnel that would have killed him. But then, crossing the Siegfried Line, he ran out of luck when an incoming shell cut him down along with fourteen other men. He spent the rest of his life wondering if the shell with his name on it had been a short round, a burst of "friendly" fire.

"We had thirty casualties on that day before we fired a shot . . . and one of them was me."

Ears ringing, Red looked down at his foot. It was twisted around, hanging from a scrap of flesh and a piece of bone near the shin. At a hospital in France, a doctor told him another eighth of an inch and the shell would have blown off his foot.

"I wish it had've," Red said.

"Are you crazy?" the doctor asked him.

Red said, "You go up on the front line, sir, one time and you'll find out what I'm talking about."

"You really took me the long way around, Bro."

Dennis peered through the windshield, resetting his compass. Bob needled him.

"I took you the short way. It's that thirty miles per hour you're going that's making it so long."

"I know."

"Thirty miles per hour and your foot ain't movin'."

"Okay, okay, We'll get there, though."

There was a bearish guffaw in the backseat. Bob had his big brother's number. Riffling through Red's box of memories, I pulled out four small documents that were stuck together. The first was a card dated 5 April 1945, Army style, and postmarked from France. On the flip side was a fading message: "Pleased to inform you that your husband's making normal improvement." The message had been slapped onto the card with a rubber stamp. By then casualties were running at anywhere from 12,000 to 18,000 men killed in action each month, with the number for the wounded sometimes topping 40,000. The only way the clerks could keep up was with rubber stamps.

Ditterline was put aboard a hospital ship, where many of the other casualties were men he had known in basic training. They had started the war together, had been blown up at about the same time, and were coming home together, if you didn't count the pieces they were missing. The Army sent Ditterline to Northington General Hospital in Tuscaloosa, Alabama, where his foot was reassembled. The second document in my hand was a doctor's report that read, "Making normal improvements perforating wound left calf." After that there was a form requesting the soldier's rate for a Pullman berth and a train ticket, marked September 1945, from Tuscaloosa to Chicago.

Red Ditterline went back to his old job in the foundry, and Myrtle Ditterline moved out of his bed. "You couldn't sleep with my dad," Dennis said. "You couldn't touch my dad when he was sleeping. He'd go crazy. I'm the same way now from being beaten. You touch me when I'm asleep, I'll knock you right out. My kids used to wake me up with a broom. When we go to Canada fishing, I tell the boys, 'If I fall asleep in the truck, holler at me, scream, whatever. Just don't touch me.' "

Ditterline's rages came from the far side of the moon. Dennis said there was no way of knowing when his fuse would blow or what would make him furious. "Whooo, Dr. Jekyll and Mr. Hyde. You'd wake up in the middle of the night and he'd beat the hell out of you. I don't mean just a thump with a belt a couple of times. He used his fists. If he was in an extremely good mood, he'd let you go out and cut your own switch, and then he'd beat you with it until your back was bloody. That was when he was in a good mood." Adjusting the rearview mirror, he glanced at his brother.

"I hate to say this but that's me, too," Bob admitted. "I have a very bad temper. It flares up and I'm off like a rocket, and thirty seconds later I'm fine. I'm not the guy you want to get in road rage. I'm the guy who stops in the middle of the street and asks you to step out of your car so I can beat the shit out of you. My wife says, 'You know, someone's gonna shoot you one of these days.' She's probably right."

Dennis's first memories went back to the days when his parents were fighting and they parked him and his older sister with their grandmother. He had kept an old photograph that showed him in bib overalls, his pet squirrel and chicken sitting on his lap. "I was a little bitty feller. I mean *little* bitty." He could remember drinking out of the bucket from the well and going to the outhouse. And he could remember the first time his father took him to Chicago. "Dad was into selling junk for Christmas money. He'd buy cigarette lighters, things like that, and then sell them at the foundry to get enough money to buy knick-knack Christmas presents—if he didn't drink it up. He'd always told me never to take anything from strangers. When we got up there, this guy I didn't know from Adam wanted to give me a dollar and I wouldn't take it. So I got my ass beat for turning down that dollar." To say Red Ditterline's signals were mixed is an understatement: They were so enciphered even he couldn't read them.

Red drew no distinctions between Dennis and his sister, Sandy. He beat her, too. When they were little, Dennis would cover her with his body and take the blows when Red was too drunk to see he was missing his target. "The only early memories I have about my dad that are worth a crap are vacations." And even those had sharp edges. On one vacation time, when Dennis was about ten, Red slipped on some ice and broke his arm. His mother told him to go find his sister. He tracked her down and told her they needed to get back home right away.

"Did he die?" Sandy asked him.

"No."

"Then we don't have to hurry."

Eventually Dennis revolted. "The thing that pissed him off the most was after a while I refused to cry. I said, 'I don't care. Beat me 'til I die. I'm not gonna cry no more. I'm done.' I learned to be somebody else. When you get a beating, you just take yourself completely out of it. Then when it's over, you can come back and be who you are."

Behind Dennis, Bob cleared his throat.

"I know it sounds weird. I just refused to let him hurt me. He could hurt somebody else. He couldn't hurt Dennis. Dennis wouldn't give him the pleasure no more. Took that away from him."

That's the way it went until both Dennis and Bob were eighteen and cleared out of the house. There were a few interludes when Red did make some progress. "He gave up the sauce when I was sixteen," Dennis said. "That was a positive change." Red didn't go to Alcoholics Anonymous. He got religion and joined Grace Baptist Church. One day he came home and said he'd had his last drink. "That was it. Cold turkey. Forever. Bam. 'I'm done.'" He was a chain-smoker. Lucky

Strikes had gone to war with him the same way they went with Ron Martinelli's dad, and they stayed with him for twenty years. Mrs. Ditterline was also a heavy smoker. In the 1950s, their American Dream drive was to climb into their Ford station wagon and take the kids on the road. While they fired up, filling the Ford with clouds of smoke, in the rear seat Dennis would crack a window halfway, sticking his nose out like a snorkel, while Bob pulled a blanket over his head and stayed in the air pocket. Then Red had a heart attack. He deescalated to Winstons, then to Merits. When he finally went off the weed, his wife told him he was on his own. Counterattacking, he hid her smokes.

He became almost obsessively religious, looking for an inner peace that always eluded him. If he didn't mellow, he warmed up at least a degree or two. "He was a better dad, somebody you could live with," Dennis observed. "I didn't like going to church three times a week, but I fathomed out in my mind that going to church was a lot better than an ass-whipping. I could take church. It had its benefits. You could meet girls when you were young and your hormones were going overtime." Away from the foundry, Red studied Scripture. He got in touch with the Moody Bible Institute and started to work for a minister's certificate.

Even so, this transformation came too late to undo the war's collateral damage on his relationship with Dennis and Bob. After finishing high school, Dennis said to his mother he'd had enough and was moving out. He got a job at Inland Steel. Hardworking, extremely acute, he spent the next four decades steadily working his way up, marrying along the way and becoming a man with his own son. Bob, following his brother's lead, not his father's, did much the same. He got a job switching for the Indiana Harbor Belt Railroad, eventually rising to supervisor. He, too, became a father, with a son. For years he lived within a few blocks of Red in the same township. "I can't tell you how many times I've driven by my dad's house and not stopped. You tell yourself, 'I'll stop by tomorrow' but you keep on driving."

So Red and his sons circled each other warily until Dennis and Bob reached their forties. "I would go to see him out of respect," Dennis remembers. "Did I feel warm and fuzzy going over there? No. I really didn't want to be there. But I didn't want to deprive my father of his grandchildren and I didn't want to deprive my family of their grandfather. So I did what I had to do because in my mind that was what was right." If anything, the thaw, when it came, began from Red's grandsons and moved up.

Dennis Jr. is the grandson who will get Red's uniform, when his father finishes the presentation case. As a little boy he always liked visiting his grandfather, and today he has few inhibitions about needling his old man. "He's thirty years old," Dennis said with a fatherly sigh. "He's been bugging me to get the case done and I've just been procrastinating."

"Same with my little guy," Bob called out from the rumble seat. "He was younger but he loved his grandpa."

"You have to *learn* to love your father," Dennis said suddenly.

Seeing my surprise, he explained that he and Bob didn't really see into their father's mind until they themselves suffered a catastrophe. The story stunned me. Sandy Ditterline grew up to marry an odd guy obsessed with inflicting physical pain. For a long time the quirk looked like an annoyance, but then it grew more and more weird. One day he made the mistake of sneaking up on Red in the kitchen and pinching him hard. In an atavistic, reflex spasm, Red garroted him with a kitchen towel. If the attack of rage hadn't passed, Red would have killed him. "No more playing around," he said later. "I can't control myself." After that, everyone in the family thought Sandy's husband would straighten up.

They were wrong. One day when Dennis was at work, he received a call telling him that his sister had been hurt. When he drove to her house, the ambulance was already taking her to the hospital. When he reached the hospital, they told him his sister was dead. "Jesus Christ," he thought. "What happened?" He drove back to Sandy's house.

"There was blood all over the place. In the middle of the night, my brother-in-law cut my sister's throat."

Dennis told the horror story calmly, as if it had lost any power over him "My brother-in-law marks the calendar, he leaves a damn note, he kills her, and then he tries to kill himself. And they give him Manslaughter Two. Something about his mental state. If they'd let me at him I'd have got his mental state right, but they put a guard over him the whole time he was in the hospital. Sandy used to say, 'If anything happens to me, take care of my kids,' so I did that. The mistake I made was trying to save money on the lawyer. The lawyer cut a deal with the prosecutor, and when they got to court the judge said, 'I'm really sorry I can't do any more to you than give you the maximum.' Ten years. He was out in three. Then he had a heart attack and died. I was really happy about that."

Dennis and Bob had to clean their sister's blood from her waterbed. The trauma burned into them much the same way combat had seared Red. When Dennis saw that he couldn't deal with it anymore, he made an appointment with a psychiatrist.

"I'm sitting in his office. He wanted to know what it was all about. I told him I was having problems with my sister dying. He asked a very pointed question: 'If there was one thing in the whole world that you could possibly do that you think would alleviate the weight on your shoulders, what would it be?' I said, 'Well, you want the truth?' He said, 'That's why you're here.' So I said, 'If I could take my brother-in-law, string him up to a tree, slowly skin him and gut him and take a week to kill him, I'd be happy.' The shrink looks at me and says, 'You're sick.' And I said, 'The fuck you think I'm doing here?' "

For a while, Dennis felt nearly as unhinged as Red. Unlike his father, he got on his own case early. "The shrink tells me one thing that really rings true. He said, 'If you did something really bad to me, I can hate you right? But do you care? No, you don't care if I hate you. Your brother-in-law doesn't even know you hate him and he doesn't care, so it doesn't bother him. The only one it bothers is you. You're the one paying the price for all that hate.' I thought, 'Damn, I'm stupid.' "

Dennis leaned over the wheel. "Should be about here."

"Just up the road," Bob said quietly. "Turn left."

"Long story short, all my childhood, when my sister and I would get beat on, I would hold her and we would huddle in the corner. That way she didn't get it. She cried a lot. It broke my heart to see her cry, so I took the ass-whipping. The psychiatrist told me my biggest problem was that I blamed myself for not being there to protect her. That I had to get over that. Accept things the way they were. You can't protect people when they're older. I guess he was right, but it still gets you where you live. I came to deal with it. After I got my mind right, it was easier to live with me. Ask my wife."

Dennis suddenly spun the wheel and we came to a stop at the front gate to the cemetery. The gate was locked. "They can't keep us out," he said with a shrug, and he drove around to the far side of the graveyard where there was no fence. He turned off the engine. "Up to then," he said, "I had never really known what was going on inside my father. I don't know if you really follow me. Unless you have something horrendous in your life, you don't know shit. The worst moment in my life was when I had to go wake my poor father up, my father who's been through so much shit that you couldn't absorb it in eighty-five lives, and I gotta tell him that his firstborn child has been murdered." He stopped for a moment, throttling back. Then he said, "When Sandy was murdered, everybody told me, 'Oh, your sister's dead. I know how you feel.' Bullshit. Nobody knows how you feel. Nobody knew how my dad felt all those years. Now I knew."

The sun had fallen below the horizon. I got out of the car and followed Dennis and Bob. Red was buried somewhere under the thick grass on a gentle slope that ended at the edge of a small lake where a fountain was laying out a plume of spray in the warm summer twilight. The markers were laid flush with the earth, almost invisible at first glance. We spread out and started to search. After a few minutes, Dennis called, "Over here." By the time Bob and I reached the grave, Dennis was kneeling on the lawn, pushing the thick grass back from the edges of a simple granite stone. Underneath it, the sons had buried their father next to their mother, Myrtle Ditterline.

The marker gave Red's dates: 1917–2000. Nothing in his life had come easily. One of its brighter moments arrived in 1995 when the Army sent him a Bronze Star that had been missing in action since 1945. Audie Murphy had recommended him for the decoration. Dennis said the delay wasn't entirely the Army's fault. "Dad was a hillbilly. He didn't turn in his paperwork. When he got back from the hospital in Tuscaloosa, he was supposed to go to the Army base nearest his home and file some documents bearing on the medal. But the last thing he wanted to see was another Army base and he never got around to it. In the middle of the 1990s, a local minister heard about the lost valor award; so did a retired Army major, who was a friend; and, Red being Red, so did the local police chief. They got in touch with the Pentagon. Records were searched. The medal arrived in time for Dennis and Bob to see their father receive it.

It was dark now. Mosquitoes came buzzing off the lake like teeny Stukas as we walked back to the car.

Audie Murphy was killed in a plane crash when he was forty-six. Red made it to eighty-three. His death, like Murphy's, was an accident. Nearing eighty, he developed Alzheimer's along with a neurological disorder called sundowners. "When the sun goes down, their minds shut off and they're locked somewhere," Dennis told me. "A lot of time Dad thought he was locked in a junkyard under Griffith. Remember that, Bob?"

"Yeah, he was a prisoner."

"You ever hear of a junkyard *under* a city?"

Dennis took his father into his own house and cared for him as long as he could. In the end he had to arrange for Red to move into a nursing home. That worked for a while, until Red broke his hip and had to sleep on a low-air-loss mattress. The mattress had a system for pumping air back and forth so no matter where a patient was lying on the bed he wouldn't develop bedsores. But Red's bunk was too small for the mattress. It flopped over the sides. Then one day he slipped and fell between the mattress and the bed rail. His neck and chin got on the rail, the mattress deflated. The bed hanged him.

In a final act of honoring their father, Dennis and Bob sued and won enough money to buy 263 new beds for the nursing home.

"I didn't want anybody else to lose their life," Dennis told me. "And I didn't want my dad to die for nothing."

The drive back to Bob's house went faster than our pilgrimage to the cemetery. Dennis seemed relaxed. He even put the metal down all the way to forty miles an hour. No family I'd met had gone through a harder time than the Ditterlines, father and sons. Certainly not me with my old man. But the gap between us was as wide as ever, where Dennis had bridged it.

"What did you mean when you said you have to learn to love your father?" I asked him. "How did you figure it out?"

"Interesting question," Bob said out back.

"Being an asshole," Dennis said philosophically, "I wasted too much of my life. When I grew up, I had to get rid of that 'heinous' disease. You know, that head and anus disease when you have your head up your ass. So I did get over it, though it still comes back on me a lot."

He stopped and thought a while. "It takes a long time to learn to love them. It's a process. It's hard to do. But first, I started thinking, he's my biological father, the reason I'm here. Everybody has a dad. No way to get around it. Now, what you choose to do with him, that's on you. So then I could say to myself, 'Pops had a sickness. Why don't you start from there?' He set me and raised me and I guess in his eyes he did the best he could. Alcoholism *is* a sickness, and an intelligent person would understand that. I classify myself in that category. The changes in Dad's life were positive after he gave up the sauce. He admitted a lot of the beatings that we got were from his drinking. You can learn to deal with that."

We stopped for gas. Bob went into the minimart. "For nails," he said ruefully. Whatever else had gone wrong for Red, he'd had better luck than Bob at giving up smoking. He came out with a pack of cigarettes and a few soft drinks for the last leg home.

Dennis twisted the cap off a Pepsi and handed it to me before pulling out onto the road. When we were back up to cruising speed, he said, "Look, if you have bad memories about your dad, that's all they are. Memories. You can't get a damn thing for 'em. You can't change one iota about anything. I can't change one thing about taking the grass off his grave back there. I can't put one blade back and I can't take one more off. It's done. I can't change all the beatings I got. Ain't nothing I ever do will ever change a beating. None. Never. But you gotta get rid of it. It's garbage. Throw it out on the curb and walk away. The only thing you can do in this life is take comfort and be the best person you can be. I had to learn this on my own because no one tells you shit like this.

"You have to talk yourself into it. It can't be just hype. I guess that's the best thing I can tell you. You have to want to love your dad. If you don't want to, you won't. It's like anything else. But if you don't, you lose. *You* lose. Your dad loses, too, sure. You're punishing him, but you're wasting your life. To hate drags you down, causes you anguish. Hate is a bag of garbage. Toss it out on the curb. Jesus, how can I explain it in a way that will really make sense? It's like being really cold and putting on a coat. And you get warm. It's that much difference."

He turned off Indiana Route 8 and a few minutes later pulled in to Bob's driveway. The house was dark. Bob's dog barked at us as we got out of the car.

"Nobody home," Dennis said.

"We chased 'em out," Bob said, pushing open the door.

Inside, he turned on the lights and we sat for a while at the dining table, repacking Red's box. For most of the evening, Bob, jammed into the amen corner at the rear of Dennis's car, had concentrated on steering us to the cemetery. In spite of his road rage confession, he was a quiet man, a very good one. Now, sitting at his own table, he took the trip in a new direction.

"Forgiveness," he said. "Let's talk about that. I had a pastor who said to me after my father passed, 'You still have to forgive him. If you don't offer that forgiveness now, how are you going to forgive when you're in heaven?' I hadn't forgiven my father for things that haunted me. So I had to give them up. The pastor talked about digging wells. He said, 'Fathers dig wells for their children. If you show your son that temper of yours, that's how he's going to be. That's what happened between your father and you. Now what you need to do for your father is fill in the wells he dug. Bury them. If you don't, those wells will continue to flow.' "

When Bob finished, Dennis looked at me and said, "You know what we're talking about. Look at your dad." I told him I thought I was a long way behind the Ditterline brothers and going maybe ten miles an hour.

Dennis laughed. "You're wasting your time," he told me. "That's what you're doing. Not for me to tell you what to do. You're a grown man. All I can tell you is what I did. And I can also tell you that you will really, and I mean really, really regret what you didn't do when it's too late. That's the best advice I can give you. I don't know any simple way to put it. If he passes, then all the unsaid words will never get said. If he's in good enough shape, hell, you can do things with him. I'd give anything to have my father back for a day. Anything I have. For one day."

One day. I hadn't seen my old man for years. How about one week? I asked myself on the way back to the motel. How tough could it be?

Chapter 11

Rover Joe and Horsefly

The high noon flight from Zurich was due in Rome half an hour late. Leaning against the maroon rail at the International Arrivals gate of Leonardo da Vinci Airport, I felt like a spy in a bad wig. My father was the last man out of customs. When he emerged at 12:45, I saw two guards escorting him and my tachometer started to rev. But the guards were laughing: The old soldier was just shooting the breeze, feeling his way back into Italy. I raised my hand. He beamed and picked up speed. At the rail, he hesitated for a microsecond, then he leaned over and thumped me on the back. Giving me a soldier's hug, he said, "We've found each other."

Remembering how Steven Greenberg and Josh Vincent had pursued their fathers only to lose them, I felt a tingle of good luck. The old *paisano* was dressed right for the land of *bella figura:* a dark blue blazer, light blue cashmere turtleneck, soft brown corduroy trousers, and hiking boots. He was walking with a slight limp and he had put on some weight. That made two of us: I had a mutinous hip and was hiding my love handles in baggy pants. Neither of us was in any shape to bolt from the starting gate. A hundred yards down the corridor, he pushed the handle of his carry-on into my hand. "All right, Brigham," he said. "You pull the wagon."

I laughed. At least we had made it to the same airport: two fallen sons of the pioneers, a living disgrace to Brigham Young's vision of the Good Mormon but still putting their shoulders to the wheel. At the Ciao fast-food stop, a beverage cooler loomed up like a water hole on a salt flat. "What'll you have?" I asked, making a grab for a bottle of mineral water.

"A beer."

I hesitated. If he was drinking, things were going to get complicated pretty fast. Should I try to kid him out of it? Or should I join him. I hadn't had a beer since 1981. Maybe we should start the trip with a good warm glow. I looked at the lines of bottles and felt a pleasant fuzziness: What the hell? Then my inner 911 started to ring off the wall. Compromising, I pulled down a bottle of Heineken and another of mineral water and headed for the cash register.

My father had taken up a position on the far side of Ciao. He was sitting on a rust red banquette and as I approached, I could see that his eyes were hooded and he was talking to himself under his breath. Next to his hand were two empty Dewar's miniatures—empties from the plane, or had he just tossed both of them down and was waiting for a chaser? I sat down across from him, the question written all over my face. He was too good a poker player to miss the sign, but he ignored it.

"Your hair is good," he said, pouring the beer into his glass. "You do anything to it?"

My hair is salt-and-pepper, the pepper running out fast. His was fox silver with a pale yellow highlight at the back of the neck. "Mine's good on the sides," he went on, tossing down half the Heineken.

I grinned lamely. Where were we heading? Trying for some small talk, I reminded him of the call I'd made on his eightieth birthday. "You have no idea how important that call was to me," he replied. And then, his face flushed and a beam of unhooded rage shot from his eyes.

"Chickenshit," he said. "You thought I was chickenshit."

He had it right. During the two years I refused to talk to him, I had seen his divorce and remarriage as a case of chickenshit in the first degree, one more example of an old fool trying to beat Mother Nature. The way I had it framed, as death started moving up the hill, he had run off, deserting my mother. "There was nothing I could do," he said across the table. "I couldn't get at you."

To do what, I wondered. To argue? To bump me off?

He now stepped up the heat. "In our tribe, chickenshit is the worst thing you can say about any man: 'Chickenshit. He was chickenshit.' The worst. The absolute worst. Your grandfather felt that way. I felt that way. *You* felt that way."

All of this was true, but what difference could it possibly make to him? He was the boss. He had made his choice. Why should he give a damn now? And then it dawned on me. Somewhere between the dog-house and Ciao, he and I had reversed magnetic poles. In 1945 he had told me that no son of his would be a coward. Today, from the look of him, he thought I was now telling him that no father of mine would be yellow.

Which, of course, I was.

"How did you know?" I asked, interrupting his monologue.

"Know what?"

"About the chickenshit."

"Your brother told me."

Fink, I groaned inwardly. Snitch. The diversion worked. My father stopped talking and his temperature appeared to go down. The point was obvious: If no son wants to look like a wimp in the eyes of his father, no father can stand looking like a wuss in the eyes of his son. Only two blind men could have missed this for so many years. Why not knock it off? Saying none of this, I left the next move to my father. He had come to deliver a message, the unspoken subtext being, "If you think I'm chickenshit, fuck you." Would he take the next flight home?

"Well," he said reflectively. "What do we do now?"

"Get the car?" I suggested.

"Good idea."

———

In the parking lot, we dumped my father's bag into the trunk. I turned the key and our little Fiat mewed to life. My father settled into the passenger seat. If nothing else, we had both survived round one. Beyond the airport, we turned up the coast road. As we drove north, a gray overcast hanging above the Tyrrhenian Sea, he took out his glasses and bent over our map. *"Andiamo,"* he said. "Let's give 'em hell."

The plan was to follow the 10th Mountain Division's march over the Apennines and across the Po Valley to Lake Garda and the Alps. The division's advance guard had shipped from Newport News in December 1944, passing Point Comfort and reaching Naples just before Christmas. The rest of the division arrived a few weeks later. From Naples, the troops had moved north by sea and rail to Livorno and Pisa, then by truck and on foot to the Apennines, the Winter Line, and the Germans. A few miles north of the airport, we picked up the coast rail line. "How did you get to the mountains?" I asked him. "Boxcars," he said vaguely. "I think it was boxcars. Maybe some other way. Christ, I must've lost 3 billion brain cells."

Jet lag caught up with him, and for the next hour he dozed. At one point he sat up abruptly, his face quite red. It looked like something might be wrong with him, and it worried me.

"You okay?" I said.

"Yeah, yeah, sure. I was just looking for the map."

For another twenty minutes, he nodded out. Then he bolted awake again. "I thought I was back home," he said. "You're going to like it in Virginia. I've done a lot of bragging on you. My show horse. Gotta show him around."

After that, the kilometers fell behind us pleasantly. Near Livorno, rain began to splatter on the hood. Through the streaked windshield, the exit sign for Pisa loomed up. Craning around to look at the sign, he said, "The fighters I directed were stationed in Pisa." To this point, although we had been driving for five hours, he hadn't volunteered a word about the war. Having broken the code, he immediately resumed radio silence. As we nosed into the Apennines, the rain started coming down in sheets. Around eight o'clock, the town of Bagni di Lucca rose through the downpour. I'd booked two rooms at the Albergo Bernarbo. For dinner, my father ordered a Chivas, a glass of white wine, and a sole. "I have to warn you about something," he said, waiting until the waiter ducked into the kitchen. "The last thing on earth I want to do in front of you is gild the lily on the war."

I nodded. It was the armor plating I needed to pierce, not any gold leaf. He put down his scotch and said, "What I do want you to know is how I had to fight like hell to get into the 10th Mountain Division." I asked him why he had to fight to get into a division that had scoured the country for volunteers. "Because I was so small. The captain told me no way was I going to get in. I asked him why not, and he said, 'Because you're too goddamn little.' " The 10th Mountain Division used 75mm pack howitzers hauled by mules that could kick a small man halfway across the Alps. Standing five-six in his stocking feet, he had kept arguing until the Army gave in, and he wound up with the 10th at Camp Hale in the Colorado Rockies with his friends—Jack Sugden, Dev Jennings, Ted and Jack Major, Bill Lenz, and Jake Nunemacher. Skiers, rock climbers, innocents, what they also shared was their youth, their idealism, and a bond stronger than fear. "We all wanted to go," he said. "And we wanted to go together."

The others joined the 10th Mountain Division as enlisted men. My father reached Camp Hale through a detour. In Officer Candidate School at Fort Sill, he had trained for the artillery. The 10th was originally a light division with no heavy artillery batteries. Then the oversight was corrected and he reached the snows of the Rockies in 1944 with the 605th Field Artillery Battalion. "I was no more an officer than a bird dog," he said, shoving aside the Chivas. "At Camp Hale, I used to take off my insignia so I could go drink with my friends. I want to go up to Lake Garda. Jake Nunemacher got killed up there and that's where I almost . . ."

And then he slammed on the brakes. I waited, hoping he would start up again, but he just shook his head, so I called for the check. As we headed for the door, he put his arm around me. "It was important for just the two of us to do this together," he said. Back at the hotel, he stopped on the landing. "I'm going to work all night on what we've been talking about," he told me. Then he went to bed. When I was a small boy, he would break into GI Italian whenever he felt sentimental, as if emotions were so dangerous they could be expressed only in italics. The tic had always annoyed me. But all day, in spite of the drinking, he'd been straight, and as the door swung closed, I felt a little surge of sentimentality myself. "*Buono notte*, Papa," I told him—but only after I heard the lock click shut.

The next morning, the sky over Bagni di Lucca was gray, and the Lima River, swollen by the previous night's storm, was roaring in a brown torrent under the stone bridge near the village square. My father slept until noon. He rose looking fresh. We drove down the hill from the hotel and stopped at a small café bar next to a news kiosk. We were out of range of the *International Herald Tribune*, so for a while we sat at an outside table, nursing a four-alarm espresso and watching the wind blow yellow and brown leaves across the cobblestone square. After a long silence, he leaned over the table and put his hand on my arm. "I want to tell you everything that happened," he said. "I want to give you all the salient points."

There was no longer any belligerence in his voice, no challenge. The word salient sounded a little formal, as if he had been preparing for a long time to reveal whatever was going to come next. I thought it would be the war, but I was misreading him. "I'm not going to say anything bad about your mother," he told me. "Bonnie is a heroine. She stayed with me through my drinking, through all the collapses. But we were two scorpions in a bottle." The direction he was going surprised me, but I had to admit that the word man in him could still turn a phrase. He went on to say that he and my mother had circled each other dangerously from the day they met. All my life I had ranked "Tom and Bonnie" as a love story on par with "Robin Hood and Maid Marian." As a tiny homunculus, I suppose, I could be pardoned for failing to see the first fact of our three lives: The night they had grappled beside the tennis courts and produced me, they were driven by something a little less cosmic than eternal love.

I went into the café to buy some rolls and orange juice. When I got back, he took up the thread of the story. He said that sometime right before he had gone to Italy, or just after, he couldn't quite remember, he had discovered that my mother was keeping a diary. He opened it and started thumbing through the entries. After a few pages he came upon one where she had confided to her diary that what she was really looking for in life was the "blue bird of happiness."

This detail made me smile. The "Blue Bird of Happiness" was a song that tenor Jan Peerce started singing during the Depression, and he kept singing it right through World War II until it reached the hit parade in 1948. From my childhood, I could still remember a few fragmentary lyrics about life being no abyss for those who keep faith with the blue bird of happiness. I had always thought of the song as high camp. But when my mother wrote the Bird into her diary, she wasn't in a kidding mood. My father told me he had confronted her with the diary, demanding to know what the entry meant. Her answer, he said, was succinct.

"She told me I wasn't it."

When I told him it served him right for reading a woman's diary, he said there was more to it than that. All their lives they had loved and fought, wandering beyond marriage from time to time. I grimaced again. If there's one thing worse than hearing from your parents that they have sex, it's hearing that they sometimes don't have it with each other. "She didn't discover that I *was* her Blue Bird of Happiness until we'd been married thirty-five years," he said. "By then, it was too late. I was worn out." So in the end, the Blue Bird of Happiness lost the Wild Goose, who had just enough energy left to fly the coop.

What followed, he went on, was a misbegotten experiment in trying to love two women: Ann Anderson in the East, Bonnie Mathews in the West. "I began to lead a double life, one week in Washington, three in Utah. Every time I left, it tore Ann up. Every time your mother caught me, the deceptions, the discoveries, I wanted to kill myself." For the first time I could remember, he seemed to be delivering the goods without revarnishing them. I didn't like what I was hearing, but his intensity and directness moved me. Pressing ahead, he conceded in ascending order his "recklessness," his "extravagance," his "deep personal flaws." In his mind, he told me, he had pinballed wildly for many years, bouncing off the bumpers of the irreconcilable: Bonnie, the wife who was always his hero, and Ann, his mistress, who had become his savior.

"Then Bonnie kicked me out." He paused.

"I loved your mother. I still love her. I still dream about Bonnie."

Tears began to stream down his cheeks. Under the bridge, the Lima was running chocolate brown. "Christ, I'm turning over the mud," he said bleakly. "I've never done anything like this." The burst of genuine passion stunned me. Awkwardly, I stood up, intending to pay the bill. He motioned me to sit down. "So what do you think?" he said.

"I think you're telling me a love story, a very complicated love story."

It was the best I could do: A Boy Scout, I hadn't wanted to believe that he loved anyone but my mother. Hoping for more, he looked disappointed, but this time he didn't go on the attack. Instead, he asked if I remembered our last showdown.

The shootout at the OK Rehab Center was not something I could forget. After my mother had caught him at the airport waiting for Ann, he had done some time drying out in an expensive clinic for addicts. One of its features was a family weekend. During one excruciating afternoon, a facilitator organized a little psychodrama for the two of us. We were sitting in a large room with perhaps forty other patients and relatives. The idea, she told my father, was to arrange a human tableau that would show why he had broken down, and how he hoped the crisis would end. He could use people from the audience as his actors. In response, he had choreographed the following scene: On his right side he placed four stand-ins to represent his wife, my sister, my brother, and me; on his left he arranged three actors to play Ann and her children. In the center he placed himself, a double-barreled patriarch surrounded by love.

"You told me it was crap," he said.

His memory was accurate. I had said that, along with a number of other slashing things you say only in the splatter-scenes of encounter groups. The afternoon they let him out, we had gone to Salt Lake City's old municipal cemetery, where he and my mother had shopped for my name and where my grandfather was buried. That day he couldn't find his own father's grave. Poking around the headstones, he had suddenly rounded on me. "Who the hell gave you the right to come out here as the family drill sergeant?" he had exploded. Reminding him of that low point, I asked him now what he had really wanted me to understand that day. "I was torn," he replied. "The deception had exhausted me."

At the time, I hadn't heard the love story he had just told me. Now, correcting for the omission, I had to admit that the tableau in the clinic had represented quite honestly the blood issue between us: He had wanted it both ways—I had wanted to force him to choose, sublimely arrogant in my assumption that the only choice was to dump Family Two and return to us. Rather than conceding him the right to his own life, the bare minimum for any understanding between fathers and sons, I had thrown a fit. And wasn't I still in fit mode?

"Look," I said, angling for a compromise. "You told me last night that war is not what people expect. What about love? What happens when a love story breaks from the script?"

"You're losing me."

"You spoiled the happy ending I had written for you, Pop. The way I wanted it, Tom and Bonnie was a love supreme. You would break out of the triangle and fall more deeply in love than ever. At the end of the story, you would die in each other's arms and float up to heaven side by side, proving that love was stronger than death. I was full of crap, Pop, but I needed that story. It was my security blanket. When you tore it away, I was furious. That wasn't your fault, Pop. It wasn't on you—it was on me."

Now both of us were wrung out. I found the barman and paid the bill. When I came out, my father was stretching his legs, looking up at the ridge tops surrounding Bagni di Lucca, where the 10th Mountain Division had fired a few preliminary rounds against the Germans. We got in the car and spent the rest of the afternoon cruising the ridges. "Rugged," he said when we stopped at one strong point. I wasn't sure whether he was talking about the terrain or the skirmish back in the square, but once again our luck seemed to be holding.

When the sun began to dip below the ridges, we turned back for the Albergo Bernarbo. On the descent into Bagni di Lucca, he started to talk about the house he and Ann had bought in Virginia. It was small, he said. "I'm getting rid of some stuff. I'd like you to have my fishing rods. Do you want them?"

Merlin's wands? The offer startled me. This was the way old men talked when they started getting squared away for eternity.

"Sure, when the time comes, but not now, for Chrissakes. Not for a long time."

He then said that he also wanted me to have a gold railroad watch that had belonged to his great-grandfather. I told him a watch like that was a fine thing to own.

"There isn't much else."

"Good," I told him. "I'd say you've organized everything just right."

He looked out the window, watching the fading light filter through the trees. There was one last salient point he wanted to cover.

"From the point of view of stewardship," he said, "I didn't abandon your mother."

Like salient, the word stewardship was oddly formal, old-fashioned, an echo from the Mormon ethos of family responsibility. There was something touching about it, as if he were casting about for extenuating circumstances to lay before a court that was still in session somewhere within his mind. To finance the divorce, he had sold the house he and my mother had built on an empty mountainside later populated by millionaires. The house, he said, had accumulated its own mountain of equity, which they had split. He insisted that my mother stay out of the stock market, investing instead in an annuity. She also came away with the rent on a small store they owned on Main Street in Park City. With the annuity and rent, the tanking stock market had not left her as a bag lady. He turned away from the window and looked at me. "You could say I bought my way out, if you want to take that bullshit point of view—or you could say I did the right thing."

He was pushing all the chips out on the table, risking it all. The tone of the challenge was different from the one he had used at Ciao in Rome, no furious indignation or bullying; he sounded more like a man who had heard the two-minute warning and knew there weren't many more plays left in the game. This wasn't a bluff.

"Look, Dad," I said. "I'm a hard-boiled guy. I hate fake emotion."

Shifting his stance, he raised an arm in front of his chin in mock self-defense.

"You're telling me."

"All right. You weren't chickenshit. I was wrong."

"Christ," he said. "I feel a hundred pounds lighter."

"We need to work out a better division of labor," I told him. "I'm the one who needs to do more for my mother. Not because you are a colossal shit, but because I haven't done anything but bitch."

"You have finely developed radar," he replied, grinning at me. I had to laugh. We were both the same kind of asshole—just as John Nelson had said. Took one to know one.

We went back to the hotel, where my father slept for an hour. Then we returned to the café-bar to kill some time. Nursing a scotch, he started talking about World War II. "I hated the Germans," he said. "I wanted to kill every one of those bastards." Pushing on, he said that the Army had picked him to take part in an experiment called Operation Horsefly. The idea was to use a small plane to direct artillery and aircraft fire, getting the forward observer off the ground and up in the sky. "I was small and light, so they put me in a plane," he said, adding that he and the Piper L-4 that carried him were built to the same scale. The little aircraft had fabric wings and fuselage. Its seventy-five-horsepower, flat-four piston engine could churn out a top speed of ninety-two miles per hour, just enough to make fighter pilots laugh. The L-4 was too slow to be hit by a fast-moving fighter and just fast enough to make it hard to hit from the ground. It had a range of 250 miles and no guns. "I was up in the air fluttering," he said, waving his hands comically. "A butterfly."

The code name for the Thunderbolts he directed was Rover Joe. The fighter jocks roaring in from Pisa would buzz the L-4, toss it in their prop wash, laugh at the lieutenant giving them orders from his kite. For a second the memory made him smile, but then another image welling up from the past blindsided him. His forehead creased and his face darkened, as if the sun had just passed behind a tower of clouds. "The fighters were P-47s," he went on, and all of a sudden I could see that he was losing altitude: "Thunderbolts. Very, very effective. Rockets, bombs, napalm . . ."

He stopped and couldn't go on.

I tried to prompt him. "You had a code, didn't you? All of you."

"We didn't want to be phony," he said. "None of us. No braggadocio. No false glory."

He closed down again. I pushed harder.

"False glory?"

"It was private," he snapped. "We didn't want to open it up."

From his head to his feet, every part of him was wildly signaling to me to shut up, let it go. I leaned toward him.

"What was private?"

His face, his neck, his shoulders, his chest—all of them tightened simultaneously, as if he were clenching his entire being into a fist. And then, from behind the armor, a spasm shook his whole body. The most terrible thing about this spasm was that it was silent. No cry, no wail of pain, just a horrifying dry heave, a convulsion.

He looked up wildly. You could hear the armor clanging as it fell to the ground.

"I killed a lot of people," he said in a strangled voice that turned to a sob. "Jesus Christ . . . I killed so many people."

Across the bar, four men playing cards were looking at us curiously. Tears began streaming down his face. I put my arms around him. "Wasn't your fault, Pop," I whispered as he buried his face against my chest. "Wasn't your fault." After a few minutes he shook it off. "I'm okay," he said. "Let's get out of here."

We drove across the bridge and stopped at a restaurant overlooking the Lima. On the way, he looked at me as if he'd just come out of electroshock. "What happened back there?" he said. "I've never voiced that stuff. Never." His voice was very quiet.

"Never," he repeated softly. "Not to anyone. Not to myself."

At the restaurant, he was silent for ten minutes. Then he signaled the waiter and ordered fish and a split of champagne. "I think I see it," he said over the bubbling flute. "The thread. What it is that connects all of us." On his fingers, he started ticking off names: "Sugden, the Majors, Bill, Dev, Jake—all of us. All that youth, all that spirit, all that courage. And then what you see is that you've turned into a killing machine. I hated the Germans. I did hate them. But it doesn't matter. You look and you see something you hate in yourself, something atavistic, something deep in the bottom of the cortex. You don't feel right. It doesn't make sense. You should feel victorious. You should feel triumph. You don't. Too much has happened. All you know is that you're a killing machine."

From the same cortex, a dart of free association prompted him to switch the subject to his own father. What he'd admired most in my grandfather, he told me, was his intelligence, his endurance under hardship, and his sense of humor.

"Did I ever tell you his cake and carfare story?"

"No."

"He was working for the Western Pacific railroad and he wound up broke in San Francisco. That's where he had his one prizefight as Kid Salt Lake. He told me the prize was a cake and carfare, and the fight lasted two rounds. What he said was, 'The other guy kicked the shit out of me, but when it was over I had the cake and enough money to get out of town.' And then he winked at me."

We both laughed. Wes Mathews was where we both came from.

But then, the narrative took a darker turn. Putting down the champagne, my father said that during the Depression, when he was about sixteen, his father had come home one night lit up like the Mormon Temple. As my grandfather stood swaying in the living room, my father had called him a stupid lush.

"He was small but he had fists like a blacksmith. He spit on his hands and he said, 'You want to take a swing at me, come on.'

"I said, 'No, Pop. You'd kill me.'

"And he said, 'You're goddamn right.' "

"So what happened?" I asked my father.

"What do you think happened? I backed down."

The confrontation had taken place less than eight years before my father and I had squared off at the doghouse. In that period of super-compression, he had gone from the scrawny adolescent terrified of his father to the returning soldier who had scared the hell out of me. Why did this story come spilling out right behind the bombs and rockets and napalm? Had he come away mortified from his own failure of nerve in front of his father? Had it dogged him all the way into the war? Was that why he had fought like hell to get into the 10th Mountain Division—to prove that his old man was wrong? Eight years. Only eight years. Were both of us still living out the same mistake?

The next morning we set off for the Winter Line, retracing the route taken by the 10th Mountain Division to the front. The Apennines were wrapped in gray fog. "Last night—I never talked like that before," my father said, peering out the window. "Things in there I wouldn't want Ann to know. I wouldn't want anyone to know." The windshield wipers scraped at the drizzle. "You're a good fisherman," he said, smacking me on the shoulder. Like the father in *A River Runs through It,* my old man ranked fly-fishing next to godliness. He'd never said anything like this to me before. I tried not to glow.

Beyond Lizzano, the road snaked up a hill and into Vidiciatico. During the winter of 1944–45, the village had been within range of the German guns. Now it was lined with ski lodges and chalets. "More primitive sixty years ago," my father grunted. We didn't stop. Near Querciola he saw a stone building at the center of a farmyard, and I pulled off to the side of the road so he could get his bearings. "We parked a howitzer in the barn," he said, pointing to the edge of a field leading off toward a deep ravine. "I was bivouacked over there."

Just above the small village of Querciola we found a restaurant with a picture window commanding a spectacular view of Riva Ridge, a rock face that rose fifteen hundred feet straight up above a small river. The Germans considered it impregnable. In February 1945, the 10th captured the ridge in a night climb that took the German defenders completely by surprise. For a long time my father stood at the window looking at the ridge.

"Jesus, those guys . . ." he whispered. Scanning the terrain, he picked out the side of a hill next to a narrow valley. "I went on my first and only ski patrol from right here," he said, as if everything had just come back to him. And he started telling a war story. "The mission was to reconnoiter down the valley between Riva Ridge and Mount Belvedere. We were to keep going toward Rocca Corneta until the Germans started shooting. So we put on our skis and set off on the shoulder of that hill. The slope was gentle enough and we didn't have to make any fancy turns. We were supposed to be very stealthy. No noise. But we were skiing on broken crust and I said to the lieutenant leading the patrol, 'Christ, we sound like a herd of elephants.' Then star shells started arcing into the sky. The whole valley lit up with bright white light and the Germans started firing. The lieutenant said, 'Gentlemen, that's it. We're going back.' I said, 'How are we going back?' He said, 'Fast.' And I said, 'Well, then, we better take off these fucking skis.' So we took off the skis we'd been training on for a year and a half and got the hell out of there."

It was a good story, the real thing. In legend and song, the 10th Mountain Division had entered my imagination as the United States Army's invincible soldiers on skis. When I was a small boy, I always thought of them as men in white parkas, schussing northern Italy, shooting from the hip. The truth was something different. Over the next few weeks, he told me, as the weather got warmer and violets began poking up through the spring thaw, the ski troops wound up like everyone else—regular infantry fighting in the mud.

After Riva Ridge, the 10th's next objective was Mount Belvedere. Following the ski patrol, he said, he had been ordered to Poretta Terme, ten or fifteen kilometers behind the front, where there was a small airstrip, and he became Horsefly. The night before the assault on Mount Belvedere, he wangled a jeep and drove up to Querciola to find Jack Sugden, who was a sergeant in the company assigned to lead the night assault. Horsefly was to provide close-air and ground support, but my father and the Thunderbolts couldn't join the battle until the sun came up. "Suggie was in the 85th Regiment. I knew they were going to attack later that night. I said, 'Look, Suggie, you're going to be down here and I'm going to be up there. I don't feel good about that.'"

"Christ, Tom," Sugden told him. "You look like a fucking pheasant up there. No one down here wants to be with you. Anybody could shoot you down."

"It wasn't true—I was safer, sanitized—it was a very decent thing for him to say."

The next morning, picking up a radio from a fallen soldier, a decision that made him a prime target for the Germans, Sugden cleaned out a German machine gun nest and won the Silver Star. As my father was telling the story, it reminded me of what Louis Simpson had said about the GI who had won the Silver Star for doing something "extraordinary" with his BAR: how much he had admired him; how deeply, despite his own Bronze Star, he felt that he had not done enough. Had the word chickenshit been running somewhere in the deep cortex when Lieutenant Mathews set off to find Sergeant Sugden? In World War II, nothing was enough until you were killed and stopped wondering. If you made it home, how much would ever be enough?

Later that afternoon we checked in to the Hotel Roma at the center of Poretta Terme. Before dinner I found him in his room poring over the combat history of the 10th Mountain Division's 87th Regiment, the volume with blue-and-white binding I had spent so many hours over when I was a small boy. Something in the book had caught his eye, pleased him. Pointing to page 25, he said, "There's a paragraph in here you may have missed." He showed me a section called "Holding the Gain." The passage covered the morning of the assault up Mount Belvedere and the days that followed:

> "Rover Joe" started operating the morning of 20 February . . . Under the direction of the aerial observation plane called "Horsefly," the front line troops came to love Rover Joe. Jerry was forced to keep his weapons silent while the planes were in the air. Typical "Rover Joe" reports were like this one at 1100: "One bomb near hit—building demolished, remainder of bombs within target area; five or six Germans fleeing from buildings; three or four killed; observed flashes from mortar in another area; will bomb at once." The sight of the diving plane, the falling bombs, or flash of rockets, and the following sound of strafing or the tremendous bomb blast, was a heartening one to the soldier lying in his hole.

"Here I am," my old man said, and for the first time all day he was smiling. He hadn't let Suggie and his friends down.

That night we went across the street to a trattoria, where the owner-impresario, a beefy giant, came over to the table and sat down next to him to talk. The dining room had a series of long tables. At each table sat an extended Italian family, out for a night on the town. When the owner asked why we had come, my father said in his best fractured Italian, "*Soldato Americano. Americano Alpini.*" Slapping him on the back, the owner told him that his own father had fought alongside the Americans.

"Soldato," the giant roared across the room. *"Americano."*

From every table, people put their thumbs up, waved their forks in the air.

And then they cheered an American hero.

From an airstrip near a stream on the outskirts of Poretta Terme, Horsefly had stung the Germans. The next morning we set out to track down the field. My father and the pilot, a Texan named Darnell, had slept in a tent next to their drafty little plane. Warming to the hunt, Horsefly said, "The Germans were experts at camouflage. They wouldn't move during the day and they set out a lot of decoys. It was hard to spot the targets. So Darnell and I started flying at night, when you could see the gun flashes. No one had done that and we were very effective. But the Germans figured it out and stopped firing at night, so it got very frustrating."

I asked him how many missions he had flown. He said one hundred and twenty. "Sometimes Darnell and I went up four times a day. The artillery wasn't the worst of it. The worst came from the Thunderbolts. We didn't want to make mistakes, so we got in very close. You could see everything. The strafing, the rockets, the bombs."

"What about the napalm?" That was where he had stopped in Bagni di Lucca. The original intent of the Army was to use napalm only on the Japanese, not white troops. The fine print was forgotten after the real fighting began in the European theater of operations. When the jellied gas exploded, it stuck to flesh; there was no way to shake off the flames. "It was lousy," he said. "You'd see men running—burning alive." A grimy little industrial park filled the stretch of level ground where he had once taken off to direct the Thunderbolts and the napalm. The airstrip was gone.

From the valley we drove up the eastern shoulder of Mount Belvedere then moved along the ridge tops: Mount Gorgolesco, Mount della Spe, and on to the village of Castel d'Aiano. According to the 87th Regiment's combat blue book, the fighting along this line of advance had been "bunker to bunker, hill to hill, objective to objective for three bloody days against prepared positions heavily mined." To the thunder of explosions and the rattle of small-arms fire, 909 men had been blown away—203 killed, 706 wounded. Now, in mountain meadows once planted with mines and enfiladed by machine guns, cows browsed and small birds sang.

The fall of Castel d'Aiano cut the German lines of communication and supply to the broad valley of the Po River on the far side of the mountains. On April 14, 1945, the 10th Mountain Division launched the final spring offensive in Italy by punching through the German defenses at Torre Iussi and Tole. When they reached the top of Mount Avezzano and Mount San Michele, they could see the Po Valley. The view cost them 1,349 casualties—290 men dead, 1,059 men wounded.

We wound past killing fields like Punchboard Hill near Pra del Bianco. At Torre Iussi my father put down the map. During the worst of the fighting, he said, a green replacement lieutenant had stood up to order Dev Jennings and the rest of his platoon forward. "Let's go," the officer yelled. At that moment a German sniper shot him. The round went cleanly through both cheeks, sparing his teeth and his life. As the lieutenant fell, Jennings turned to the next man in the platoon and said, "Maybe that will teach the sonuvabitch to keep his trap shut." That's what they all did when they got back to Salt Lake City. To open your trap was to break the code.

Just beyond the crag of Rocca Roffeno, advancing through a forest, I drove around a bend and a silver star flashed behind us. "The hell was that?" my old man said. "Stop the car." I cranked into reverse and backed up for fifty yards. The star was affixed to a very large rock in a very small park at the side of the road. He got out, walked over to the rock, and stood there so long I finally shut off the ignition and went over to see what was going on. What we had seen was the white star of the U.S. Army and U.S. Army Air Corps. The rock was a war memorial. Under the star, written in Italian, was an inscription that read, "On these mountaintops, American mountain soldiers, together with Italian partisans and Alpini, fought and died in eternal glory defeating the evil of the Nazi Reich and saving the world for Justice." My old man was working out the words.

"Look at that," he said, sending out more kilowatts than Con Edison. "I'll be goddamned."

Piling back into the car, we started down a long, winding grade. The mountains gave way to gentle hillsides. Far off on our right flank, we could see Bologna. Like the 10th, we debouched into the Po Valley and advanced north toward the river. As we picked up speed, I handed my father a chronology compiled by John Imbrie, a veteran from C Company of the 85th Mountain Regiment. The account read, "In a struggle to keep up with one of the fastest drives of the war, German trucks, cars, horses, wagons, carts, bicycles, motorcycles, and Italian Fiats were pressed into service to ease aching backs and tired feet."

"That's right," he said. "Just like that."

Kicking our Fiat into fifth gear, we shot through flat, dusty farmland, bearing down on the division's old bridgehead on the Po. Above us the clouds broke and the sun warmed the broad valley. Around noon we stopped at a bar off the main square in San Benedetto Po. While I scouted for sandwiches, my father drank a beer and read the blue book. When I got back with the tray, he was chuckling over the morning report for 22 April 1945, by a general at Fifth Army headquarters:

"Gentlemen, this morning the Armored Division has lost ground in the mountains; while on the other hand, the Mountain Infantry is racing across the valley!"

He unwrapped a soggy prosciutto and cheese sandwich and examined it dubiously. I had read the histories. There had been stories about armored units losing their edge, hanging back, staff officers fulminating about "cowardice." I asked him what had happened, and he said that not one soldier he'd ever met "needed any lessons from fucking generals about guts." The armored units had been fighting for more than two years, since the beginning in North Africa. If they kept their heads down now and then, it was only good sense. I asked whether it made any difference that by the spring of 1945 everyone knew Germany was collapsing. What point did it make getting killed when the Germans were on the brink of defeat? He snapped the book shut. "They weren't anywhere near defeated enough for me," he said. "I wanted to kill every last one of those bastards." Then he said, "What are you really looking for. I don't think I get it."

"What do you mean?"

"The nexus," he said. "Why did we come here? What does the war have to do with fathers and sons?"

Stalling, I suggested we leave the nexus for the end of the trip. Out in the square, I slipped behind the wheel and turned the key. He was still deliberating. "You raise a son, you want him to be like yourself," he said. "You set standards based on who you are, what you've just been through." He paused. "Maybe those standards are too fucking... what... unhealthy? Is that it?"

He was way ahead of me, advancing like the 10th, moving fast and not worrying about his flanks. In the war diaries of Gen. Fridolin Rudolf Theodor von Senger und Etterlin, the German commander in the Po, I had read that he considered the 10th Mountain Division his "most dangerous opponent." Just beyond San Benedetto, von Senger had been forced to swim the river to escape the Americans. As we approached the bridge, my old man cracked open the blue book. "Hey, look at this," he yelled exuberantly. He had found a section full of mountain infantry songs, the same songs the whole Mathews family had sung at the top of its lungs in the late 1940s, whenever we drove up to Brighton in the snow.

"There are systems and theories of skiing," he sang.

"But I can remember just one," I answered.

"The skiing's confined to the wintertime." Was he going to yodel?

"But the drinking's good all of the time," I sang back.

WALLA, WALLA, WALLA, WALLA, WALL, we both roared, and the rest we did as a duet:

The skier must dodge all the trees he sees.
And the rocks that lie hidden in the trail.

> *But the thing he fears most are the heebie gees.*
> *And the snow snake's loud hideous wail.*

"Especially those fucking snow snakes," I yelled. The bridge loomed up and we careened across the current where von Senger had done his dog paddle.

"We got 'em on the run, Dad," I shouted.

"You're goddamn right," he yelled back. "We'll dust their asses for miles."

Below Verona we picked up a four-lane highway that skirted Villa-franca, where Gen. George Hays, a Medal of Honor winner in World War I, had drawn up the 10th Mountain Division before the final lunge to the Alps. Earlier I had asked my father what he thought about Gen. Mark Clark, the Ultimate American commander in Italy. Instantly he had snapped, "I thought that bastard was a vainglorious fucking butcher." Now I tried out Hays. "Not so bad," he said. "I liked him." One day toward the end of April, on returning from observing the German line of retreat along Lake Garda, he had received orders to report to General Hays. Surrounded by staff officers, Hays was studying a large map of Lake Garda. "He said to me, 'Lieutenant, you've been up there. What do you think?' I said, 'General, I think there are too many Germans on the west side of the lake." Hays dismissed him. The next day the 10th advanced along the east road. "Only time in the whole war I made a difference," he said, instantly taking it back—"What difference?" It was along that line of advance that Jake Nunemacher had been killed.

Half an hour later we passed through Lazise, and started up the same road. On either side of the lake, rocky crags rose thousands of feet, disappearing into a dark, overcast sky. The road, carved into the rock, ran through a series of tunnels. The sun was going down now. North of Bardolino, I turned off and followed a road about a thousand feet higher above the lake to a village called St. Zeno of the Mountains. The village was dark, and a cold wind was blowing through the streets. Only one hotel was open. The owner was a friendly woman who fussed warmly over my father when she discovered that he was an old soldier. It was still dark when I woke up the next morning. Across Lake Garda, the lights of Gargagno, where D'Annunzio composed poems and Mussolini set up his last government, twinkled above the water. I read for a while. Around eight, just as the sun began to gild the highest peaks, my father knocked at the door. He was up early and eager to move out.

From St. Zeno of the Mountains we descended to the shore road and began to work our way through the tunnels toward Riva. We started from a point on the lake where a full platoon from his company had capsized in an amphibious DUK and drowned. Out on the lake, the wind was churning up whitecaps. I started counting tunnels as we headed north on the road. In the after-action reports, tunnel five had gone down as the Tunnel of Death. On 29 April 1945, Germans defending the tunnel had touched off an explosion that dismembered dozens of their own men. The following day, as elements of the 86th Mountain Infantry Regiment were moving gingerly into the hole through the rock, a catastrophically lucky round fired from the head of the lake struck the far mouth of the tunnel, splattering American body parts on top of the dead Germans. More than forty men were wounded and five were killed, including Jake Nunemacher, Jack Sugden's brother-in-law. When I reached five in my count, I looked over at my old man. His face was set. He looked straight ahead, said nothing as the wheels of the Fiat grazed the spot where Jake's luck had run out.

Coming out of the tunnel, we passed through Torbole, where a random 88 round killed Col. William Darby, legendary founder of the Army's 1st Ranger Battalion. Naively, I asked if losing such a figure had demoralized the advancing Americans. "We'd just lost twenty-five men from drowning in the fucking DUKs," he said. "Jake was dead. I didn't give a shit about any colonels. Nobody did. I don't think we even knew."

Pushing on through Riva, we followed a narrow road that turned into a cow path meandering along the western crags. He kept checking the sky, as if measuring the distance between the cliffs and the valley floor. At one point two Italian carabinieri in a tiny cop car met us nose to nose on the path. The four of us got out. When I explained what we were doing, they saluted, backed off the road, and waved us on. "There," my father finally said, pointing a few hundred yards down the cow path to where a stone bridge crossed a narrow stream.

The valley narrowed to a choke point at the bridge. I pulled off and my father started across. In the middle he stopped and looked up at the sky. He had been saving one story for last:

"This is where I thought I was going to die."

And so it finally came out. On the second day of May, 1945, he had flown up Lake Garda to draw a bead on the retreating Germans. Beyond the village of Riva he spotted a huge troop concentration: tanks, trucks, artillery pieces, long columns of foot soldiers, all trying to squeeze across a little bridge and up a narrow valley toward Trento and the Brenner Pass. It was the fattest target he had ever seen. While the pilot circled, he called in the coordinates and waited for the valley to go up like the Fourth of July.

Nothing happened.

He shouted into the radio again.

Nothing.

"What's the matter with you guys?" he yelled. "We've got the whole German Army up here."

"Return to base."

"Are you out of your fucking mind?"

"Return to base, Lieutenant."

The pilot kicked the rudder, and just at that moment the sky exploded around Horsefly. From the ground, every antiaircraft gun the Germans had left opened up on the little plane. White puffs of smoke from the 22mm ack-ack the Germans called *pom-pom* burst in front of them, behind them, over the wings, above the fuselage, under their balls. "It was like being popped in a popcorn popper," he said. The pilot yanked the stick, wildly bobbing and weaving. "I don't know how long it lasted, thirty seconds maybe. The whole time I was bouncing around thinking, 'This is it.' "

The view from Cocksucker Bridge: Tom Mathews Sr. returns, Garda, Italy, 2003

By some miracle, Horsefly buzzed out of the flak. When they landed at Villafranco twenty minutes later, he jumped from the plane and ran across the strip, intent on killing every artillery captain he could find. An officer came walking toward him.

"What the fuck . . ." Horsefly started to say, but the officer cut him off.

"The war's over, Lieutenant."

Lieutenant Mathews pointed to the Alps.

"Why don't you tell that to those cocksuckers up there?"

In the precise moment he had missed his best shot at the Germans, he nearly lost his life—and in a war that was already over. Now, walking over to the rail, he dropped his pants and, from Cocksucker Bridge, took a flying piss at the romance of war.

The Brenner Pass between Italy and Austria was the next mark on our map. When I was a boy, one of the songs my father sang after a few drinks was called "Please, Mr. Truman, Won't You Send Us Home?" He sang it to the tune of "Lili Marlene." After pointing out that the U.S.

Fifth Army in Italy had conquered Napoli, taken Rome, and subdued the Master Race, the words went, "Let the boys go home—let the boys at home see Rome." Given the right kind of dork commander, a soldier could be court-martialed for singing them. Mark Clark thought the song was defeatist. In fact, it was just weary, like the sentiments in "Tenting Tonight on the Old Campground" ("Many are the hearts that are weary tonight, waiting for the war to cease"). During the Civil War, Union generals also thought that old standard smacked of defeat. Some people can never get enough of war, but those people very seldom are the soldiers who do the dying. I didn't understand any of this as a child. What I liked was another line that said, "We met the Seventh Army at the Brenner Pass. We got hepatitis and a bullet up the ass." For a long time I thought the Seventh Army were the Germans and hepatitis was some sort of medal. The bullet up the ass was the best part because singing the song was the only time I could get away with swearing in front of my father. Although I had always dreamed of reaching the pass where the 10th Mountain Division met the U.S. Seventh Army, after the view of my father at Cocksucker Bridge, even the Alps looked like an anticlimax. So we piled in the car, hit the Autostrada, and turned south.

In 1945, it had taken my old man 114 days to make this round trip from Naples. After that march, 3,849 men in his outfit came home with Purple Hearts. Another 975 returned in coffins, or they didn't come home at all. The others, alongside the equivalent of five battalions of Fifth Army dead, were buried on the shoulder of a hill south of Florence. I had stopped at the place the day before picking my father up in Rome. Some military cemeteries are as regimented as the Army itself, the graves arranged in stiff ranks and files, as if the troops six feet down are still at attention. In this memorial, a less martial eye had softened the symmetry with gentle curves, and the soldiers beneath the stones were lying at something closer to parade rest. A broad mall led to the top of the hill, where the names of another 1,409 Americans were cut into the granite Tablets of the Missing. For the chapel, someone short of commas had carved a few lines once delivered by Pericles in praise of the dead. The sentiment had impressed Thucydides, who bookmarked it for history: "They faced the foe as they drew near him in the stretch of their own manhood and when the shock of battle came they in a moment at the climax of their lives were ripped away from a world filled for their dying eyes not with terror but with glory."

The words were carved in stone in a graveyard next to a road tramped by Roman legions, the words of a Greek soldier-spinmeister on an altar raised to American GIs who had fallen twenty-four hundred years later. I preferred the hepatitis and the bullet up the ass. Not so inspiring, I suppose, but surely closer to the truth. These soldiers hadn't just made a sacrifice. They *were* the sacrifice, burnt offerings.

What was it that Ron Martinelli had said?

Nothing ever changes.

In the mountains to the east of the American Battle Memorial was an old hilltop farm called La Capraia—the goat. I had booked us two rooms for the weekend, thinking that we might make a visit to the cemetery. To get to La Capraia, we left the main road south of Florence, passed through some vineyards, then wound our way up a terraced hillside planted with olive trees. La Capraia, a jewel of Italy's *agriturismo* program for travelers, was the last farm on the road.

From the top of the ridge early the next morning, I could see halfway across Tuscany. While my father was still sleeping, I went back down the hill for supplies: apples, pears, melons, cheese, salami, bread, juice, bottled water. On a shelf in the *minimercado* I saw a jumble of bottles: beer, wine, whiskey. Along the road my old man had been keeping his tank topped off; nothing too serious; but now we were going to spend two days alone on a hilltop where the restaurant and bar were both closed for the season. If I picked up some moonshine, would I be feeding a bad habit?; if I didn't, would I be a prig? Striking a compromise, I bought four bottles of beer and a liter of white wine and left the scotch on the shelf.

Back atop our hill, I cut fruit, sliced bread, poured juice, and put plates on the table. Around ten, the sun, burning away the morning fog, lit up the windows. I heard my father rustling around in his room, and after a while he came out. "Well, lookee here," he said, pleased. "What have you done?"

All I had done was fix breakfast, but the question was better than he knew. As I thought about it, I couldn't remember the last time I had done anything for him. Maybe never. It wasn't a good thought. Beyond that, I still had a hidden agenda for the next forty-eight hours. We had made our way safely through the divorce, through the battlefields, but there was plenty of dangerous ground we still needed to cross; other happenings after the war: little things like the doghouse, the rucksack, the broken leg, big things like malingering and guts, trust and love. There would be no second acts. I knew that. This was a trip you didn't take twice.

Above the hilltop farm later that morning, the sun was floating like a balloon by Botticelli. For an hour I sat outside in a chair taking notes. When I finished, I found my old man in the kitchen, and we spent the rest of the afternoon over the table exchanging stories. Peeling an apple with a paring knife, he started talking about his boyhood. "I felt weak. Small, scrawny, badly educated, poor." Putting down the knife, he dropped into a flashback—to the night he'd called his father a stupid lush. "I was pathetic. Or maybe I just mean lame. The plot does run into pathos when the father is weak and strong at the same time and the son feels called upon to do the impossible: replace him—and then he fails."

He wasn't being sly. He was talking about himself, not me, but the parallelism ran as deep as the snow on Mount Millicent that day, at eight, when I had tried to steal my mother from him. Had I really been furious because he seemed to be indifferent to my broken leg, or was it simply because my impossible effort to replace him had failed? It had never occurred to me that the two of us might be partners in pathos. I asked him if he remembered that day, the ski patrol shack, the splint, the long drive down the canyon, my bleating.

"You said I was malingering."

He leaned across the table, and to my total astonishment, his eyes filled with tears.

"How could I have said that to you?" he whispered. "How could I have done that to my own son?"

All my life I had been trying to extort an apology, but now as I saw the multiple possibilities of my own little game and watched him crying, I felt rotten. Wiping his eyes, he cleared his throat.

"I thought the best that could happen on this trip was for us to come out as two wisecracking pals," he said. "I wasn't expecting anything like this." He patted my arm. "I'm hoping you can see me the way I see myself as a father. On the one hand the heroic side, on the other side, the agony of uncertainty."

I had never seen him that way. Why did the poles have to be so extreme? Instead of heroism and agony, why couldn't it be something more like not too hot, not too cold, just right. Oh sure, I told myself. Just like Goldilocks and the Three Bears. How lame.

My heart began to drum and I felt sweat dripping down my cheeks. Not tears. I was returning heat with cold, and the transaction set off my fight-flight machinery so powerfully I could feel my chair shaking. This wasn't a fight. I rose and went out to stretch my legs. For a while I walked up and down in the garden. When I got back, my father was in his room sleeping. Bending over him, I couldn't hear any breathing, and for an instant I felt a stab of panic: Don't die on me now, Pop. As I leaned closer, his chest heaved once and he started to snore.

That night we went to a restaurant down the hill called The Rooster. It was full of upmarket destination diners from Florence. My father knocked back an aperitif and a scotch, and over the antipasto we picked up our conversation where it had broken off at The Goat.

"I'm so goddamned proud of you," he said, reminding me of a long ago night I had spent in Beirut with Yasser Arafat twenty years earlier, the closest I had ever come to a battlefield. I saw that he was overheating some, and it put me on guard.

"What?" he said. "You can't take a compliment?"

I explained that I'd only spent a few days in Beirut, and as a junketing editor, not as a reporter who'd risked his neck for years. There was another thing. That night in 1981 was the last time I'd fallen off the wagon. Arafat's operatives had called for me long past midnight, armed to their headdresses with rocket-propelled grenade launchers and AK-47s. No way to be certain whether I would be interviewing a target of opportunity or serving as one, so I'd tossed off three gins before getting in the van and putting on the blindfold.

My very last drinks. Maybe the best.

This, I did not confess.

A bit testily, my father ordered a bottle of wine and switched his attention to it. I wasn't keeping up my end, so I asked him if there was anything I could do to help him with Ann, to let her know after we got back that we'd closed out our war.

"She needs to know she's worthy," he said slowly. "She needs to know I love her. She needs to know I won't leave her."

"Wait a minute, Pop," I said. "I can't do that. That's your job."

"We know how far to go, don't we?" he said, glaring. "We push it pretty far, but we know where to stop." His face had gone red the way it had flushed in Rome. Was he going to spit in his hands and say, "Come on, kid"?

And then I saw that he was cooked to the gills.

Signaling wildly for the check, I settled up and staged a tactical retreat. It was very dark outside in the parking lot, so I took his arm. "Thanks," he said, easing into the car. "I haven't been this drunk in five years."

Before dinner I hadn't seen him drink any more than he'd put away the rest of the trip. Perhaps I had misjudged his maintenance level along with some other things: the fast pace, the captive intimacy of the road. Back at La Capraia, he fell into bed. I was still hungry, so I opened the refrigerator. The last of the fruit and cheese was still there, but all four bottles of beer were gone. When I pulled out the plastic garbage pail next to the sink, I found the empties jammed next to the upended liter wine bottle, also empty. While I had been out sunning before dinner, he had polished off the entire weekend stash.

Outside the room there was a small courtyard with stone stairs leading down to the edge of an olive grove. I went out and sat on the stairs. Across the valley, the lights of villages sparkled on the near slopes of the Chianti Mountains. Sitting in the darkness, I rewound the tape.

How could I have done that to my own son?

He had said that to me and he had cried. Had I risked anything so dangerous? No. Had I even wiped my eyes? No. So what the hell had I done? I had bought the alcohol and put it on full display. The answer made me feel sick. I knew the game as well as he did: Once you started, you didn't stop until the last bottle was empty. I rocked forward and stared at the stone beneath my feet. This was worse than stupidity. It was a test. I hadn't had a drink since that night in Beirut. By fits and starts, he had been drinking ever since he opened his secret life with Ann. Was that it? At Ciao with the beer, on the road with the scotch, at the *supermercado* with the bag of booze, had I set out to poleax him? I knew what alcohol did to both of us. I might as well have bought him Drano. Was that the idea: to see him wobble without actually *saying* anything—his own father had showed how fatal the direct approach could be—so I could write him off forever as a lush?

How could I have done that to my own father?

What was this merciless drive for the upper hand, this obsession with seeing my father as a tyrant whose statue I had to pull down? What kind of son would reach middle age still treating his father as if he were Mussolini?

A chickenshit?

A coward?

A fall wind blowing through the olive trees swirled up the stone stairs. I shivered, wrapping my arms around myself like a small boy. Life scared me. Everything scared me. The armor I girded on every morning was even heavier than his: clank, clank, clank—amazing that

I even made it to work all those years, amazing so few noticed all the rattle and bang. I was heavy, very, very heavy, too heavy to make any leaps toward life.

Jump to me. I'm your father.

Wasn't that where it had all begun, the day I didn't trust him? Would he have caught me? Of course he would have caught me. What was I really afraid of that day? Was the real problem where I wouldn't jump from, not where I wouldn't jump to?

Wasn't that the nexus?

For those 114 days, Italy, to my father, had been *The Inferno*. On me, World War II had bestowed the Mill Creek *Paradiso*. The fall I had been afraid of was the loss of that paradise, so I didn't jump. From that day on, I had never forgiven him for returning alive, evicting me from my little Eden, and restoring me to what was only, after all, the real world.

The moon sank behind the mountains. I started to shake, but it wasn't the cold. My cheeks felt warm. I raised my hand and felt tears. If I hadn't touched them with my fingers I wouldn't have known they were there. The rest of the night I spent staring at the ceiling in my bedroom until the light began to pour through a crack in the shutters. There was something I had missed the night before: I was still here. My father was in the other room. No one was running away. Neither of us was chickenshit.

In Tuscany the next morning, the air was so sweet and clear you could see all the way back to the Renaissance. I was sitting at the kitchen table working on a fruit compote for breakfast when my father came out of the bedroom. He looked a lot better than I felt.

"I've been thinking about everything that's happened," he said, pulling his chair next to me. He was speaking slowly, choosing his words carefully, steering clear of anything that might sound like exaggeration or faux sentimentality.

"I'd like to be able to describe what's happened between you and me," he went on. "It's beyond paraphrase, but I want to be able to tell it in terms that are not . . . operatic."

Honor and a Code of Silence: A war memorial in the Apennines between Torre Iussi and Rocca Roffeno

I'd never heard him talk like this.

"I guess I'd say that when we started, you saw me as sort of . . . a villain. And I saw you as being in such a mindless rage that we were on entirely separate planets. I thought I'd lost you. I didn't want to die lousy, but I couldn't see anything to do about it. Now, I don't want to sound pretentious, but . . ."

He paused, and then he bet the farm.

"What I feel is redemption."

For a moment I was speechless. There was only one question left.

"You remember the day you came home from the war, the day you put your arms out and I wouldn't jump?"

"Yes."

"What were you thinking?"

"I wanted to be embraced."

Not, "My son is a coward."

Les Ware had been right. All I had to do now was jump.

I couldn't speak. I put my arms around him and this time I was crying.

"Hell," he said, squeezing my shoulder awkwardly. "We're on the same planet again. I'm proud of us."

Us.

Not him, not me, but us.

The next day we packed the car and set off for Rome. I drove south the slow way, past the American Battle Memorial. Somewhere near Siena I told him how if all else had failed on the trip, I'd planned to sandbag him at the cemetery. No need now. "Where is it?" he asked me. I pointed to the rearview mirror. "About forty kilometers back."

"You were right," he said. "I couldn't have taken it. No more wringers."

He pointed up the road.

"Sempre avanti," he said, calling out the war cry of his old outfit.

Just keep moving.

Acknowledgments

Col. David H. Hackworth, United States Army (ret.) made me see how war changes men's lives and warned me I was running out of time to understand how combat had shaped my father. Lester Ware, Personal Best, got me in mental and physical shape to pick up the phone. My father, Tom Mathews Sr., took an enormous risk when he agreed after a lifetime of silence to retrace the 10th Mountain Division's advance through northern Italy in the winter and spring of 1945.

It is sometimes said that men can't or won't talk openly about their deepest feelings. Anyone who still believes this should ask a son about his father or a father about his son. This book was only possible because Michael Savino, Louis Simpson, Richard Vincent, and Col. Spann Watson, all Greatest Generation stoics like my father, decided to tell me their stories. Hollace Ditterline, Murray Greenberg, Frank Martinelli, Arthur Nelson, and Edgar Persan were already gone when I started—an immense loss that grows each day as the veterans of World War II depart—and before I finished, Michael Savino and Richard Vincent joined them. But their stories survived in the memories of their sons—Steven Greenberg, Bob Persan, Joshua Vincent, Erik Nelson and his own son John, Richard Savino, Weyman Watson, Ron Martinelli, Dennis and Bob Ditterline—who talked openly and passionately, sacrificing the usual cloak of anonymity because they believed candor offered the surest approach to the mystery of their fathers.

These weren't stories of men without women. My mother, Bonnie Mathews, was generous and enthusiastic in filling out the years beyond my own memory, and fair-minded about what followed in spite of my parents' divorce. My sister Anne Aoki supplied crucial family records and irreverent insights. My sister-in-law, Lois Beachy Underhill, explained her husband Richard Vincent in ways that never came easily to me. She also read the entire manuscript and corrected more flaws than I'm eager to count. Dianna Everett, Doris Hartheimer, Renee Martinelli, Irene Nelson, Deborah Rossow, Mary Savino and Mary Quinn Savino, Laura Storch, Maria Vincent, and Edna Watson all helped explain blanks that had eluded their husbands or brothers. My daughter Clea Mathews and granddaughter Lucy De Souza took on the same assignment for me.

Alexandra Penney, force of nature, was in at the creation. Steve Rubin, publisher and gentleman, told me to give him stories, not sociology. Gerry Howard, good cop among editors, taught me that books are not therapy and put me back on course every time I veered off. Rakesh Satyal kept count. Alice Martell, agent-counselor and Lady of the Swamp, pulled me out of all puddles.

I also want to thank Laura Anderson, Dennis Ashbaugh, Elizabeth Barnes, John Brannen, Bryant Brown, Maryann Calendrilla, Harry Campbell, Dean Curtis, Mike deNardo, Eilhys England, Ed Furey, Bob Graham, Pete Greenberg, Dawn Hedberg, John Hillendahl, Alan Kaplan, Jimmy Kavanaugh, John Kavanaugh, Michael Kinsey, David Lebwith, Tom Mac, Colin Mathews, Sean Mills, Tracy Sheehan, Claude Soffel, Chris Stubelik, Kathryn Szoka, Christian Villeneuve, Larryann C. Willis, the Audie Murphy Research Foundation, Black Cat Books, and Canio's Books.

Lucille Beachy above all.

About the Author

Tom Mathews, an award-winning journalist, served as Senior Writer for National Affairs, Foreign Editor, and Arts Editor at *Newsweek* magazine. *Standing Fast*, the biography he wrote with civil rights leader Roy Wilkins, was a *New York Times* Notable Book. He now writes about soldiers and war. Mathews lives in Sag Harbor, New York.